Made in Florida

UNIVERSITY PRESS OF FLORIDA

Florida A&M University, Tallahassee
Florida Atlantic University, Boca Raton
Florida Gulf Coast University, Ft. Myers
Florida International University, Miami
Florida State University, Tallahassee
New College of Florida, Sarasota
University of Central Florida, Orlando
University of Florida, Gainesville
University of North Florida, Jacksonville
University of South Florida, Tampa
University of West Florida, Pensacola

University Press of Florida

Gainesville · Tallahassee · Tampa · Boca Raton

Pensacola · Orlando · Miami · Jacksonville · Ft. Myers · Sarasota

MADE
IN
FLORIDA

Artists,
Celebrities,
Activists,
Educators,
and Other Icons
in the Sunshine State

Art Levy

1434593

Printed in the United States of America on acid-free paper

This book may be available in an electronic edition.

24 23 22 21 20 19   6 5 4 3 2 1

Library of Congress Control Number: 2018950629
ISBN 978-0-8130-5626-5

The University Press of Florida is the scholarly publishing agency for the State
University System of Florida, comprising Florida A&M University, Florida Atlantic
University, Florida Gulf Coast University, Florida International University, Florida
State University, New College of Florida, University of Central Florida, University
of Florida, University of North Florida, University of South Florida, and University
of West Florida.

University Press of Florida
2046 NE Waldo Road
Suite 2100
Gainesville, FL 32609
http://upress.ufl.edu

To my family—wife, Sharon, and sons, Andy and Zach,
the three who mean the most to me

CONTENTS

MADE IN FLORIDA

INTRODUCTION

Shortly after his interview ran in the April 2018 issue of *Florida Trend*, Greg Asbed sent me an email.

Greg, who cofounded the Coalition of Immokalee Workers and helped create the Fair Food Program, is not a person who craves attention. It's true he's a MacArthur genius grant winner, but he's not the sort to revel in limelight. He just wants to help farmworkers. In fact, the only reason I suspect he agreed to talk to me for two hours back in December 2017 and answer more than fifty questions was the possibility that the interview might draw attention to his work and, in the process, convince Floridians to care a little more about how their produce gets from field to table.

After reading his own words—accompanied by a glaring-into-the-camera portrait photographed by Brian Tietz—Greg worried that the interview made him look like a "self-focused man who jumps from topic to topic, mainly about himself, without too much rhyme or reason."

He's right that the interviews flit on topics like a butterfly looking for nectar, jumping from family to work, joys to worries, failures to triumphs, and dislikes to desires, with a whole bunch of Florida insight mixed in.

Amid the avalanche of quotes, for example, you'll learn what happens when Burt Reynolds goes to Costco and Chris Evert goes to Publix.

You'll learn what it was like for prominent artist James Rosenquist to work in rural Aripeka. You'll hear Carl Hiaasen talk about Florida's challenges and Steve Spurrier make a case for paying college athletes.

From Mel Tillis, you'll learn what it was like to grow up a stutterer in Pahokee, and from Shaquille O'Neal, you'll discover why he never complains.

During his interview, Apollo 14 astronaut Edgar Mitchell talked about the likelihood that space aliens have visited Earth. Fight doctor Ferdie Pacheco explained why he never flossed his teeth, and botanical gardens founder Don Goodman revealed what it was like to lose an arm to an alligator's jaws. And, from *A Land Remembered* author Patrick Smith, you'll hear about the time he researched a novel by posing as a migrant worker in a labor camp near Homestead.

There's way more. You'll see.

A few days after his email, Greg contacted me again, noting that, with time, he was starting to feel slightly better about the interview.

"It's an interesting form," he said, "like you're dropping in from time to time on a conversation while wandering through a party."

I hadn't thought of it that way before, but it's true. It's the accumulation of thoughts, feelings, and opinions that tell the story.

For someone as altruistic and unassuming as Greg, the process was a bit of a grind to endure, but hopefully, at least, it'll be a good read for you.

ADVOCATES

GREG ASBED

Cofounder of the Coalition of Immokalee Workers and Fair Food Program, winner of a 2017 MacArthur genius grant, interviewed in December 2017, when he was fifty-four, Immokalee.

Greg Asbed

I tend not to be the person who looks for explanations for why you do what you do based on your background because, frankly, I think anybody who has seen the sorts of things that I've seen through the work that I do—you know, slavery, beatings, sexual assault, the kind of stuff that goes on in the fields—I would hope anybody would respond to it, no matter who they were, no matter their background.

Being born poor shouldn't be a life sentence.

Have you read *Devil in the Grove*? You should. It should be required reading for all Florida high school students. And for all Floridians. It talks about Florida, not the one we know today, but the roots of what we are today.

In the early 1990s, when we first got here, the conditions in Immokalee were pretty shocking. You would see people getting beaten up out here in this parking lot on payday, and it was because they complained about their pay being short. Or they complained about not getting paid at all. We realized that these conditions were not put here on two rock tablets—thus shall it always be. The conditions have reasons that have roots that we could analyze, and we could see how we could change them. We started to ask: Why are farmworkers so poor? Why are farmworkers so exploited? Why are they so abused? Why do they face so much violence at work? That was the beginning of our organizing.

At some point in life, the most fun you can have is being with your family. I love the hell out of my wife and son, and we have a great time together.

All this data was coming in, and we could see that there were forces beyond the farm gate itself that actually influenced conditions on the farm. And those forces were the consolidated, multibillion-dollar retail food companies that leverage their volume purchasing power to drive prices down. So, if that power is the thing that's driving farmworker poverty, then we had to address that power in some way. We realized that these retail food companies don't care if farmworkers protest, but they do care if consumers protest. We don't think of ourselves as the boss of the companies we buy from, but that's only because we abdicate our power. If we choose to use our power, we can demand that our tomatoes are picked by workers whose rights are not trampled on every day.

My son and I go to the FGCU [Florida Gulf Coast University] basketball games. It's the best ticket in town. It's nine bucks for him, twelve bucks for me, and no parking fee. And you can get food for like five bucks. They have a really fun team. It's a great time.

The fair food agreements that we were finally able to achieve—first with Taco Bell, then with McDonald's, Burger King, and Subway and these other food service companies and supermarkets—resulted in two simple things: They would pay a small premium, known as a penny more a pound, to help improve farmworker income, but much, much more importantly the corporations would only buy from growers who comply with a human rights–based code of conduct that we developed. Wendy's and Publix and Kroger—there are a lot of companies that are still not part of this. But there are fourteen companies now that are, including Whole Foods and Walmart.

In Florida, in the 1950s, '60s, and '70s, farm labor was, in many cases, the compelled, forced labor of African Americans in small towns throughout the spine of Florida, where sheriffs would offer them essentially the opportunity to either go to jail or work in the fields. And anybody who rose up against it, anybody who tried to organize, would be brutally dealt with. The only reason this changed was because, at some point, agriculture was no longer the most important industry in this state. That became tourism, and tourism could not handle the connection to that kind of political reality, and so Tallahassee changed its stripes.

Eighty percent of farmworker women report being subjected to sexual harassment or sexual assault at work—80 percent!—a much higher percentage than any other occupation.

Gerrymandering has things on lockdown. We have to fix that first before we fix anything because it's the motor. You can have a beautiful car, but if the motor is broken, you're not going anywhere.

On my little, less-than-a-quarter-acre property in LaBelle, I have mango trees and some old-style Florida tangerines, the really delicious ones, not the ones you get in the store, and some other citrus that's struggling as hard as it can against the greening. I've got bananas, pineapples, pomegranates, guava, Meyer lemon, Key lime—all that and some that I'm probably forgetting. And I've got a garden, with greens and everything else. Eating what I grow, it's one of my favorite things.

I'm the son of a Syrian-Armenian refugee immigrant. He was the son of a woman who was thirteen years old when she survived the Armenian genocide. That was my grandmother. She survived after seeing virtually everyone in her family killed. The young women were taken on marches called caravans—death marches—through Turkey to Syria. She was sold by the Turks to the Kurds for two goats and a bale of hay and a gold coin. My father always insisted on the gold coin being part of the story.

We stopped dealing with Tallahassee. We did at the beginning. Lawton Chiles was there when we started, and Chiles was a reasonable human being. He was a good person who cared about people. But, ever since, it has just been a succession of people who don't care.

I could have just as easily been in neuroscience—PhD, teacher, researcher. That was the path I was on. But after studying neuroscience at Brown University I went to Haiti to live and work there for a few years before going to graduate school. And that changed my life entirely. I saw everything from kids dying of starvation—the swollen bellies, what's called kwashiorkor, the word for malnutrition to the point of death—to people being shot dead in front of me by the government because they wanted to have a voice in democracy.

In the morning, I'll go out and water the garden and grab a fistful of leaves—kale or arugula or whatever—and eat them, and then I'll go to the tangerine tree, which is ripe now, and grab one or two of those, and they're still cold from the night, and they're delicious, and you feel like you're eating pure goodness.

Gay Culverhouse

Founder of Players' Outreach, an organization that assists former NFL players who have brain injuries, former president of the Tampa Bay Buccaneers, interviewed in October 2010, when she was sixty-three, Jacksonville.

IF I PUT MY MIND TO SOMETHING, I'm going to do it. My children learned that very early on. If it was bedtime, you were going to bed.

I've got three blood diseases, all of them extremely rare—and I mean extremely rare. My doctors have never seen this before. It's from I think being exposed to the air at 9/11 because I was on the sidewalk near the towers.

When I found out I had myelofibrosis, I got my will in order, told the kids, bought a cemetery plot. I got my headstone all done. Then I didn't think anything more about it. That was seven years ago. My life expectancy at the time was five years.

I have so much going on in my life, the last thing I have time for is to think about being sick. Being sick is a fact of my life, just sort of like I wear size eight shoes. You buy the shoe that fits and keep going.

For four years in a row, up until this year, I was the top amateur rider in the country in the Paso Fino horse world.

I've broken a lot of bones. I've broken my back. I've broken my ribs. I've broken my tailbone. I'm a disaster because I ride really hard, and I take risks that no one else does, and I ride horses that no one else will ride. Because of that, you have to expect certain things to happen, but that's why I've been a top-ranked rider. I will push the horse to the absolute extreme. Most people are very tentative, but I'm not tentative. I'm either going to have a major crash or I'm going to win.

The majority of Americans have jobs that are just hard work and stressful, and they need a break. That's sports.

I probably have twenty-four Paso Fino horses. I breed them. They are born with brio, and if the horse doesn't have brio—or fire—you sell him to someone who wants a trail horse. I breed them for fire, the hottest to the hottest. It's like driving a Ferrari versus a Ford Focus.

The average, normal, run-of-the-mill person never interested me and doesn't interest me today. I just choose to be around people who have faced challenges, overcome them, and if they haven't overcome them, I'll be glad to help them become independent. I have a doctorate in special education from Columbia. That's my field, so when I started to hear about retired players who were in trouble, I said, "OK, I'll find them and help them." It's just a natural progression of what I've always done.

I have a preponderance of platelets, which either leads to clotting or bleeding, and you never can tell which. I also have something called cold agglutinin disease, which means if I get cold, if I drink something that's cold or if I physically get cold, I kill red blood cells. So I'm anemic, and I kill red cells when I get cold. It's a bad combination.

In the winter, I go south. Last winter, it was cold in Florida, so I took a place in Key West, and it was the coldest winter ever in Key West. So I went even farther south into South America. I have also spent time in Africa because it's nice and toasty in Africa. I just move around and look for warm places. In order to live, I should be in a place that's 98.6, but that's like impossible, so I just get as warm as I can. Most people don't like to come into my home because it's really hot.

When I spoke to Congress last year—I testified to the Congressional

Judiciary Committee on Brain Injuries—they asked me, "What are you going to do next?" And I told them that I was going to find Jerry Eckwood. I remembered Jerry when he was with the Buccaneers. I remembered Jerry walking to the wrong huddle, and I remembered him walking to the wrong bench. That stuck in my mind, so when the concussion stuff started coming out, I thought about Jerry. We tracked him from Arkansas to Tennessee. He has dementia. Now, he's in a phenomenal living facility, with his own mini-kitchen. He says the most exciting thing about it is he has a closet. He's well taken care of. He's clothed. He's fed. He lives near a mall he can walk to, and he's happy because it has a Cheesecake Factory. We gave him a life.

I'm a super grandmother. I've done my tour of duty at Disney World. I go visit the grandchildren, but I don't hover above them because I don't want them to think I'm weird. I want to leave them a legacy so they can say: "Man, my grandmother did this and my grandmother did that. She never stopped." Yeah, they may say that or they may say, "God, she was really funny and couldn't do Legos worth a shit."

When my grandson was seven, he started playing football, and of course he made the all-star team his first year. He plays both ways on the line. He's a little tank. He has lived in the South, and he's moving to the North, and so his mother not only has him in football, she's also enrolled him in ice hockey. So I say, "Great, not only won't he have a brain, he won't have any teeth either."

I went to school with all the kids who got hit with the polio epidemic, so I went to school with kids on crutches and with all sorts of limbs atrophied and everything else. I thought they were really cool. I thought they were interesting. They were like old souls. They had been through a lot more than I had. These kids were like troopers, and I found them fascinating. I knew then that I was going to work with people who were different.

Years ago, my daughter and I were targeted in a kidnapping plot. That incident still has an impact on me and on my children. I keep a very low profile. You will find that I have many addresses in many places. I am always on the move, and my phone doesn't reflect the number where I live. I assure you I have a trained attack dog. I carry a concealed weapon, and I would kill. There would be no doubt about it. I'd kill you just as soon as you moved. Don't think you're going to intimidate me. You walk in my house unexpectedly, you're going to get plugged.

You know, I've never given a thought to what my dad [Hugh Culverhouse, the former owner of the Buccaneers] would think about what I'm doing now. I guess he'd probably be thinking that I'm just doing what I always did, that I'm out there trying to save the world.

LOUISE GOPHER

Former director of education for the Seminole Tribe of Florida, interviewed in September 2014, when she was sixty-nine, Okeechobee. Gopher died in November 2016.

I WAS BORN IN AN ORANGE GROVE because that's where my parents were working at the time, so that's where they established their camp. I was born in a chickee. Sometimes we would live in a trailer or some other structure. I must have been almost finished with school before I actually moved into a house with all the comforts—indoor bathrooms, indoor showers, running water.

When I was a kid, I only spoke my native language: Creek. No English. I guess my father knew a little to get by at work, and my mother probably did, too, but I didn't learn English until I started going to school.

I like football games. I'm a fanatic.

My daughter Carla was FSU's first Seminole Indian graduate back in 1996. While she was there, I guess I made a lot of contacts. I started taking kids up there, like on spring break. We would tour Gainesville, too, and go on up to Florida State, tour, and we'd always meet Bobby Bowden. They always rolled out the red carpet for us.

Don't forget our ancestors. They went through a lot to get us here.

I was the first female member of the Seminole Tribe to earn a bachelor's degree. I lived in Fort Pierce, and a junior college had been built, Indian River Community College, and I finished two years there and then went to Florida Atlantic University. After a while, people kept saying, "She's been going to school forever," but I knew the education was helping me.

We were so into pushing our kids into the white culture and catching them up that we were forgetting about own culture. We were trying to fix this for years, trying to teach the Native American language and history to our young people, and the effort became a charter school, which opened on the reservation in 2007. We call it Pemayetv Emahakv, which means "Our Way School."

The traditional foods are still my favorite foods. I like fry bread and sofkee. Sofkee is a drink that we drink all the time, any time. It's made from grains, like rice or grits or oatmeal. In the old days, it was made from roasted corn, which was a long procedure. We still make it that way, but not often, so when we do have it, everybody jumps on it.

We lived in camps, near Fort Pierce, with a lot of other families living nearby. My parents did agricultural work. It seemed like every evening there was a big bonfire or campfire, and we sat around, and that's when you listened to the stories and legends and learned the history.

Somebody told me a while back, "Education is your gold mine," and I would spout that to kids, everywhere I went. What you learn stays with you. The gold mine is in your head.

The mascot thing has been a big issue for some teams, but I don't mind FSU's mascot. The outfits and everything are correct. There's nothing cartoonish or ugly. I think FSU understands our history.

Being a little five- or six-year-older, I didn't realize what problems my father had to deal with getting me into school. He had to go to the school board to get us enrolled in St. Lucie County. This was back during segregation. You had the white students and the black students. Native Americans, where did we fit in? Finally, they put us in with the white kids.

Living on the reservation feels comfortable and safe. I can't imagine having family living across the country. Here, they're right down the street.

We have two dialects in the Seminole Tribe. It's like having two languages. One is the Creek language, and the other is Miccosukee. I speak Creek. The languages are so different, a lot of people who understand one can't understand the other.

I own beef cattle. I like to ride out where they are, where it's peaceful. They call to me, and I talk to them.

My grandfather Desoto Tiger, he was killed when my mother was two weeks old. He's a history story. Did you ever hear of the John Ashley gang? They ran up and down the south Florida coast in the 1910s to about the 1920s. They were outlaws. Where my grandfather fits in, he was their first victim. He was a fur trapper and was taking some otter hides down to Miami in 1911. John Ashley killed him and took the hides.

Public education always needs improvement. I know it's a budget thing, but we need more teachers and smaller classrooms.

Gopher is a Native American name, I guess. I don't know what it stems from. My sister's name was Smith. In fact, we had brothers with different last names: Frank Shore, Oscar Hall, Sam Jones. They just gave us names.

NICOLE JOHNSON

Former Miss America, health-care educator, diabetes advocate, interviewed in March 2016, when she was forty-two, St. Petersburg.

THE LEVEL OF GUILT THAT I FEEL—as a mother with a disease—is profound. My daughter watches me struggle with diabetes. She experiences the highs and lows of the disease, and it forces her to be much more mature than she should be at ten. That is the mourning that I often feel in my heart. But, at the same time, watching Mommy with a disease has given her such a beautiful respect and sensitivity to people who are hurting.

Standing on a stage in a swimsuit is very not-normal. But what I learned after the fact when I was a judge at Miss America that I wish I had known back when I was a contestant is that the judging of the woman who is standing before you in a swimsuit has nothing to do with the swimsuit. It has everything to do with how she can command the audience when stripped away of everything that's convenient to her.

I met one of the local TV news reporters in a McDonald's, and I think I was about ten. It was Gayle Sierens. I went up to her and said, "Oh, you are on the news!" She was just so sweet and kind to me. I left that encounter thinking to myself: "That's what I'm going to do. I'm going to be a TV news reporter."

On my last day as Miss America, I rode in a parade that's legendary in Atlantic City, the shoe parade. People all along the parade route waved at me and held up insulin pumps, and they had signs saying, "I'm like you." That's the most beautiful picture I keep in my mind.

Our lack of progressiveness in some of our statewide policies is hurting people with diabetes and other diseases. I'm not making a judgment about anybody, but I would hope in the future that we'll make decisions that would benefit more of the citizens of Florida, especially those living with chronic illnesses. Our decision to not expand Medicaid has really hurt a lot of people.

Growing up, I fantasized about being a Broadway actress and musician. I never really put action behind that because, sadly, as a child, I lacked the confidence to try.

At Bringing Science Home [a medical research group], we've taken a social-ecological view of life with diabetes. What I mean by that is at the core is the person with the disease, but there are these concentric circles that go around the person: immediate family, close friends, business associates. We started working on that second-tier circle, looking at parents and the stress they experience around caring for their young person with diabetes and how that fractures families. And we're also looking at romantic relationships—spouses, partners of the individual with disease—and how they feel often isolated and alone.

I feel really good about the things that I've accomplished so far. I'm open to God surprising me with whatever's next.

When it came down to it, my goal was to get on the Miss America stage and be in the top five because the top five women would be interviewed and got to hold the microphone on national television. I wanted to talk about living with type 1 diabetes and how that was OK and that discrimination against anyone who has something different about them is wrong.

I have to calculate how many carbohydrates are in each meal, how much insulin I'll need, how much fat is in the meal because that determines how long the meal will affect my body. There are many elements of eating that make it not fun. That might be one of the most unfortunate parts of life with diabetes, especially in our food-obsessed culture.

Everything crosses your mind when you are diagnosed with a chronic, lifelong illness, so I thought about how could I end it all. At times, the pain and the frustration seemed too much to handle. I'm so grateful for my early years of learning to depend on my faith because I think that was the most important element in helping me see my way through the darkness of depression and feeling like everything was torn away.

We're Disney lovers. We go there frequently, especially in spring and fall. The holidays are unmatched there. We're not crazy. We don't go in the summer.

I was in a local preliminary pageant, Miss Sarasota. I was a student at USF at the time. They called my name as the first runner-up and instead of stepping forward, I fell backward. Another young woman caught me and they took me off the stage, and that's when my family took me to the emergency room. After I was diagnosed with type 1 diabetes, I was forced to understand who I was with this disease. It was very difficult to feel frail, to feel broken in so many ways.

When I was Miss America, I never cut a ribbon to open an establishment or anything like that. I spent 365 days speaking before health-care audiences—patients and professionals. The people I met influenced me and made me want to do something where I was giving back to the health and well-being of others in a bigger way than I thought I was prepared to do at that point. That's when I altered my plan from becoming a journalist taking the *Good Morning America* route to going back to school and studying public health.

Food, for me, is not a motivator. I fuel my body to do what I want to do, but I don't live to eat. A great dinner is not a win for me because I don't look at food as this wonderful experience. For me, it's a means to an end.

You can always make strides toward delaying or preventing. It's proven that if you lose between 5 and 7 percent of your body weight and you walk thirty minutes a day, you can prevent the progression of diabetes by up to 58 percent.

Being judged is frightening. There's no other way to say that.

Barbara Mainster

Early childhood
education advo-
cate, interviewed
in October 2014,
when she was
seventy-three,
Fort Myers.

I KNOW WHAT HARD WORK IT IS TO GROW THINGS.

My mother and father both influenced me. They were not formally well educated. I think my mother probably went through the eighth grade. I think my dad attended what would be technical college now. They were avid readers. Both were avid political observers and very into social justice.

If you're a phony, I think everybody knows it.

I went to the job interview at Redlands Christian Migrant Association, and that was it. It was like being back in the Peace Corps. The job was education coordinator. I said to them, "If you don't hire me, I'm going to come back and volunteer for you anyway," which was a stupid thing to say at a job interview! That was forty-two years ago.

Early childhood is the most important time of anybody's life. When I meet people, it's pretty easy, when they're outstanding people, to know they had a good early childhood and that they had parents who thought they were the greatest thing in the world.

I know how to use a pickaxe. I had somebody tell me, "You're the first woman I've ever seen use a pickaxe right." And I said, "What? You pick it up and you swing it!"

The older I get, the more I can get away with, I think.

Right now, 30 percent of the kids we're serving at our migrant Head Start are indigenous-language speakers. That means they don't come in speaking Spanish or English. They speak an indigenous language. It's from the mountains, an Indian language basically.

I love gardening. I love being outdoors. I have learned to appreciate Florida's seasons and the nature. I have a bromeliad jungle. My bougainvillea are happy. This is where they want to be.

We actually had kind of a nice little house in Long Island, with a garden and all those trappings of the beginning of middle class. I was ten when my folks moved us to upstate New York to become farmers. We moved to this place that had an outhouse. The house had been vacant and was falling down, but the farm had 50 acres. My parents' thought was they wanted to be independent. They wanted to raise their own cows, their own chickens, pigs, and have gardens and all of that good stuff. They never made a lot of money on that farm, but the milk they sold put us through college.

I am terrified of what will happen if we don't wake up about water quality and water. The notion that we'd consider fracking in this state is absolutely insane.

For me, life was never about how much money you're going to make or how important you're going to be.

Kids make me laugh. The honesty of kids is just so refreshing.

By the way, I read Patrick Smith's book—he was one of your Icons— *A Land Remembered*, and I loved it. Fabulous.

Wendell N. Rollason, who was RCMA's executive director before me, is the one who recognized that to make a strong organization, two things had to happen: one is that the board needed to be made up of both farmers and farmworkers, and the second was the staff needed to come from the community we're serving.

I'm not a micromanager. You have to trust people.

The Mennonites started us, so we are not faith-based. We are non-sectarian. The Christian in our name means "love thy neighbor," plain and simple.

I feel good after every day. I do worry, but I have to tell you that's another blessing about how I was raised. Little things make me happy.

The kids go to school and get tested in English, and that's grossly unfair. That's not what should happen. That's not testing what the kids know. That's testing what they know in the English language. If you really want to know what they know, test them in their own language.

I am not patient, so I have to force myself to listen and seek first to understand.

The immigration issue affects us hugely—not in funding, not in any of those things—but emotionally. We have kids everywhere being raised by their moms alone because dad was deported because he drove without a driver's license. You talk to some of our elementary kids and they will tell you they worry about their parents being deported.

In agriculture, people really do value hard work. They respect it.

You have to lead by example. You have to follow the golden rule and treat people the way you want to be treated. You have to be willing to do yourself what you're asking other people to do.

JOHN WALSH

Anticrime advocate, television host, interviewed in December 2008, when he was sixty-two, Fort Lauderdale.

FLORIDA WAS THE FIRST STATE to have a missing-child clearinghouse and one of the first states to have mandatory background checks of teachers. The Justice Department did a survey of state sex-offender registries and how states deal with the exploitation of children. Florida was the only state that got an A. Florida is my model state.

The Adam Walsh Child Protection Act was signed by President George W. Bush in the Rose Garden on the twenty-fifth anniversary of Adam's abduction—a horrible day for us that was turned into a very positive day. It mandated a national sex-offender registry. It mandated that every state have a sex-offender registry. The problem with Adam's law is it hasn't been fully funded by Congress.

People come to me with sad things because they know I've walked in their shoes. My wife puts it more articulately than anyone could. She says this is a color you've never seen, a color you can't explain, and a color I hope you never see.

Ottis Toole, the man I believe killed Adam, died in jail for other crimes. He was a horrible, horrible person, convicted of many other crimes. And if there is any kind of justice in the next world, which I believe there is, he'll be held accountable.

I tell parents: Be street-smart. Be informed. Be educated. Open those lines of communication with your children. They'll be all over that internet, and they'll know how to use it better than you ever will.

Adam was our only child, the light of our life. I had a great father. I named Adam after my father. My father died at fifty-four. I wanted to be a father, and I thought I was a great father.

I have been so blessed, Reve and I, that, despite all the troubles and problems we've had, we have had three children since Adam. They are street-smart. They don't live in Adam's shadow, but they know about his legacy. They always speak about how wonderful it would have been to know him.

Lots of parents of murdered children never have another child. Eighty percent of parents of murdered children end up in divorce. All you have in common is the terrible grief, the stress. It drives you, no matter how good your marriage is, apart. We've had some really, really unbearably tough times. It generates behavior you never dreamed you were capable of.

I don't care what party you are, Democrat or Republican. It's the person. It's the woman or the man. It matters how you do the job.

Reve, my wife, is the one who said, as we were spiraling down into hell, that we can't forget who the real victim is. Adam went through the kidnapping, the horrible death. We can't let this beautiful boy's death be in vain.

Lots of people we put on *America's Most Wanted* hate me. They don't want to be held accountable for their actions. They vent their anger and vengeance at me. Those are things I never dreamed I'd be dealing with. I have no choice.

Crime victims sometimes can't get their life back. But justice is the way to change.

It's the strangest thing that a guy who was very successful at a young age in the hotel business has a son who is murdered, who just tries to change a few laws out of anger, becomes the host of the first reality television program on a network that in 1987 was one night with a guy named Johnny Depp. [Walsh is referring to *21 Jump Street*, starring Depp, which aired on Fox from 1987 to 1991.]

When they came to me and said they would like me to host this program, that there's a media mogul named Rupert Murdoch who is trying to create this show, I said: "Who's Rupert Murdoch? What the hell is Fox?"

Cops have told me some of these guys would be out killing people if not for your show.

I loved the hotel business. It was my passion. I was a partner with three other guys. We were building a $26 million dream project hotel in the Bahamas. I was very successful. I was living the American dream. That dream turned into a nightmare one day when I went to work and never saw my son again. I lost 30 pounds. I couldn't function. The hotel business was irrelevant. The opening of that dream project was irrelevant.

I love Florida. It's my residence. I don't blame what happened to Adam on Florida.

I'm an avid, die-hard polo player. I've gotten hurt really bad. Horses crash. You go down. It's dangerous. I've fractured my skull on a motorcycle. I broke my leg. I have a big plate in my leg with nine screws. My ankle is screwed on. I don't think you can live life by sitting on the bench. I don't think you can live life on the sidelines. I like to be in the game.

I like any kind of dangerous, high-adrenaline hobby I can have to take my mind off all the dark stuff.

Charlie Crist I met years ago when he was the education commissioner, a good one, and then he became a kick-ass attorney general. Almost the first thing he did when he became governor was he got the anti-murder bill passed, and he had me at the bill signing. That's a man who keeps his word.

The internet has become a big hunting ground for sexual predators. Now they don't have to take the chance of following the school bus and trying to grab a kid off of a playground, although they still do that. Now, they can talk to forty children and find the one that's the most vulnerable, the one they can lure.

Kiss your kids every day and tell them you love them. I've known thousands of people who have gone to work or somewhere and have never seen their kids again.

CARLTON WARD

Photojournalist, Florida Wildlife Corridor advocate, interviewed in October 2015, when he was thirty-nine, Tampa.

FLORIDA IS NOT LIKE COLORADO, where you can look and see the Rocky Mountains and know that the snowmelt is a source of your water and those high, beautiful places are where wildlife can still roam. We have an amazing, wild interior that is the source of almost all of our drinking water. It's the source of our $100 billion agriculture economy. It's where all of our wildlife in any significant scale can still survive, but it's hiding in plain sight. We have to treat these vast wild spaces as our sacred mountains that are the source of our life and economy.

I grew up in Pinellas County and was fortunate to spend a lot of time on the water. My family also has some ranch land in Hardee County, near Limestone, and something I often say is I kind of had one foot in the suburbs and one foot in the woods growing up, which I think had a lot to do with my perspective on conservation.

There's no doubt that Florida is an eclectic and weird place, but I think that gets amplified further in the media. And that is a challenge. If we want to foster a true sense of place and identity, rooted in the real Florida, we're having to overcome a lot of stereotypes.

The way I look at it, it's not necessarily an argument against more houses and roads in Florida. It's an argument for where to put those new houses and roads.

My mom always encouraged a sense of wonder in me about things, like picking up seashells and learning the difference between univalves and bivalves.

I feel like there's a tendency to portray the world of *A Land Remembered* as if it's in the distant past, but, in fact, that world still exists in Florida today. You get out on a cattle ranch with a fifth-, sixth-, seventh-, eighth-generation cattle rancher whose family has been working and managing that same land for, in some cases, two centuries, and you'll see that the Florida frontier still exists but needs our appreciation to continue to exist.

Photography is definitely a selective process. The first lens in that whole equation is the photographer's eye, deciding what to focus on. My eye is focused on natural heritage and the environment.

There's this myth that the Florida Forever program is just a government land grab and it's just there to buy more public land, to take it off the tax rolls and to strap the public with the long-term management burden. Well, the Florida Forever program also invests significantly in conservation easements, and I think that is a real common ground that even the most conservative lawmakers can see value in. It's not a matter of the state having to pay the full price of the land and then manage it forever. It's actually a way to buy the development rights so the landowner can afford to keep owning the land and continue operating it for agriculture.

It's a challenge to find the discipline to stay working within your purpose.

I have such awe and respect for the people who, every morning before dawn, saddle up their horses and coil up their lariats and whips, and ride out to work the herds. They are almost like knights out there because of their commitment and connection to the land. They ensure that those lands still serve as habitats for wildlife and remain the watersheds that we all benefit from downstream. Those cowboys and ranchers are heroes to me for what they're doing for our state.

One of my big concerns has to do with changes in the media landscape. As circulations of newspapers and magazines shrink along with budgets, I worry about the future of in-depth journalism that is so important for our democracy. There are so many public-interest stories that need widespread attention. But without sustained investment of time and money that allows journalists to focus on the issues, these stories could go untold and unseen, at a great loss to our society.

I'm an eighth-generation Floridian. My great-grandfather was Doyle E. Carlton, the governor of Florida from 1929 to 1933. He was also one of the founders of the Carlton Fields law firm in Tampa.

Apalachicola Bay is a magical place.

The people who are the most vocal opponents of land conservation will give you statistics about what percentage of Florida is already in public ownership and, therefore, why do we need any more? I want to show them a map that shows them why. We need more because this amazing national forest that we protected decades ago and this beautiful state park are not connected to one another and if we can just help this rancher through a conservation easement or help expand this wildlife refuge so everything fits together, well, that's just a clear, common sense, pragmatic approach.

There's something always nostalgic and adventurous about being in Everglades City and going by the Rod & Gun Club, just to see the old wooden bar where all these past presidents have been during fishing trips.

I'm encouraged by something the Department of Agriculture has started under Adam Putnam—which is bringing school lunches under the purview of the Department of Agriculture rather than the Department of Education, which gives schools a chance to source produce locally. That's really cool. It's healthy. It helps educate kids about the source of their food. And it also gives farmers one more reason not to sell out to a housing development.

The Florida Wildlife Corridor project is a life's work. I hope to spend the foreseeable future of my career on this, telling these stories of the corridor. I want to be able to, in thirty years, take my daughter to revisit some of the places we've visited on our expeditions and have those places still be there.

ARTISTS

ROMERO BRITTO

Artist, interviewed in January 2011, when he was forty-seven, Miami.

WHEN I WAS A KID, I loved watching soap opera television, and I dreamed that my life would someday become like that. It was so different from how I actually lived.

I grew up in a family of nine, and my mother was a single mother. We lived in a part of Brazil called Recife, and we lived in a very poor part of the city. It was very difficult, very challenging. I was child who didn't understand where the food would come from, where the money would come from. I started painting to bring light and color into my life.

Color is a universal language, like music is a universal language. Yellow and blue is yellow and blue anywhere in the world.

With the way globalization is today, people can see how other people live across the world, and this makes some people feel left out. They feel jealous, and then they want to take things from the other people because they feel like they deserve it. That's when the problems arise.

A lot of times, people go through difficult times and they become angry. I went through difficult times, but I'm always trying to see the best in the world.

I was studying law, hoping to be a diplomat. I wanted to travel the world and be an ambassador for Brazil and learn about people and countries and everything. But then came a moment that I realized it was not through this that I would find happiness. So I gave up the idea of being a diplomat, and I gave up studying law. I quit everything, and I said: "You know what? I'm going to just paint."

I don't watch television much anymore because I don't have time. But when I was a kid, when I had the time to watch television, I thought it was very cool.

When I create, I put together shapes and colors and then I use the shapes and colors to create a kind of vocabulary that everybody can understand.

There is some negative stuff happening around the world, but I still think that there's more beauty happening, and I focus on that beauty. When I look at my work, I feel happy. I feel content. I don't have to drink a bottle of anything. And hopefully people who see it have that same feeling of joy without having to fill themselves full of alcohol or drugs.

Miami influences my work definitely. The people. The weather. The atmosphere. The special energy about the place. The water. The sky. The light. The city has such vitality and happiness.

When the people who gravitate to darkness and negativity criticize me, it doesn't mean anything. Their words I can't hear. I just keep doing my work.

I think there are more people who understand what I do than people who can't, so I'm not focusing on what the art critics say. At the end of the day, the people fill up their walls with what they like.

It's not difficult to run a business when you love what you do. I love what I do. I'm excited about waking up in the morning, and I'm ready for the challenge. Plus, I have very good people around me. I have a loyal staff.

I have a great opportunity to walk and talk and feel and see, but I'm here not that long. In another fifty years I'm going to be gone, so why not do something interesting? Why not fill my every day with colors? To have this opportunity and not do anything, that would be such a waste.

The mothers will tell you, having a baby will hurt a lot, but she loves the child. That's how I love my paintings. I love what I do, but sometimes the process of creating hurts.

Miami is a city of choice. Most of the people who live here, it's their choice to come here and to live here.

It would be a wonderful thing if we could somehow forecast our lives as we do today with the weather, that we could know a little bit ahead of time what we will become. That way, we wouldn't waste time doing things that would be a waste of time. We would just focus on the right thing, but unfortunately we don't have that yet. We don't have a manual to tell us how to be a human being, how to be a husband, a wife, daughter, son, or friend. So, sometimes, we make mistakes, but I'm happy to be here learning from my mistakes.

I like to look at art with a positive image, something you can look at on the wall and not feel scared and want to run away. I leave the horrible paintings for people who feel dark inside, to enjoy seeing themselves reflected on a painting.

If everything was the same, life wouldn't be fun.

There's this beautiful thing about happiness that we all want so much. The world wants it, and that's what our struggle is all about. Sometimes, happiness gets confused with power. That's the biggest problem we have.

I like to drive. When I'm driving, I'm thinking about who is ahead of me, not who is behind me.

Artist, only female Highway-men painter, interviewed in July 2007, when she was sixty-eight, Fort Pierce.

I MET HAROLD NEWTON by the road in Fort Pierce. He was one of the first Highwaymen. It was his car that attracted my eye. There were flames painted on it. He did that for attention. He told me what he did, and he showed me his paintings in the back seat. I watched him paint. He wasn't my teacher, though. He showed me how to mix oils, but when I was a child I could already draw anything I saw. Then, I started going on the road with the guys. I was probably eighteen when I sold my first painting.

When I was young, the options I had were cleaning house, babysitting, picking fruit, nurse's aide. Basically, that was it for a woman. But

I wanted to be a painter, and there were things I had to do to support my art. I never picked fruit. I did some babysitting and I did some housecleaning. I worked in a gladiola field when I was younger, cutting the flowers with a pocketknife.

My husband left me and the kids when the youngest was five, so I had seven children to raise and I had to have money. They had to eat. They had to have a place to sleep. They had to have clothes. I had to provide. I raised seven kids as a single parent.

A lot of the times I went on the road, I would take my kids with me. If I went on the road when they were in school, I made sure I got back before school got out. The painting enabled me to be momma, daddy, caretaker, and all that I had to do.

I didn't worry about my safety. I used to be thin, and I could jump high as a house. I was strong. I was so happy. I wasn't afraid to walk anywhere. I wasn't afraid of breaking down along the side of the road. I'd have a gun, maybe a .22 or a .38 in the car, only for my protection. I didn't really feel like I could find a person who I couldn't take care of as long as they would fight fair.

Newton was good. His finished product was almost unbelievable. It inspired me. He was nice to me, but all of the guys were nice. Harold was my friend, but he was not my boyfriend. He was the first person who ever took me out to dinner at a restaurant. That was a treat. He was that kind of guy. We had ox tails and chicken. It was a little restaurant called the Town and Country, and it was the fanciest black restaurant in Fort Pierce.

I would do at least two 24-by-36 paintings a day. It was hard work, straight through. An 18-by-24 would sell for $18.00, a 24-by-36 for $35.00. A 12-by-24 was $12.50. People commission me now, and the price depends on what they want me to do.

These landscapes are true Florida scenes, and a lot of these things I paint, you don't see anymore. Treasures are being destroyed. That's why I like painting landscapes. It's painting history.

I have peace of mind when I paint. I'm content. My mind pictures what I paint. I go to these places in my mind.

The thing about my diabetes, I have to eat properly, sleep properly, but I don't.

I want to paint a masterpiece, but I don't know what it would be. People say my trees, the poincianas, are what I do best, but I say whenever I can feel what I'm painting, like I'm there, those are the best.

It actually kind of breaks my heart to think about things that aren't here anymore. I look across the street from my house and see houses where I used to see trees. What I'm going to do, by the grace of God sometime soon, I'm going to paint that scene, but I'm going to take all those houses out of there and I'm going to bring back the trees.

I feel blessed. I don't say lucky, because luck comes from the devil.

There were years when some of the guys stopped painting, but then Gary Monroe, he wrote that book about us, and the Highwaymen came back. I call it the Florida art rush. That book turned the tide.

I've painted thousands of pictures. I just wish I knew where they all are so I can go and look at them sometime. But I'm glad they're out there, glad that someone still sees something in them.

MIKE PETERS

Cartoonist, creator of the *Mother Goose & Grimm* comic strip, interviewed in February 2009, when he was sixty-six, Orlando.

WE LOVE LIVING so close to Disney World. My wife and I sometimes go there for breakfast, at this little shop where they sell rolls and breakfast things. Then we sit at one of the tables right at the end of Main Street and watch all of the kids coming in. They're so excited. It's so wonderful to see their faces. They're exactly the way I was the first time I visited—and still am each time I go.

I wake up whistling. I'm happy. I'm not a depressed person. I don't wake up going, "Oh, God, no . . ." Well, I did during George Bush.

My mom [Charlotte Peters] had a TV show for about twenty-five years in St. Louis. She was an amazing lady, but also crazy. She's the reason I am the way I am. I would wake up and if she was not in a happy mood, I would start working on my cartoons and not be involved in whatever the tornado was that day.

My dad was a traveling salesman, very quiet, very sweet, but he was gone most of the time.

Growing up, I had a horrible stutter. I couldn't pronounce anything. My mom would get me in front of people and say: "This is the future president of the United States. This is my son Mike. Say hi Mike!" And I was like, "H-h-h-h-h-h-h-h-h-h . . ." It was so embarrassing. That's why I started cartooning. It was something I could do without speaking.

At school, people would laugh whenever I started saying something, and so I thought, "Well, at least I can make people laugh."

My mom sent me to an all-boy military Catholic high school. It was the kind of place that taught you to love people and then shoot them.

I was too much of a ham to withdraw from people. Every Friday, I would get on the intercom, for all the classes to hear, and then the student council president would ask me what was coming up that day. And I would say: "T-t-t-t-t-t-t-t-t . . ." and you would hear the laughing all through the school. I was kind of proud of this. I played it up a little, just for the laughs. So three weeks before I graduate, my mom gets called to the school, and they tell her: "All of the brothers agree. Mike is retarded." She comes home and says, "What the fuck have you been doing at that school?"

One time, Mort Walker told me that he thinks of the brain as a well, and whenever he gets a good idea, he thinks, "Is that the last good idea

I'm going to have?" That scared the hell out of me. But I've realized that the brain isn't a well. It's a river, a river that's always moving.

A buddy from college said he thought he could help me. He said, "Every time you speak, I'm going to tell you to speak lower." So, every time I spoke he'd say, "speak lower." This took my attention off the word and slowed down my brain, which was going beyond where my mouth was. It was taking the attention off my fear of saying the word. It changed my life.

The NRA has damaged our country as far as safety. Everybody needs to have a gun? Give me a break.

I didn't realize how much work a comic strip was. It's unrelenting. It never stops. There's no end. You have to do it every friggin' day. I haven't had a weekend off in twenty-five years.

Hypocrisy drives me up the wall.

When I was coming up with a strip, I thought I would do a dog. I've always related to the dog, even though there were like a thousand dogs out there, Snoopy and Marmaduke and all of them. But when you do a comic strip, you try to do something you're familiar with and can relate to. It's like being married to a nymphomaniac. It's really fun the first three weeks, and then you go, "What, again?"

I wanted a dog that would be looking and seeing things but actually acting like a dog, like drinking out of toilets and knocking over trash cans. One thing I thought of was Robinson Crusoe and this dog living on an island, but then I could only come up with like a thousand coconut jokes, and I could tell that wasn't going to work.

I get writer's block two or three times a day.

When you do this kind of job, especially when you do humor, you do it for yourself. I don't think about anybody who reads it. I think: "Is this funny to me? Will I be ashamed of this a month from now or will I be happy?"

I use humor as my weapon.

Whenever I go to St. Louis, I take two or three hours and visit Dogtown, the neighborhood where I grew up my first ten years. I went back last year and knocked on the door of my old house to ask if I could sit a while on the front porch. It's an odd thing, I know. The man who answered said they'd just bought the house and they were told that a cartoonist would come and ask just to sit, and to not be afraid.

I think I'm a better political cartoonist than I am a comic strip guy, but when I go into crowds, people know the comic strip. If I didn't enjoy the strip so much, I'd be, "Oh God, so I'm going to be known for this?" But I'm having a blast doing the strip.

Grimmy is my inner child. I'm the dog.

I get myself in trouble, and it's usually when I think something is funny—and if I think it's funny, I think surely everyone else will think it's funny, too.

As a political cartoonist, it was like Christmas every morning with George Bush. He was for sure the worst president of my lifetime, if not ever. Obama hasn't really made a mistake yet, but when he does, I'll blast him.

I don't have fears about the newspaper business. I just know it's changing. The papers that can stay around are going to do great. There's still work to do. There's just not as much money.

Before we moved to Orlando, we lived in Sarasota, and I would tell people that Sarasota is a great place to live if you can take losing your home twice a year for those two days you might have to load up and leave because of a storm. The other 363 days are fabulous.

I'll tell you exactly where I want my ashes spread after I die, at Disney World, right at the statue of Walt Disney holding Mickey Mouse's hand.

James Rosenquist

Pop Art pioneer,
interviewed in
June 2009, when
he was seventy-
five, Aripeka.
Rosenquist died
in March 2017.

IMAGES ARE EXPENDABLE. What's left over is your new idea. Images really only promote a spark of an idea.

I'm not a commercial artist. Commercial art, you do something for somebody for money. Painting, you do for yourself.

The light in Florida is so beautiful for an artist that, when you cry down here, your tears either turn to broken glass or diamonds.

Sometimes an image in my mind occurs and then, after a long time, titles, many titles, come about. Or a title appears and no images, and I go, "What the hell am I going to do about that?"

I didn't meet Andy Warhol or Roy Lichtenstein until 1964 and became friends of both those guys. They were very nice people. I'm also very good friends with Bob Rauschenberg and also knew Jasper Johns, but he was very acerbic, not too friendly.

I make dozens and dozens of sketches. I'll change sketches, change them and change them and change them, throughout maybe a year. Pin them on the wall. Keep looking at them. If they start to look pretty, maybe I'll start to paint them. It's a progression of working on sketches for a long, long time. If they look good this big, they might really look good 25 feet long. That's my method.

The hard question is ideas. I never paint anything unless I have an idea. Painting, I can do. Ideas are difficult.

My mother would say: "Well, you're always drawing. Maybe, you could make some money at it." So I answered an ad in the paper from a sign-painting company. I made $1.50 an hour painting Phillips 66 emblems on gas tanks and stuff around North Dakota, South Dakota, Iowa, Minnesota, and Wisconsin.

I was an only child. I had to entertain myself a lot.

In New York, my first job was painting Hebrew National salami signs on the Flatbush Extension in Brooklyn.

I painted signs on Times Square. I had to paint good enough to sell. That was the first criteria. Never mind the art part. My audition was an 8-foot-tall painting of Kirk Douglas's head for the movie *The Vikings*. I gave him beautiful blond hair, saliva on his lips, tears in his eyes. I got the job.

I started clipping images out of magazines that I thought were really peculiar, ridiculous, contradictory, and so forth, and I started making what's called Pop Art. One was the front of a Ford and two people whispering to each other in a field of Franco-American spaghetti.

Color and form are the same thing.

There are a lot of influences in Florida. The scenery has an effect on me. In New York City, I'll see a handsome woman, with a briefcase, wearing a business suit on Madison Avenue. Here, I'll see a girl and her little bathing suit walking through the palm fronds, and from that I've developed paintings with slices of women going into palm fronds. It's like they're morphing into something else.

I had my first show in February 1962 and sold out. In 1963, all the work I did went to the Museum of Modern Art. In 1964, I had another show—sold out. Painting prices were 350 to 1,100 bucks. You weren't getting rich, but I felt very lucky to paint any damn thing I felt like.

My only mistake, if there has been a mistake, is not judging professional people correctly. You think they're good, and they're terrible. That's a mistake.

Before being called a Pop artist, I was called a new realist. I was also called a Russian realist. In my first show in Paris in 1964, Edward Jaguer invited me to be a surrealist. He was the head of the surrealists, and El Lissitzky says, "No, he's a new Russian realist," and El Lissitzky socked this guy on the jaw and knocked him on the floor. I said: "Holy cow, this Paris is an amazing place. They hit you for an aesthetic reason!"

I have a lot of friends in Miami. There are a lot of superwealthy people there, and I usually stay with them. I have a room there anytime.

The '60s, the creativity part was try everything and anything, whatever came into one's mind. That's the feeling I had. I had nothing to lose and didn't know if I had anything to gain.

Andy Warhol, he had this thing called The Factory, which was a place covered in aluminum foil. He would attract the runaway people as they came out of the Lincoln Tunnel, crazies, real crazies. He used to tease people a lot. He'd make people angry. People would try to hurt him. I traveled around with him when we were both in the same gallery, the Stone Gallery in New York, and a couple of times people tried to push him into traffic. Someone tried to push him over a balcony one time. He made enemies. He put people on. But otherwise, he was a nice likable guy.

What you do is at night, you go out drinking at bars with Bob Rauschenberg until late, wake up with a hangover, start working at about eleven o'clock, work until seven or eight o'clock at night, rent a tuxedo, go to an art opening at a museum, drink again, wake up with another hangover, and keep doing that. I did that one time seven days a week for seven months in a row.

I went away for the day and came home in the afternoon and the place was gone—[Rosenquist's Aripeka studio was destroyed by fire in 2009]—the studio, the house, everything completely burned to dust. Machinery. Cars. Things are unrecognizable. It's melted and gray. There's no color. The trees are dead. There were only a few things that really hurt, the print archives and the 133-foot mural. That was rough, and I lost my mother's scrapbooks. Emotionally, it's vacancy. Big vacancy.

Now, I can see why some fellow artists aren't more well-known or not known at all. Seems to me they're not outgoing enough. I don't know how to put it. They're like turtles that stay in their shell and think that something is going to knock on their shell and take them out of there. That doesn't happen.

If a person can see an advantage, do it. Recognizing opportunity, that's what you have to do. There are opportunities galore, but, whoosh, they'll just go right by.

I've been living and working in Aripeka for thirty-two years. I like it here because there are no interruptions. In New York, there's nothing but interruptions.

I'd like all of my paintings back, so I can apply for a grant from the Ford Foundation to study my own life.

JERRY UELSMANN

Fine art photographer, professor, interviewed in June 2013, when he was seventy-nine, Gainesville.

Jerry Uelsmann

If I have an agenda, it's to amaze myself.

When the word processer first came out, was there a glut of fine literature? No way. So, we have the digital world now, but it's not like suddenly there's better art. It's the image that still counts.

My father was an independent grocer. After school, I'd help him in the store, which introduced me to hard work. In those days, people would call and say, "Can you bring by a dozen eggs?" and I was the kid who'd go to them pulling a wagon.

I have a friend who likes to date younger women because their stories are shorter. Old men like us, our stories are longer.

When I was a student at the Rochester Institute of Technology, one of my teachers was Minor White, who spoke of the camera as a metamorphosing machine. It opened all kinds of doors for me in terms what photography could be.

I got involved in photography in high school and in retrospect it helped me socially. I was overweight and shy, but if I photographed for the school newspaper I could give people pictures. It gave me a basis of interacting.

The day I figured out I could go into the darkroom and blend this tree into this building, that was a leap of faith. You strive for those kinds of moments.

I loved teaching, but more in the old days. We used to have this mimeograph machine, and you'd get one memo or maybe two a semester, telling you the things you had to do. Then they got a Xerox, and you'd get more memos. Then came email and even more memos. The part I liked was interacting with students.

When you see any nineteenth-century picture with clouds in it, that's a combination print because the material was so blue-sensitive that when you photographed for tones in the landscape, the sky would be white. You'd have to do a second exposure of the clouds and print that in later. So, for technical reasons and then later for aesthetic reasons, there's a whole history that's been kind of ignored of people manipulating photographs. Today, nearly all of the people manipulating photographs are using Photoshop. There might be a few still doing things like me in the darkroom, but I feel pretty much alone.

I don't like things that are too casually done. I'd rather see that this person has some technical skills to support the work they are creating.

There are places you're born and places you're supposed to be. I'm fortunate to have ended up in Gainesville.

I'm a big fan of the blues, and I used to be blasting blues away in the darkroom. Now, as I get older and some of my images are getting more complex, I can't blast the blues anymore because it makes it harder to concentrate and remember what's in each enlarger.

In Micanopy, we go to Pearl Country Store. It's in a gas station, but you can get your collard greens, your beans, catfish, and chicken, and in big heaping amounts.

The thing that I tell people—and students never like to hear this—is there's sort of a way in which quantity produces quality. You produce enough images and then you edit back to the ones that rise above.

The camera basically is a license to explore.

I got restless with trying to have the primary creative gesture being when I clicked the shot, then going in the darkroom, where there was more or less a prescribed ritual that you followed to make a print. The painter, the sculptor, the printmaker, they go into a studio to work on their images. There was a point at which I felt my darkroom became my studio and allowed me to explore visual options.

The University of Florida was way ahead of its time. It was one of the few places in the country that in the late 1950s, early 1960s had photography in the art department.

If you talk to writers, people in the arts or music, there's a point in which you get to the fringes of your own conscious understanding and things begin to happen. You have to sort of intuitively go with it.

The darkroom to this day—even though the computer world has emerged—has an alchemy aspect for me. It's magical watching an image come up in the developer. I've spent so much time in the darkroom that it's a part of me.

Our water supply. Protecting our springs. Those issues concern me.

The simple act of having a camera, not a cell phone, but a camera-camera, there's a kind of a heightened perceptual awareness that occurs. Like, I could walk from here to the highway in two minutes, but if I had a camera, that walk could take me two hours.

We have three dogs. All of them are white. The veterinarian calls them Alachua terriers because they're mixes.

Florida affects my work. It's a strange environment. The trees. The plants. The Spanish moss.

Early on, when I showed my photographs to photographers in New York, one of the comments I consistently got was, "This is very interesting, but this is not photography." That's because my images were not camera-conceived images. It was the decision of the camera that was primary then, and that's what I was sort of challenging. As long as I was in the context of fine art, there was support. It was the photography world that was not so sure. But after I had my one-person show at the Museum of Modern Art in 1967, all kinds of doors opened in terms of acceptance of what I was doing.

A lot of times, I'll go to bed and the next morning, I'll think, "You know, a different cloud in that image might look better," and I do it. Why? Because art cannot afford compromise. Why would you compromise on this thing that's coming out of you?

ATHLETES

JOEY CORNBLIT

First American-born jai alai star, interviewed in April 2017, when he was sixty-one, Plantation.

JOEY CORNBLIT

JAI ALAI WAS MY LIFE. It's all I did from the first day I started playing when I was twelve—every single day—and it's all I cared about.

My dad fought in the war for Israeli independence alongside Moshe Dayan. He was born in Poland but immigrated to Israel. He had a pretty rough young life, escaping from the Holocaust.

When I first started, everybody said I was too skinny, that I wasn't strong enough, and that I would never make it because I was an American. As a kid, hearing those things, that gave me an awful lot of motivation.

The game back in the day was basically catch and throw and catch and throw and volley back and forth until somebody missed. Well, I never had the patience for that. I wanted the game over and done with as quickly as possible, which is why I became extremely aggressive. The first opening, the first opportunity I got, I would go for the kill shot. I put in the work, practicing all these different kinds of kill shots, and I felt that I would win the point seven or eight times out of ten if I played aggressive and threw my shots.

It was pretty cool being the best at something, but it's not easy staying there. There are always kids coming up to take your spot. Every single day, I had a tremendous amount of pressure. When you get 10,000 people in the stands, and you know that about 9,500 of them bet on you, and you're the favorite every single game that you play, you feel the pressure.

People don't realize, the transition from being a professional athlete to all of a sudden not being one is very difficult. Unfortunately, we never made the money that athletes make today. I never had an endorsement contract. I didn't have a pension or anything, so I needed to get a job. You hear throughout your career: "Hey, when you're done, you'll come work for me. I'll take care of you." Well, those people aren't always around at the end.

Today, there are some great jai alai players, but they're playing in front of so few people. It's disheartening. They should be playing in front of 10,000 people a night like we used to.

Aside from being an American, I was the only Jewish jai alai player.

It was funny. Every condo owner in Miami Beach, they loved me to death. They could relate to me.

Growing up, you think all the old people say the same thing—how hard they had it—but you're a kid and you don't really understand. I'd complain about something, and my dad would go: "Never, never complain. You don't know what it is to go through hard times."

The other players weren't too fond of me at the beginning. I was an American in their sport. Deep down, I really believed I wasn't too welcome, but you know what? My philosophy was I was going to be the best player in the world, and I didn't care if they liked me or not. After I became pretty successful pretty quick, they respected me, and that's all I could ask for.

I always felt like Tampa was like a "Little Miami." It has that Latin flavor.

When I started playing professionally, I was still going to high school, so I went to school from seven o'clock in the morning to eleven o'clock, and then I'd get in my car and I'd drive down to the fronton. My mother would get up every morning at five thirty and cook me steak and eggs for breakfast because she knew I didn't have much time to eat after school.

Obviously, I had a lot of Jewish fans, but I had many Latin fans, too. The Latin community in south Florida really took to me. When I left Miami Jai Alai and went to Dania Jai Alai, the fans followed me. Some athletes complain about the fans, but I could never do that.

For two years, I was out of work, and then I met my angel—the CEO and founder of Ultimate Software, Scott Scherr. He was so excited to meet me. Him and his dad used to go to jai alai every single night to watch me play. I love that man so much. He changed my life. I've been working in marketing and sales for him for seven years. It's a great company, and I love working there.

What happened to jai alai? Several things. Back in the day, south Florida only had the Miami Dolphins, and now you've got three more sports teams competing for that entertainment dollar. Also, the Florida Lottery hurt jai alai and the rest of the parimutuel industry probably 20 to 30 percent. People think for a dollar or two they can become a multimillionaire. And the final dagger—casino gambling.

I play golf anywhere I can. I love it. I play for fun, but I don't just go out there to hack it around. I go out there to shoot a good score, to have a good round. I'm very competitive.

Of course, there were times when I'd come pretty close to getting hit by the ball, but you can't play jai alai scared. When I went out on the court, I knew I could get hurt, but I wasn't scared. You can't play scared at anything.

Phil Esposito

Former hockey player, cofounder of the Tampa Bay Lightning, interviewed in April 2014, when he was seventy-two, Tampa.

I loved playing hockey. It was orgasmic. Seriously, I felt such elation when the puck went in the net.

My forte was being mentally strong. The only thing I wasn't disciplined at was marriage. I was terrible. I was. I admit it. Nothing came before hockey—not my wife, not my kids, not my mom and dad. If it's wrong, it's wrong. I don't regret it. It's the way I am.

Everybody thought I was nuts trying to bring hockey to Florida. But to me, Florida is paradise, and why wouldn't you want to be in paradise? People told me it's football country. They love football. They love wrestling. They love boxing. They love car crashes. Well, we got all of that in hockey!

My daughter was tops, no doubt about it. It's coming up on three years from when she died. How do I deal with it? You just do. Was I the best father? Probably not. Could I have been better? Absolutely. We can all say that. I had to live my life, and she had to live hers. That's how I deal with it.

I liked John Kennedy. His brother Teddy, I didn't care for too much, and I knew him personally. I knew him a little too personally.

Last Christmas Eve, I'm shopping at the mall, and I see these two kids, thirteen, fourteen years old, and they're keying my car. They're maybe 40 or 50 feet away, and I yell. They start taking off, and I start running after them. Then I stopped myself. I said, "What the hell am I doing?" If I get them, and I touch them, I'm in trouble. Or, what happens if they pull a knife and stab me for Christ's sakes? I get too passionate sometimes and I've got to calm down.

I work out three days a week and walk three days a week. Then, I drink and eat and lay around as much as I want on the other day.

For me, I think we overprotect our kids way too much. The last straw for me, I was walking in my neighborhood and I see this kid, maybe three years old, a little girl, on a tricycle. She's got a helmet, elbow pads, and shin pads—on a tricycle! I said to the lady—I couldn't help myself—"Don't you think that's a little overkill?" Maybe I should have minded my own business, but when I see things like that, it just gets me going.

I'm one of these guys when I put my mind to something, I'm going to get it done. I'm going to keep on going until I've exhausted every avenue and then I'll cheat and lie a little to get it done. I guess I get that from my grandfather on my mother's side. When I was growing up, this son of a bitch would put dollar bills on a clothesline, and he'd pull it up and my brother and I would try to reach up and grab the money, and he'd pull it up a little higher. But I kept trying, boy. I fooled him one time. I put my brother on my shoulders, and we reached it.

I'm a television freak. I'm a big fan of the Discovery Channel and the History Channel.

I started working in a steel plant when I was fifteen. When I turned sixteen, I got my driver's license and drove trucks at the plant—the tires were taller than I was—and bulldozers. I did that every summer until I was thirty years old. People don't realize that we didn't make enough money playing hockey to survive, so in the summer we worked. The year I scored seventy-six goals I made like eighteen grand or something.

My daughter wasn't feeling well six weeks before she died. She needed an MRI, but she was living in Germany, and she said she had to wait nine weeks and drive an hour to get it. I said: "Are you kidding me? I'm sending you a ticket." She said, "What am I going to do with the kids?" Her husband was in The Hague coaching at the time, and the kids had hockey practice and she had to drive them all over, so she kept going. I was honestly three days from going over there and getting her myself when she died. She had an abdominal aneurysm and bled to death internally.

I never wanted to do anything but play hockey. I wasn't good in school. I didn't like school.

Think about all those lunatics, letting the pythons go in the Everglades. Who would do that? And now they got these big lizards down south, not too far from here, and they're eating everything.

You don't need a piece of paper with me. If I give you my word, I'm going to do it. It cost me my job in New York, by the way, when I was GM of the Rangers. They wanted me to trade this guy, and I wouldn't because I gave the guy my word that I wouldn't trade him, so they fired me.

I love going to Boca Grande. I can do without fishing, but I like laying out on the beach, my wife and I. I've been a lucky guy. I got married again, which I never thought I would, and she's a terrific woman. She actually works. She's the first woman I've been with who has a job.

To this day, if I could go out there and be on the ice right now, I'd be out there. I'd be out there in a freakin' heartbeat.

I like golf, although it isn't always relaxing. It depends how I do. Some days I play like Ray Floyd. Other days I play like Ray Charles.

CHRIS EVERT

Professional tennis
player, broadcaster,
interviewed in June
2011, when she
was fifty-nine, Boca
Raton.

I WAS IN KINDERGARTEN, and every day after school I would go to
my best friend's house and go swimming and have barbecues. I was
having a pretty fun life at that time, and then all of a sudden my dad
plucked me away and started bringing me over to Holiday Park. He
put me on a tennis court with a shopping cart full of tennis balls and
started hitting balls at me. I was like, "This is no fun." I wasn't happy
about it, but, you know, it worked out well.

There are a lot of worthy charities out there, but twenty years ago,
after I retired, I was trying to figure out one to support. I grew up in
Fort Lauderdale, so I knew drugs were a big problem in south Florida.
I didn't have any personal experiences or anything like that, but I knew
it was a problem. So, we started raising money for drug treatment

centers. After visiting the centers that we fund and talking to the moms and seeing the hope in their eyes and seeing them go from a drug addict on the street to a responsible mother, I knew we were doing the right thing.

The way I took losing was probably not really normal. I would probably be a therapist's dream. For a while, winning and losing was part of my identity and how I felt about myself, which, again, isn't the healthiest way to feel. It's not really a normal way to grow up knowing that every day, at the end of the day, you're either a winner or a loser and the whole world is writing about you.

When you are given a lot, you should give back. It's a responsibility. It's an obligation.

It's very difficult when you're famous at a young age and you get labeled that you are a certain way before you are developed as a person. You're confused. You haven't formed any sort of foundation as far as the person you are, because you're so young. And then the press calls you "Little Miss Ice Maiden" and "Cinderella on Sneakers." I was labeled as sort of being goody-goody and not having emotion. It puts you in a little bubble. And sometimes you have a tendency to act that out because you know that's what is expected of you.

The attention puts pressure on you. I was just a normal girl who liked boys and had dates and cussed every once in a while and, after twenty-one, liked to have a glass of wine once in a while. I was just normal.

Florida was the best state to grow up in as a kid. The ocean. Playing tennis all year. I'm glad I grew up in Florida.

It was great being coached by my dad. He never got mad at me once in my whole life after losing a match. He never yelled at me. He was tough, very tough, on all of us as far as putting in the hours and practicing. I practiced a lot. I didn't always enjoy practice, but I knew it was the only way to improve. I was hungry. I enjoyed winning.

The trademark of my game was the mental part and my concentration. I was pretty tunnel vision when I was out there. I didn't let anything affect me. I was known to be unemotional, the Ice Maiden, but I was unemotional on the court because that worked for me. Off the court, it was a lot different.

There's a Publix near where I live, and I can go in there and go about my business. I don't have the kind of celebrity where people rush up to me and get breathless.

The top tennis players today, I'm older than their parents.

There was no question whatsoever that I would play tennis. I was born into a tennis family.

Every November, we put on the Pro-Celebrity Tennis Classic to raise money for our charities. We invite celebrities and professional players, and we all play together. We're microphoned on the court, so it's pretty entertaining. The event takes all year to produce, but we make around $500,000 or $600,000, and the State of Florida matches it. Every year, the state comes through. As far as this year, we won't know. When the economy was healthy, there was never any question.

Nowadays tennis players have entourages. The women, I don't think, are as close as they were in my day. Billie Jean King, Martina Navratilova, Virginia Wade, and Rosie Casals, we were all close. We practiced together, had dinner and socialized together.

I talk about all of these things I do, but the number-one priority is still to be a full-time mom. All of my work, like the Chris Evert Tennis Academy, the Chris Evert Children's Hospital, the Pro-Celebrity Tennis Classic, everything is here in my hometown. So I can work on that during the day and then when three o'clock rolls around, I'm 100 percent here for my kids. I just want to continue to be a hands-on mom until they're out of the house.

You have to realize that at the end of the day you are just like everybody else, but it's kind of hard when everybody is telling you how great you are and you're the number-one tennis player in the world.

What helped me was just having such a normal family life. When I went home after Wimbledon and I was seventeen years old, I still had to do my chores, empty the dishwasher and fold the clothes and make my bed. I was not treated any differently than any of my other siblings, so I think that really helped me keep things in perspective.

I'm not an extremist, like I can never see myself running a marathon. I'll jog three or four miles and then if I feel a twinge in my knee I'll stop.

I go in and out of happiness. Isn't that true with most people? I'm dealing with children and high school and getting older. I would say I'm at peace.

My whole life, I've nearly always been married. This last year and a half, I've been by myself as far as not having a partner, and I think the result of that has been a lot of growth and a lot of just dealing with myself and dealing with my issues and coming to peace with it. Let's put it this way. I could be happier, but I could be unhappier, too.

ARTIS GILMORE

Former basketball player, special assistant to the president of Jacksonville University, interviewed in March 2016, when he was sixty-six, Jacksonville.

PICKING COTTON, that was just an incredible process. You'd get up early in the morning, like around three o'clock, and you would go out and stand on the corner and the trucks would come by and take you out to the fields. Most of the time, it was $2.50 for every 100 pounds. Most families could pick 300 or 400 pounds a day. I could get close to

100 pounds a day myself. I was about twelve, thirteen, fourteen years old, and I was already pretty tall, so to get low enough to pick the cotton, I had to get down on my knees.

Growing up in Chipley, the schools were segregated. The movie theaters were segregated. The public bathrooms, the toilets—you had men's and women's toilets and colored toilets. There were water fountains we were not allowed to drink from. You didn't look a white man in the eye.

The crowd cheering, that's helpful and very nice, but it's really about the competition between you and your opponent. That's the focus. To compete at the highest level, you have to beat the guy in front of you.

My dad was about five eight. My mother was six two.

Money was an issue for my family, absolutely. Just the basic things, we didn't have. No electricity, for example. We used kerosene lamps. There were a number of days I remember getting up to go to school and there was no food in the house.

When I talk to student athletes, I stress the importance of getting an education.

Having the proper equipment, that was a problem, like having shoes to play basketball in. My mother and father had very little money, and even a pair of sneakers that probably cost a dollar and half, that wasn't in the budget. In high school, I played in a pair of shoes that had a rubber strip across the top and flat bottoms. The sides would start ripping, and you'd put some cardboard in there, and you tried to play.

I'm not bitter whatsoever. Being bitter is not healthy.

My coach at Jacksonville University, Joe Williams, he had a tremendous influence on me. During my early years, my relationships with white people were none, just none—the environment I lived in was totally black. And then I went to Jacksonville and tried to make this transition, and I found it very difficult. But after meeting Joe, he was so personable and he treated me so special. He opened me up and helped me develop my personality.

Intimidation is really just about being better.

I played eighteen years of pro ball. Physically, I had a little bit of a knee surgery and a broken orbital bone—I caught an elbow in the eye—but for the most part I held up pretty well.

I wanted to play football in high school, but you needed financial support for that. The school was not able to finance uniforms and shoes, so you had to buy those. That wasn't an option for me.

Dan Issel. Bob Lanier. Wes Unseld. Kareem Abdul-Jabbar. Bill Walton when he was healthy. They were all a challenge to play against.

My father was not able to communicate with his kids and share with us his experiences as a youth growing up, but I try even now to share with my kids to make sure they understand the history of what I experienced.

Every day, I try to enjoy my life. I have my health. Every day when I go to work, I have a smile on my face. Every day.

I returned to Jacksonville after basketball because of the success I had here as a collegiate athlete. There were business opportunities, as well, but I love Jacksonville. It's a great place to live and raise a family. So much has changed here, and the city continues to grow.

I'd love to see racism be eliminated from the face of the earth, but, realistically, that's not going to happen.

My heart is here at Jacksonville University.

I'm seven two, and that can be difficult. The airlines, I guess because of cutbacks, the space on the planes is so limited. The leg space is practically zero. Even now if you go to a sporting event, the space is limited. As far as clothes, it has always been challenging. There's no store really where I can walk in and buy something that fits. I wear size 18 shoes. There's a place in Atlanta, though—it's called Friedman's Shoes—for all the guys with big feet. I'll go there and buy shoes.

I don't get into politics—other than voting.

When I played, I was considered media-shy. I guess I was shy, but, really, I was just uncomfortable.

Shaquille O'Neal

Former NBA basketball player, broadcaster, entertainer, interviewed in January 2013, when he was forty-one, Orlando.

Four years ago, I went to Walter Reed hospital to see some of the troops. I saw a guy with both of his legs cut off, and he had the biggest smile on his face. He told me in front of everybody, he said, "Hey, I'm waiting for my legs to come back"—he was waiting on some of those robotic legs—"and then I want to go back to Iraq." I was like, "damn." From that day on, I decided I'm not complaining about nothing.

I don't worry about my privacy. I don't promote myself as being perfect. I think it's the people who promote themselves as being perfect who have to worry about privacy.

A friend of mine was running for sheriff in Lake County, Sandy Carpenter. He unfortunately lost. If he had won, I was going to apply for the undersheriff's job.

I've always wanted to own a law firm, so I'm thinking about going to law school. Not to be a lawyer, but just to own a law firm so when I hire other lawyers I can have educated conversations with them and not just be the guy who owns the building.

I like the mayor of Orlando. Buddy Dyer. I like what he's doing. Every time I leave for a couple of weeks or months, there's something new going up. We have one of the best arenas in the country, and the nightlife is the best it has been in twenty years.

I've always tried to make people like me for me and not for my size. I was always bigger and more intimidating than everybody, but my sense of humor enabled people to see that I'm a regular person and a cool guy.

One time, my father took me to a basketball game. He really couldn't afford it. He had to scrounge to get some change to take me to the game. When I played, I remembered that. All these fathers and mothers and families that are struggling, but they take care of their kids and want to give them some entertainment for the night. It's my job to give them a great show. So, you play in pain. I never wanted anybody to waste their money when they came to see me play. If I could walk, I could play.

I have six kids. They changed my life. I had to cut down on 90 percent of the nightlife and watch what I did. I'm more like a play friend to my kids. I let their mother do all the yelling and screaming. My job is just to teach them, comfort them, and show them the way.

As a leader, you have to answer this question: Are you focused on the task or are you focused on the relationship? With the people who work for me now, I focus on the relationship. But on my athletic side, I was always focused on the task—and when you focus on the task, your relationships can be so-so. People always thought me and Kobe Bryant had a problem. But as a leader, I was only focused on the task of winning a championship. They said me and Kobe didn't have a good relationship, but our relationship was good enough to win three championships. That's what mattered.

I'm a law-abiding citizen. I try to do things right, but if I do happen to make a mistake, I don't want people to judge me. Especially the kids, I want them to learn from my mistake.

When I want to get wild and crazy, I take a three-hour drive down the turnpike to Miami. Hang out for a couple of days. Get in the ocean. Go to the beach. I like the Fontainebleau in Miami Beach and hanging out at Prime One Twelve and Prime Italian.

If I didn't play basketball, I would have probably joined the military or gone into law enforcement.

When I left LSU early, I told my parents I would go back and get my bachelor's. I went back and got that degree, and a master's, but then I thought: "Let me challenge myself. We don't have any doctors in the family. Let me see if I can do it." It was the most challenging six years of my life, but I accomplished it. I've got a doctorate in education.

If it wasn't for my father's discipline, I wouldn't be able to do what I'm doing now. If it wasn't for my mother's calmness and sense of humor, I wouldn't be able to be as humble as I am now. They made me who I am.

I'm a seven-foot guy. People are going to take pictures. People are going to sell the pictures to get money. People are going to print certain articles to get clicks. It's life. Things I can't control, I don't worry about.

Most of us get in trouble when we try to portray ourselves as something we're not.

I don't want to be remembered for being one of the best basketball players. I don't want to be remembered for being rich. I want to be remembered as someone who was nice and humble and tried to help others.

Juan "Chi Chi" Rodriguez

Professional golfer, founder of Clearwater's Chi Chi Rodriguez Academy, interviewed in November 2011, when he was seventy-five, Palm City.

In Puerto Rico, I started working in the sugarcane fields when I was seven years old. Now they call these kids slaves, but my daddy wanted a man and he got a man.

Meeting Mother Teresa was a great chapter of my life because I met somebody I would die for. A good friend is somebody who would stand between you and the bullet, and I would stand in front of a bullet for Mother Teresa. I spent forty-five minutes with her, and those have been the best forty-five minutes of my life.

We started the academy from a detention center. We took a kid out of the jail, really. Now, we help close to a thousand kids a year.

A lot of people believe that they are not lucky. They believe in luck. I believe that when they call you lucky, that's when you know you're good, because luck is only acquired through hard work and practice.

You might live in luxury. You might live a rich, rich life, but is it really rich? My dad was a laborer. He was the strongest man I ever knew because he worked sixteen hours every day digging ditches and milking cows and you name it. When he came home, his kids used to wash his feet and massage them and dry them off and cut his toenails. That's really rich.

We had a golf course about 200 yards from my house, and they had sand greens, and I used to sneak in and play there. The first hole I ever played, I played with a half ball. In the old days, you couldn't find any golf balls to play with, so I played with a half ball, and I made an 18 on the hole. I also used to make golf balls out of tin cans. I used to put a lead ball in the tin can, and I would hammer the can around the lead ball. Out of guava limbs, I'd make my own golf club.

I created my own choreography on the course, the dancing, the sword fighting. I figured I was a bullfighter. There's the bull. I stab the bull. I draw blood, and I put the club back in scabbard. In real life, I wouldn't hurt a fly.

Most of the fans liked me because I weighed 117 pounds and I could hit the ball over 300 yards. They couldn't believe what they were seeing.

I had tremendous club speed. When they first invented that machine that they have now that measures club speed, they put it in Pebble Beach to test it on some pros. Tom Weiskopf went on it, and he swung the gulf club 132 mph. Then they put me on it, and the machine didn't register. So they said, "No, something's wrong," so I said to put Weiskopf back on. They put him back on, and he was 132 mph, and they put me on again, and it couldn't register my club velocity. Lee Trevino said I was so fast I could steal your radio and leave you the music.

When I was a caddy—and this is a true story from the old days—if you lost a ball, they used to make you bend down on your hands and knees and look for it. I tell you, if you couldn't find the ball, they would kick you in the butt and then they'd fire you. I never lost a ball because I didn't want to get kicked in the butt. Nowadays, I pay my caddy $150,000 in one year, and I hit the ball and he says, "Where did it go?"

They say it was harder to win in my era, when Nicklaus and Palmer were playing, but I tell you what. They won more trophies than me, but I won the fans' heart. That to me is as big as anything.

In my day, all we wanted to do was have our name show up in the newspaper, so we could become the head pro at a golf course. Golf was sport then. Golf is now a business. Now, they play to make the money to buy the course.

Rush Limbaugh, they ought to send him to Siberia, and Sean Hannity, they ought to send him to Siberia, too.

I don't get pleasure from playing golf anymore, because I don't play like I used to. I'm a perfectionist. I've been a perfectionist all my life, and when I try to hit a draw, say with a five iron, and the ball starts to draw and then all of a sudden it flattens out, I don't care for that. I don't think I can break 77 anymore. People say, "Oh, you should enjoy it." No. I don't enjoy failure.

I was a very heavy smoker, and that's what gave me the heart attack. A doctor friend of mine, he wanted me to sue the cigarette company, which used to give me three cartons of cigarettes every week when I was on tour, but I knew the cigarettes were harmful. Why should I sue them?

When I first started giving golf lessons, I gave six in one day and I made eighteen dollars. I used to charge three dollars for a half hour. I brought the eighteen dollars to my father, and he was really upset. He thought I stole that money. I said, "No dad, I made it." He said: "How can you make that money in one day? I used to make that in a week." I think to the day he died, he was worried about me stealing that money.

I eat everything, but I really like rice and beans and pork chops.

Most of the pros live in Florida because of one reason: taxes. If I was a baseball player right now and I sign with the Yankees, I have to pay 55 percent taxes. In Texas or here, you get $100 million, you keep $100 million. So that's why all the golfers live here. They can give you all kinds of reasons, but that's why. No taxes.

I hit my brother with a punch, and I knocked the wind out of him when we were young kids. And that has bothered me all of my life because he was the smallest one. I talked to him about it, but I don't ask for forgiveness because I don't ask anybody but God for forgiveness. But my brother knows I feel bad about it.

I just want to be cremated, and I want them to throw my ashes here at the academy. I want them to take the little can that my ashes were in, bury it, and then put up a little plaque. I'm going to leave enough money to change the roses every week, a few roses on my tomb, and have the kids come over and say, "Chi Chi, he was our pal." That's all I want.

STEVE SPURRIER

Football player and coach, interviewed in August 2017, when he was seventy-two, Gainesville.

THE GOVERNOR OF SOUTH CAROLINA, Nikki Haley, I got to know her a little bit when I was coaching at the University of South Carolina. She was a very sharp lady and did an excellent job. When she got that Confederate flag removed from the capitol building there, I remember sending her a text, and I told her she did more for the state of South Carolina in one day than maybe anyone else had in the last one hundred years. Waving that Confederate flag, it just wasn't right.

My dad was a Presbyterian minister. He loved sports, loved baseball. He was a Little League coach, and, being very competitive, he'd always get the guys together before the season, have a team meeting, and ask how many of them believed in that saying, "It's not whether you win or lose, but how you play the game." Most all of them raised their hand, but I knew better. He'd tell them, if you're keeping score, you're supposed to win. Sometimes, some of the backup players, if it was a close game, they didn't get to play.

Heck, we really all try to recruit the best players, athletically and with the top personal traits and habits. You don't want troublemakers. If they have problems in high school, then it might be best not to recruit them, but, then again, people can change.

They put my name on the stadium here at Florida. That was the biggest honor I've ever received in my life, and I've been fortunate to receive a bunch of them.

I probably average working out four to five days a week at least, mostly the treadmill and bike. I've gotten to where I like the bike a little better because you burn more calories and get a good sweat. I like sweating.

Me and Bobby Bowden, we had a decent relationship, but when his guys bragged about hurting the quarterbacks and hurting people on the other team, I didn't think there was any place for that. He was the head coach, and he pretty much, in my opinion, allowed it.

I wish people would drive better. I don't know how you stop it, but collisions and car wrecks, they happen all the time.

On the field, everyone has to play the best they can at a full-speed level, and if they don't, you've got to remove them—no matter who they are.

My doctor said my spine is pretty ugly with arthritis, but my heart and lungs look real good, so that's good. The heart and lungs are the keys to longevity.

In 1987, I was the head coach at Duke, making $75,000 a year, and my last year, 2014, all of sudden I was making $4 million a year. So I go from $75,000 to $4 million, and the athletes are still getting the same scholarship they always got. That's not right. Let's give the athletes some money. The pot has gotten bigger and bigger. They deserve more than a scholarship.

I always tried to convince our guys that we're playing for memories. The most thrilling games for me are the ones that led to a championship, so all of us, the whole team, would have something to celebrate for the rest of our lives.

Football is really a pretty simple game. There's a good offensive play for every defense. And there's a good defense for every offensive play. So the key is how often can we call the right play against the right defense?

I've been blessed way beyond what any person deserves to be. I'm thankful every day.

Most of those cute or stupid things I said were in the off-season, during the spring and summer, when nothing was going on. We were winning, and the Gator fans were happy, and they wanted to hear something funny. But it's a fact of life if a coach wins a lot of games and has a big year, he's a little bit more talkative in the off-season. If he had a bad year, got his butt beat, he's pretty quiet.

When you're the head coach and the offensive coordinator, the quarterback coach, and the game planner, you can do any damn thing you want.

I tell people I was fortunate to play ten years in the NFL and be a backup quarterback for eight of the ten, so I didn't have to play much, so no concussions. I had a few little injuries here and there—I had four knee surgeries and a knee replacement in 2012—but nothing too bad.

The head coach is the guy who shows the players, first of all, that he cares about them.

I was big on motivational quotes.

It was obvious early here at Florida, when we started winning right away, there were a few referees that I don't think particularly wanted Florida to continue winning so much. So, every now and again, I'd have to yell and criticize the refs.

Governor Scott, I think he does a super job. I don't know what I'd tell him to do differently.

Football is a lot safer now than it used to be. They used to teach players to hit with their helmets and heads, and they don't teach that anymore. The new rules against targeting, hitting guys above the shoulder pads, is a really good rule.

If your team played pretty well and it just didn't work out and you didn't win the game, you can live with that one pretty well. But if somebody did something really stupid to lose a game, that hurts. I always blamed myself.

There's so much money involved in college sports today—to the coaches and for a successful program—that a little bit of sportsmanship may be lacking.

Coaching wasn't my entire life. It was my occupation.

Golf is still my hobby. I just don't play as well as I used to. I've got arthritis, arthritis in my fingers, but that's no excuse. I want to shoot my age. I haven't done that yet, but I've got a chance. When I get to be seventy-five or seventy-six, I ought to be able to shoot that.

If you know you've tried your best to be the best person you can be, then that's a successful person. That's all you can ask.

Doug Williams

NFL quarterback, Super Bowl XXII's most valuable player, head coach at Grambling State University, NFL executive, interviewed in December 2008, when he was fifty-three, Tampa.

WE DIDN'T HAVE RUNNING WATER at our house until I was fourteen years old. We drew water out back. We had an outhouse. Today, we'd be on food stamps, but back then we got government rations. Every month, you'd go in and pick up your boxes. I'm not ashamed of that. It helps me stay grounded.

Growing up, I was an athlete—baseball, basketball, football—but I never really dreamed of playing professionally. I just wanted to go to college, get a degree, and come back home and coach high school football.

When I was a kid, we didn't have role models. We just had people we wanted to be like. My older brother, Robert, was the guy I wanted to be like. He was fifteen years older than me. He played baseball at Grambling and got drafted in the late rounds by the Cleveland Indians in 1964. He was a pitcher, and he hurt his rotator cuff, and back then they didn't have all the modern-day surgery. Once you hurt your arm, you were done. He came back home and was a teacher and a coach. In the seventh or eighth grade, I was in his history class. He always made an example of me. If I didn't have my homework, I was the first one called up and popped upside the head.

I played to win. It wasn't about personal gain. It was about the team. I gave my body. That's probably why I walk the way I do today. Look, I've had five operations on my left knee and one on my right. I've had a separated shoulder and a broken jaw. I've had back surgery, a broken ankle, and a whole lot of headaches. Knock on wood, I can still walk. It's the price you pay to play the game.

In 1978, when I first came to the Bucs, there weren't many African Americans playing the quarterback position. It was hard probably for a lot of people to accept me. I got my share of mail over the years. I got a box once with a ripe watermelon inside and different expletives saying what I could do with it. I heard the boos. I heard a lot of things, but at the end of the day I never crawled into a shell and said I'm not coming out to play today. You have to be like a duck. You have to let it roll off your back.

Being confident in my abilities, I've always been one to say that pressure is something that an individual puts on himself. I refuse to let anyone else put pressure on me.

Some people dispute it, because they probably weren't there, but I was asked before the Super Bowl, "How long have you been a black quarterback?" I didn't take it as a stupid, stupid question because I felt like I knew what he was trying to say.

The day before the Super Bowl, I had a root canal. It was no big thing.

A lot of things came to mind after we won that game. There are a lot of things you'd like to say and a lot of people you'd like to tell where to get off, but I realized it wasn't worth it. I realized it's not about yesterday and it's not about tomorrow. It's about now.

Afterward, I thought about Martin Luther King when he talked about getting to the mountaintop. And in my profession, at that particular time, I was on the mountaintop. The rest of the stuff didn't bother me.

Both of my parents worked. Early in the morning, before school, I didn't see my mom and dad. They were long gone at work before we woke up.

My phone didn't blow up after the Super Bowl. Even today, being the only African American quarterback to ever win a Super Bowl MVP, to me it seems like it should mean something as far as advertising or being a pitch man for certain things. But at the end of the day, it doesn't.

Coaching is teaching. It's patience. You have to be able to suffer the headaches sometimes. If you don't like kids, don't do it.

If anybody tells you that they don't hear the fans, they're lying to you. You hear the fans. But as long as the fans are not attacking me personally or my family, I don't care what they say.

I always knew when I got a letter and there was no return address that it wasn't a good letter.

If you are going to move up in football as an African American, you have a better shot doing it in professional football rather than in college. I wish I could answer why. I think there's an answer out there. I think the athletic directors and the university presidents know, but they might not tell.

If you're not first, you're last, and that's how you have to look at it.

My sixteen-year-old son thinks he has the dumbest dad in the world. I tell him all the time that my dad used to be dumb, too, until I got older and realized that some of the things he told me had come to fruition.

WINKY WRIGHT

Two-time light middleweight boxing world champion, interviewed in August 2017, when he was forty-five, St. Petersburg.

BEING A BUSINESSMAN, hands down, is harder than being a boxer.

My best experiences in life have been doing stuff with my kids and my family. Don't get me wrong. I partied a lot, partied with the best people. That's cool, but the best times were with my family, going to Disney World with my kids, going skiing with my kids. That's the kind of stuff you remember.

Even as a kid, I wasn't scared of getting hit. I was so quick that I felt you couldn't hit me. For real. My biggest thing was learning how to box and gain more power so I could hurt people and knock them out. Once I did that, my boxing took off.

You're going to do things that you're going to fail at, but failure is just a way to make you work harder.

I could never be one of those parents who don't see their kids. How do you do that?

Talk is cheap. Like in basketball and football, yeah they can do all that talking, but they have other people to help them. In boxing, it's just me and you, and I love that. Man against man. You think you're better than me? Let's do it.

My mom was like fifteen when she had me, so I lived with my grandparents. My mom was always there, but I lived with my grandparents, so my grandmother, my grandfather, they raised me. They helped me to appreciate family. My grandmother made sure, whatever I needed, I got. She was the best.

I'm a big kid. I love to play. I love to joke around. I love to have fun.

My grandparents moved me from D.C. to St. Pete when I was fifteen going on sixteen. At first, I didn't want to be here—you have to remember that I was moving from a big city—now I feel blessed to be here. Within a year, St. Pete felt like home.

When I want to relax, I play golf. I play golf almost every other day. When I'm frustrated, I just want to get out on the golf course and get with some friends and laugh and joke. Take my mind off business.

Being a great person inside is just as great as being a great boxer. You've got to treat people with respect, no matter who they are. It doesn't matter if you're a billionaire or if you have no money. Treat me with respect and I'll treat you with respect.

When I was fighting, my big-money time was right before the crash. I lost money, but I also saved money, so I'm good. I would love to be a lot better, but it is what it is. I'm happy, healthy, and I got my kids.

The weird thing is I never thought about what I was going to do. When I started boxing, I was in high school and never thought about becoming a professional boxer. Even when I was at the top of amateur boxing. I was like I'm going to finish high school and find work somewhere. But when I was eighteen, a promoter came to me and said, "Do you want to turn pro?" I'm like, "You're going to pay me to fight?" Hell yeah!

My business now, I help adults with disabilities. I help them live on their own. The state wants to put them in group homes, but some of them don't function well in group homes, so we try to get them to live in a house with another client who has the same kind of disability. I like the business because you're helping these people, but it's hard. The problem is the state underpays the providers who provide this service. It's crazy because there are a lot of people with disabilities. I have clients right now who need twenty-four-hour care, but the state will only pay for eight hours. Who's going to watch them for the other sixteen hours?

Sometimes, you get drunk people who want to fight you. I don't play like that. I get paid to fight. I get paid to throw punches. I don't want to have to hit nobody with my bare knuckles. You know what I'm saying? That's going to be a problem.

It started getting hard to get people to fight me. I had to go to Europe to get fights, and then, when I started beating people up in Europe, it was hard to get fights there.

My grandmother gave me the Winky nickname. I was probably a year old, I guess, and I used to wink at people.

You may not be right when the police pull you over. You might not be wrong. But don't antagonize the police to pull out a gun. Don't give him a reason to shoot you. Get the ticket and argue about it later when you're in a safe environment. You can argue all you want. But if you're dead there's no argument.

My health is good, but certain fighters, their speech slows down, their mobility slows down, but that's part of the game. We know that going in.

I grew up fighting. I liked to fight. I was always so small, but I just liked to fight.

The world is changing. There are a lot of people who don't want that change to happen, people who want to keep a certain demographic of people down.

When you're boxing, you're amped up, hyped up. You've got the adrenaline flowing, so you really don't feel it when you get hit—until later. That next day, that's when you feel the pain.

I don't cook. I don't know how to cook. I never learned. I always had a woman, so she cooked for me. I just learned how to wash clothes.

Don Zimmer

Baseball player, coach, and manager, interviewed in February 2010, when he was seventy-nine, Seminole. Zimmer died in June 2014.

THE MOST IMPORTANT THING is to have a good wife. You're gone half the time, and the wife is home with the kids. It's a tough life. Now they have nannies. We couldn't afford nannies when I played.

Starting out, I made $140 a month, but I thought I was a millionaire. Getting paid to play baseball? That was something special.

I never squawked about my salary. I would say that's part of why I'm still in the game after sixty-two years.

You can't win if you don't have good players. If you have good players, you're a pretty good manager.

I got hit in the head in 1953 playing in the minor leagues. I had a skull fracture and was in the hospital thirty-one days. He was a big, redheaded pitcher. He wasn't throwing at me. He was just wild. We get a Christmas card from his family every year.

In 1956, I'm up with the Brooklyn Dodgers, game of the week, Saturday afternoon, and I get hit, and it shatters my cheekbone. And I've got almost like a detached retina. Al Campanis always said that he thought that I would have been one hell of a player if not for getting hit.

I'm the reason for helmets. When I was in the hospital, they made it compulsory in the National League to wear helmets. It took them about a year to make it compulsory in the American League.

Chicago, 1989, I'm managing the Cubs. Jim Frey was my GM. We're ready to leave spring training, and he says to me, "Do you think we could win eighty-one games this year?" I said, "Jim, if we win eighty-one games, we'll dance down Michigan Avenue together." Well, we win ninety-three and the division. If I wanted a double steal, they executed it. If I wanted a bunt, they laid it down. If I wanted a squeeze play, they laid down the squeeze. The newspapers were writing: "Zimmer's a genius! Zimmer's a genius!" The next year, I'm the dumbest guy in the world. That's the way baseball is.

Boston was a town I loved, but it can be a tough town. I got booed there a lot. We were winning ninety-one, ninety-three, ninety-seven, ninety-nine games, but never a championship, and I was the cause. People would come down from the upper deck hollering: "Zimmer, you're a bum! You can't manage!" You have to take it. If you fight back, you have a war on your hands.

You know who I'd like to talk to? I wish I knew him well enough that I could contact him—Tiger Woods. I would love to sit down and talk to him for half an hour, just about what you and I are talking about.

Jackie Robinson treated me great. I wasn't a great player, but I think what he respected about me is if I had to go through a wall to catch the ball or if I had to dive for a ball, I would. That's the way I played, and he respected that. We became very good friends. Jackie would call me for a golf game. That was a thrill, Jackie Robinson asking Don Zimmer to play golf with him.

Traveling in baseball, either you love it or you don't love it. If you don't love it, you're in the wrong business.

Branch Rickey had to be a brilliant man to pick the one man in the world to become the first black major leaguer. Branch Rickey never cursed, never used a bad word. But they say when he called Jackie from

Montreal, the AAA club, when he called him to Brooklyn, he told him, "Sit down, you God-damn n———." Just nasty things. He wanted to see how Jackie reacted. That's what Jackie was going to hear out in the world—and he passed the test. Jackie was a tough son of a gun.

When I go to different events where I have to talk, I always start by saying, "What's a career .235 hitter doing up here on the dais?"

I don't say much about this, but I'm sitting there in the dugout, next to Billy Martin, and there was a rule at that time that, so many inches up, that's as far as the pine tar can go. George Brett comes up with a bat, and I seen black all the way up to the label. And he hits that home run, and I said to Billy, "I guarantee you that bat is illegal by the rules," and Billy started out. I can still see it, George Brett charging that umpire. I'm not proud of it, but it was a rule.

For twenty-five years, George Steinbrenner was my friend, a good friend, but we haven't spoken since I quit the Yankees. I don't regret leaving, but I regret the way it worked out with George.

I like to go fishing. I'm a city fisherman. I have to go with somebody who knows what they're doing. I break the line, they have to help me fix it.

Buzzie Bavasi, when I got hit in the head, said, "Go to Florida and recuperate," and he gave me money to come down here. We never left. It's home.

I've been very fortunate that I've never had to look for a job. Somebody always offered me a job.

One day, somebody was doing a story and was talking to Pee Wee Reese and said, "Boy, that Zimmer has a lot of guts—hit in the head once, broken cheekbone." So Pee Wee says, "I don't know if he has a lot of guts or if he's just dumb."

The thing with Pedro Martinez, that came from a long period. His act to me was tired. He was a great pitcher, but I've seen this guy do things over in their dugout, making gestures at us. And throwing at guys. There were just so many things that irritated me. When the brawl happened, I was the last guy in the dugout. I'm just sitting there—too old to fight. I said I can't sit here. So, I started out, and I'm looking around for Martinez. Truthfully, what I wanted to do was go after him with my head in his chest, and I figured I could knock him down. As it is, he got criticized for throwing an old man on the ground, but he didn't do nothing wrong. He was just protecting himself. The next day, they wanted me to go on television, and our PR guy, he didn't want me to go on because he thought I was going to say things that I shouldn't say. Hell, I knew what to say. I said I was sorry that I did what I did.

I knew nothing else but baseball, and I didn't have to know nothing else. Baseball was my life and, after sixty-two years, I'm still here.

4

EDUCATORS

RAY ARSENAULT

Historian, writer, interviewed in January 2017, when he was seventy, St. Petersburg.

WE LIVED IN PENSACOLA IN 1957, just after the Montgomery bus boycotts, and when my grandmother would take me into town she'd always insist that we sit in the back of the bus. I can remember all the whites in the front, looking at us. Obviously, I was young—about eight or nine—and I really didn't fully comprehend what was going on. Later, I was very proud of my grandmother for doing that.

The fact that Tallahassee is so far away means that Florida's political center is not anywhere near the center of the state. There is no center, really. It's centrifugal, so I think Gene Patterson's idea to buy *Florida Trend* and make it a statewide voice was really right. He was trying to get over the parochialism that we've often associated with parts of Florida.

Historians, we say we're slow journalists. We're journalists who can't deal with deadlines.

Florida has a very heavy frontier heritage. It was underpopulated for so long. It didn't have much in the way of legal culture. Almost everybody was from somewhere else. Even today, only about 35 percent of Floridians were born here. The average state is 64 percent. So, Florida has become a place to reinvent yourself, kind of a last chance if you've failed somewhere else. Florida attracts people who take risks, which, I think, widens the state's spectrum of potential behavior.

I just shudder to think what the cultural life of Florida would be like without the Florida Humanities Council.

My father was in the Navy when I was a little kid. He was a chief petty officer, and then he became an officer the last ten years of his career and we were constantly moving. I went to twelve different schools before I graduated from high school. It was kind of a crazy quilt. I think one year I went to three or four different schools.

Florida's not really a red state. It's a blue state—but it comes out a red state because of gerrymandering.

When I need a mental health break, I'll go to Fort De Soto Park and walk on the beach.

From the age of eleven, I knew what I wanted to be. If I wasn't going to be in the NBA, then I wanted to be a historian.

I love the Highwaymen painters. It's such a great Florida story, these sort of self-trained artists, selling these paintings out on the road for five or ten dollars. Most of those paintings are worth a couple thousand dollars now.

Trump, I have to say, I've never experienced anything like this. I feel like I survived Nixon and Reagan. I survived George Bush, thinking that was the low point of the American presidency, but I was so wrong. Trump, who knows where this is going? It just seems like every day you wake up and there's another reason to be clinically depressed.

I've often said to my students, just to get them riled up, that we have to figure out a way to get seven, eight, nine million Floridians to leave because the ecosystem just can't bear all these people.

You're only as good as your legal-justice system. If you use the legal-justice system to be the enforcer of Jim Crow and inequality, then bad, bad things are going to happen. We need good judges and good policemen.

I've devoted almost my whole career to race relations and civil rights.

Many of the students that I've had over the years have gone on to be teachers. I think half the history teachers in Pinellas County were my former students. I'm very proud of that.

I'm split. I'm not sure whether I want to be buried in Cape Cod or here. I don't like to think about it, but I'm genuinely conflicted. I still feel like a New Englander—out of place in the South—and yet most of my life has been heavily influenced by Florida. I love Florida, I really do. Florida's a fascinating place, a place you can root for because it has so much potential. There's all this wacky, weird stuff, but there are also people here who really care. We have some of the best environmentalists in the country, for example, who really see how endangered the nature of Florida is and how fragile the ecosystem is. We must not kill the goose that laid the golden egg.

Sunday mornings, I play tennis on the old clay courts at Bartlett Park. That's where Chrissie Evert won her first state juniors tournament. Arthur Ashe played there in 1969. I was a good basketball player, but I'm not a very good tennis player, but I love playing tennis. It's a game you can play your whole life.

I think the gun situation is probably the most troubling thing right now. This sort of gun-nut culture, with Mrs. Marion Hammer, it's just outrageous. Now, they're talking about allowing guns on campus. The day that someone brings a gun into my classroom is the day that I retire. It's just so frightening and ridiculous.

I've had type 2 diabetes for almost twenty years. I've lost a bit of weight, but I need to lose another thirty pounds. I do swim a lot, play tennis, and go to the gym almost every day, but I love to eat—bread, ice cream, huge hunks of meat.

I feel so privileged and fortunate first of all to be a university teacher. It's just the greatest job in the world. It keeps you young. I love the kids. It's never boring. History is the only thing that never runs out. You wake up, there's twenty-four more hours of history to deal with.

The *Freedom Riders* book changed my life. It succeeded beyond anything I ever could have imagined. I worked eight or nine years on it. The book kind of rediscovered the Freedom Riders, and it was so satisfying because they were all but forgotten. Historians didn't put much stock in the Freedom Rides as a milestone, but I think I convinced everybody that the rides were a huge turning point in terms of the beginning of the '60s and direct action and ordinary people doing extraordinary things.

I loved geography and maps from the time I was a little kid. I used to memorize the almanac. One of the things I did was memorize all the populations of all the cities in the United States over 100,000, according to the 1950 census. I knew them all. Then, of course, the 1960 census came out and I nearly had a nervous breakdown.

John Lewis has become a close friend, along with many of the other Freedom Riders. We were on *Oprah* together and went on tours through the Deep South. I just feel so lucky to have known them.

JUDITH A. BENSE

President emeritus of the University of West Florida, anthropology and archaeology professor and researcher, interviewed in April 2017, when she was seventy-three, Pensacola.

I SPEND FAR TOO MUCH MONEY at Starbucks, but I can't help it. I need my lattes.

We discovered Don Tristan de Luna's shipwrecks from 1559 in 8–10 feet of water in Pensacola Bay. People are fascinated by it, and they're really curious. That's what archaeology can give to the public.

Hard work—and being a finisher—that's what I learned growing up on a dairy farm.

People love it when they see you bring things out of the earth.

In the Panhandle, we are the forgotten part of Florida, and sometimes that's a blessing and sometimes that's a curse. We're in a different time zone, for heaven's sake. But I have used the neglect of northwest Florida as a rallying cry—and it worked.

I had to put my archaeology aside. I couldn't touch it. It was difficult. But I will tell you that being a university president is so distracting, the schedule is such a killer, that you don't have time to think. I tried going to an archaeology meeting early in my presidency, and it didn't work. It made me miss it more. I just had to put up a wall.

My brother Allan is a former Speaker of the Florida House. Our mother was driven, just a real hard-driving woman. And our father was a real nice guy. Everybody liked him. And so we have a combination. If you're going to do something, go for it in spades and don't give up. We got that from our mother. And yet we have a nice side, a friendly side, which gets people to like us and we like them. Maybe that's why we've both been so successful.

After I got into middle school, I began to get interested in archaeology through *National Geographic*, seeing pictures of mummies.

We did a lot of things at UWF. We built modern, fancy dorms. We built other buildings. We grew enrollment by 30 percent. The last thing I did was start football. And my God, football is just wonderful! It's Division II, so I'm not rattling any other state university programs yet. We went to the national championship game last year. Football brings spirit, pride, cohesion, community relations. We play in a stadium downtown. It's just a fantastic stadium right on Pensacola Bay. It has been magic. There's something special about football in our culture, and, as an anthropologist, I know it.

I made a very serious attempt to bring archaeology to the public, to have the public share in the discoveries and the techniques and the finds that we so much enjoy as professionals. I've also worked to bring northwest Florida into the mainstream of Florida archaeology. Our sites are just as old.

Outside of work, I've really been enjoying for the last fifteen to twenty years restoring our family farm back in Panama City with my brother Allan. We bought another farm in Chipley, and we have turned them into productive hay farms. We sell every blade of grass that we can produce. I like turning our farms into something that's productive, not just something that's pretty.

Pensacola is a very historic town. They were doing urban renewal in the early 1980s and improving utilities in the historic downtown area, and there were those who began to appeal to me as a professional archaeologist to help them because once you destroy an archaeological site and archaeological materials, you can't put Humpty Dumpty back together again. Everybody knew we were a colonial city, but they didn't think there was anything left. But when I began to look, my gosh, there was stuff all over downtown, just a foot deep.

We don't want to be Orlando, Miami, or Tampa. We want to be what we are. What we kind of fear is the overdevelopment that has happened in the peninsula of Florida.

These are complicated and large institutions, and you have to have someone where the buck stops—and that's the president. It's not for the faint of heart. It's not for the thin-skinned. And it's not for the ones looking for a high-paying, part-time job so they can go play golf.

We are a product of our past. The fact that we are an old historic city is part of the pride of Pensacola and northwest Florida.

I thought I was doing just fine at UWF in 2006, setting up the Florida Public Archaeology Network and maybe retiring in four or five years. But we had a president who left, and it left a vacuum. The reason they wanted me for the job, I think, was because they knew they could trust me. I wasn't in it for the money. I wasn't in it for the status. Opportunity only knocks once. A lot of things the university needed to do, I could do. One is visibility. I understood that we were the best-kept secret in higher education in Florida and we needed to grow and modernize. I said I'd do it for nine months. That turned into nine years.

There's nothing like our Florida seafood. I'll tell you that. We've got a fish house called Joe Patti's in Pensacola, and it has the freshest seafood in the world. I go there at least once a week and get some grouper or snapper. Sometimes I'll just have some mullet.

WILSON BRADSHAW

Former president of Florida Gulf Coast University, interviewed in July 2017, when he was seventy-one, Fort Myers.

MAN, WE WERE BUILDING BUILDINGS. We were adding programs. I likened my job at FGCU to building a jetliner while flying it at 30,000 feet.

When I talk to young people today, and I tell them about attending segregated schools when I was growing up in West Palm Beach, they kind of gasp, and I joke that they're gasping because they think I'm so young. But, really, my point is it really wasn't that long ago.

Growing up in West Palm Beach was fun. We had a strong, strong sense of community.

I've been asked since day one if FGCU would get a Division I football program. I answer the same way now as I did when I walked in the door ten years ago—it's a matter of when, not if.

Ninth grade was the first time I went to an integrated school. It was also the first time I went to summer school to make up credits because I had failed biology, which is interesting because now I have a PhD in psychobiology.

In higher education, resources are always a challenge.

At FGCU, every single employee has an opportunity to add value to something that can be felt. You don't get that opportunity very often in higher education.

There are people who are very astute at seeing what's between the lines. For me, what's between the lines is just space.

My wife and I, we built our retirement home in St. Augustine. We have relatives who moved there, and we visited them over the years and kind of liked the flow. It has a pace that we like. It has a good feel.

Mom and Dad separated probably when I was in the first grade.

What would cause me some concern about Florida right now is mass transit, rapid transit. We have a long state. We're the third-most populated state in the nation, and we are woefully inadequate in mass transportation. We need to address that.

Attending Palm Beach Junior College was a financial decision. I couldn't afford to attend other places. I wanted to, though. When I was growing up, the place that most African Americans aspired to go was either Morehouse in Atlanta or FAMU. At FGCU, we've held tuition and fees flat for now going on five years, so, with the slow rise in wages, FGCU is more affordable today than it was five years ago. I know how important it is to have a high-quality, affordable education available. I benefited from it.

My wife and I took up fishing several years ago, and she has already caught a fish that she had mounted. I've not caught anything yet that I can mount.

I never had air-conditioning growing up.

The first full-time administrative job I had was vice president and dean for graduate studies and research at Georgia Southern University. In the faculty, we called taking a job like that drifting to the dark side. But I had just come to the point where I had to decide if I wanted to get involved in developing policy or spend the rest of my career critiquing policy.

I was the first to graduate from college in my family.

My grandson lives in Atlanta, and I want to encourage my sons to have more children. One grandchild is not enough.

When I got here, I remember awarding the ten-thousandth baccalaureate degree. This past commencement, I awarded the twenty-five-thousandth baccalaureate degree. My legacy—and I really feel strongly about this—is going to be written by those graduates who go out and improve themselves, their families, their communities, and the world. So, give me twenty years and let me see what my little darlings have done.

I'm not really politically savvy.

My mom worked at the post office. She was initially a postal clerk. She also worked at the post office window, and she was the first African American to do that in West Palm Beach.

The first time my wife and I drove on FGCU's campus—and we drove on campus before I applied to be president—I could see from the main entrance all the way to the end of campus. I saw trees, but I could also see promise.

I thought I was going to go to medical school. That's why I was taking all those chemistry and biology courses. That's what I was educating myself for, but when I became a junior in college and I learned of this emerging science—it was called physiological psychology then and later psychobiology—it pulled me in.

For a while, I sorted mail and packages at the post office in West Palm Beach. We would get carloads of shipments from the train terminal. Every Christmas, we all dreaded the cheese train. You know that people ordered that Wisconsin cheese, and there would be boxes and boxes of it. It was just awful. The boxes were heavy, and there were so many of them. During Christmas, the packages would be up to the ceiling when you got to work, and they'd be up to the ceiling when you left.

Learning is interactive.

My mom wanted me to be a medical doctor. She was not shy about that. She wasn't sure about this PhD thing. But when I was inaugurated at Metropolitan State University in Minnesota for my first presidency, my mom was there—she has since passed—and as I was coming off the dais, she whispered in my ear that she thought I made the right decision. That was very gratifying for me.

Known as "Dr. Beach," beach rater, coastal ecologist, professor at Florida International University, interviewed in April 2017, when he was seventy, Miami.

MY SON'S MIDDLE NAME IS BEACH. And my daughter's name is Sandy.

Rip currents are the most dangerous things at the beach. Not sharks. Rip currents cause the most deaths, even more than hurricanes on average every year.

Science is discovery. It's a search for knowledge. There's a joy in discovering things and a joy of being with nature and trying to figure out how things operate.

I grew up in Charlotte, North Carolina, which has red clay everywhere. I was always getting really dirty, being an outdoors boy, and my mom was very distressed that my clothes were being ruined by the clay. So, she told my dad to get me a sandbox, and my dad did something really special. He got a whole truckload of sand. He built a frame around it, and I'd tell people I had the largest sandbox in Charlotte. Everybody came to my house to play in the sand. I discovered the joy of adding water to sand. The first time I saw a real beach was a year or so later, and I fell in love immediately.

Luck largely depends on preparing yourself to take advantage of opportunities.

After one of the lists came out, I got a call from Daytona Beach. The caller said: "Look, Dr. Leatherman. We see you're a very knowledgeable scientist, but we don't see Daytona Beach on your list, the world's most famous beach! Daytona Beach is not on your top ten? What's wrong? Have you been to Daytona Beach?" I said, "Sure, I've been to Daytona Beach, and I've even driven on the beach"—and I told them that's where the problem is. I take off for that. To me, you shouldn't be driving on beaches.

Sea-level rise. I call it the dipstick of climate change.

My favorite show as a child was *Sea Hunt*, starring Lloyd Bridges. I would hurry home from school to watch it when it came on at 4:00 p.m. I just loved that show. It taught me a whole lot about the ocean, the power of the ocean, the power of hurricanes.

This past year, I ranked Siesta Beach in Sarasota as the number-one beach. Within the first couple of days, Siesta Beach got almost six hundred million media hits.

They call Florida the Sunshine State. I think it ought to be called the Beach State.

People say: "Oh you can't be Dr. Beach. You ought to be tanner." And I say, "Look, if I didn't use sunscreen, my face and body would look like my name—Leatherman." I'd look like baked leather. I use a lot of sunscreen—40 or 50 SPF. I always have that on me.

I didn't mind when my students called me Dr. Beach. I'm not a stuffed shirt.

South Florida, particularly Miami, you can hardly get around anymore because of the traffic. I don't go to a lot of events downtown because the streets are clogged.

In 1989, I got a call from a magazine, saying they heard I was the beach expert, the beach professor, and they wanted to talk to me about the best beaches. I had never thought of it that way, but I rattled off the best beaches I'd seen, and didn't think much about it. A few months later, I saw this glossy magazine in the mailbox. Within hours, the phone started ringing off the hook. That's how it started.

I go to a beach incognito. I have a clipboard. I have all my instruments with me. I have a backpack with all my gear. I measure the width of the beach. I measure the clarity of the water. I definitely go swimming because that's part of it. I have all this data, and I've developed criteria, but what it really comes down to is clean sand and clean water.

If you get into a rip current, swim sideways. Don't swim against the current. Natural instinct is to swim against the current, but that'll tire you out, and most people aren't going to make it.

I like to play tennis—and that's not related to beaches.

I really have a pet peeve with cigarette butts. Cigarette butts are the number-one form of littering on beaches. In terms of volume, it's certainly plastics, and I have a real problem with plastics, too, but smokers think beaches are like some giant ashtray or something. I've been talking to Gov. Rick Scott about trying to pass some sort of law to ban smoking from state beaches. I've counted as many as ten cigarette butts in one square meter of beach. Can you imagine? That's awful.

We have saltwater in our bodies. I think that's why we're attracted to get in the saltwater. It's a primordial urge.

Theresa Manuel

Member of the 1948 U.S. Olympic team, educator, coach, interviewed in August 2016, when she was ninety, Tampa. Manuel died in November 2016.

WHEN I WAS A LITTLE GIRL, my stepfather coached a boys' baseball team, and sometimes the boys would come by the house with a ball and bat. They taught me how to throw and catch. When my stepfather started a girls' softball team, I became the youngest member of the team. That's what started me in sports.

A good teacher gives inspiration.

My main sport was always basketball. Not track. I started playing basketball at Middleton High School in Tampa. The basketball court was outside. We didn't have lights. At night, the neighbors would set up lamps with long extension cords and flood the court with light so we could practice.

I was not someone who talked a lot. I'm just a quiet person.

The most important thing I've learned in life is to be truthful to yourself and be truthful to others.

I went to Tuskegee to play basketball. Some friends from high school used to call me Trixie, and when I got to college, they started calling me Trick Shot. I was a good passer, but I was also a pretty good shot. When I'd get the ball, they'd yell, "Shoot it Trick Shot!"

You have to always keep your body in shape.

We went to a store when I was a teenager, and there were two water fountains, one white and one colored, and I wanted to taste the water from the white one to see if it tasted the same. It did.

When people boast about themselves, I think they should leave the boasting to someone else—and not do it themselves.

At Tuskegee, we were undefeated in track when I was there. We were undefeated in basketball. We would always win. When I was a coach, I'd tell the girls that when I played, we'd never lose a game, and that we're not going to lose a game now. That's how I motivated them.

One of the most important things is to have a job.

I was the first black woman from Florida to compete in the Olympics. I was the first black woman to compete in the javelin. I also competed in the 80-meter hurdles, and I ran the third leg in the 440-yard team relay. I was happy to be there, representing my country, but I was also very hurt that I didn't win. I knew I was also representing black people. I wanted to show everyone who thought that I couldn't do it that I really could do it.

My stepfather was a porter on a train. He couldn't read or write. The color of the tickets would tell him what city the person would get off at. I taught him how to sign his name.

I never was a good cook.

It's been a while, but I like shopping and going to the mall.

Before a race, I believed I could win. You have to always have that in your mind.

I really didn't know if I was a good teacher at the time, but when students graduated and came back to see me and told me that I helped them, that's when I knew.

Jumping over those wooden hurdles for years, my drag leg would hit the hurdle and that hurt my knee. That's why I'm in a wheelchair now. I've had a knee replacement. I have pain. It hurts me not being able to get up and walk.

I wouldn't have gone as far as I did without athletic talent, but I still did a lot of practicing. I had to work very hard.

There was segregation back then. To ride a streetcar, you had to get in the back. For them to say you can't do this or you can do that, that made me feel pretty bad. But when I competed in sports, that was a good feeling. I felt like the best girl out there.

Competing in the Olympics in 1948 may have paved the way for other blacks. I was very proud to do it.

I was engaged once, but my mother was ill, so I told him that I'd have to wait before I could get married. I had to make a choice, but I couldn't leave my mother, so I never did get married. I devoted my time to my students, but I would have loved one or two children of my own.

My advice? Be a winner. Not a loser.

M. J. Soileau

Scientist, researcher, former president of the Office of Research and Commercialization at the University of Central Florida, interviewed in November 2016, when he was seventy-two, Orlando.

M. J. Soileau

I never was the brightest star in the galaxy—and I'm still not—but I grew up learning how to work. I think one of the most important things you learn in science is, if you really push on a problem long enough and hard enough, it gives up.

When I was a child and we were sharecropping, that was the only time I remember being hungry. What I remember about it, really, is the trauma associated with it. One morning, I was hungry and I started to cry because there wasn't any bread. My mom, who was a very, very forceful lady, one of the most forceful people I have ever known, she grabbed me by the hand and marched me to the company store. She asked for a loaf of bread. The owner of the store was also the person we were sharecropping from. He said no. He would not sell us bread on credit. I thought my mother was going to kill him—I mean quite literally. She grew up cutting sugarcane from the seventh grade on, so she was a person to be reckoned with. We walked out of there with a loaf of bread.

In the academic world, particularly in higher administration, if you talk bluntly, you're considered a grouch. And I speak bluntly.

Like any Cajun man, when I cook, there has to be a lot of people around to eat. I cook a wicked gumbo and a wonderful suckling pig.

My parents were very hardworking people, very good people. I was never taught there was any shame in being poor.

Particularly in the job I just left at UCF, VP of research and commercialization, I spent a lot of time with economic development people and business people, and there's a lot of happy talk that goes on in those situations. It drives me nuts. The glass might be halfway full, but, well, sometimes, the damn thing is half-empty and there's a hole in the bottom.

My family had deep reverence for teachers.

We lived quite literally in the swamp. During that time I had a sister who contracted spinal meningitis at three months old. She was an invalid. My older brother, who was two years older than me, he was mentally retarded. In those days, we used that term. Nowadays, we would call him mentally challenged. So, my brother started school before I did, and I did his homework. It was first grade, so it wasn't integral calculus or anything, but I could do math at an early age.

I have an excellent recipe for gator. No, we don't batter it and fry it. We marinate it and grill it.

The truth is, I'm a volatile character. I wear my emotions on my sleeve. I haven't been able to figure out how to be another way.

I have three acres of prime swampland on Lake Jesup. People call it the most alligator-infested lake in Florida. And I love it. It's more Louisiana than Louisiana.

I grew up as a shy little kid. Somewhere along the way, I lost that.

Yeah, recruiting companies into the state is fine, but I don't think that's a long-range strategy. I think that's a very short-range strategy. You're paying people to colonize you. We've gotta get over it. Let's invest in ourselves.

I grew up doing all kinds of odd jobs. I'd pick cotton, three cents a pound. It turns out it takes a lot of cotton to make a pound. When you're a farm kid, you work all the time anyway, but my first job, shall we say, outside the home was when I was in second or third grade. There was a little hotel in my hometown. We didn't have paved roads yet, and I would water the hotel's driveway for a nickel to keep the dust down. Then I learned the value of entrepreneurship. Some guy gave me a dime to wash his car.

You need some chaos. Otherwise, there's no creativity.

I oftentimes defined my administrative job as keeping the next level of management off the necks of the people doing useful work.

My health right now is excellent. I've lost 118 pounds in the last not quite three years. I did it through diet and exercise. The way I describe it to people is eat less, move more, and don't eat stuff that's not good for you.

My mother told me many times, "Nobody ever died of hard work."

As a teacher, if you have a student who shows interest in what you're teaching, you pay attention to that student. It's a natural response that teachers have to feed that interest. My teachers certainly did that for me when I became interested in astronomy in the fourth grade. There were people who saw something in me and provided me with help and guidance. I was lucky.

The long term for Florida is companies being born in Florida from our investment in intellectual capital at our universities. That's how you get a high-value, value-added, wealth-producing economy, as opposed to a service economy.

My mother and father learned to speak English as their second language. My ancestors were in Louisiana before Louisiana was part of the United States.

Being a faculty member at a university, for me, is the best job in the world. What a wonderful life to spend your life learning stuff. And by the way, when you teach, you learn so much more than the students.

The lady who was my first-grade teacher did a fundraiser when I graduated from high school to buy me a suit—the first suit I ever had.

Nan-Yao Su

Entomologist, inventor, interviewed in March 2015, when he was sixty-four, Davie.

Catch a dragonfly and look at the wings, with all those veins, a very intricate network of veins. To me, that's fascinating, just totally fascinating, and beautiful.

You know, I was always interested in biology, except that I hate blood. I can't handle blood. If you want to study biology—if the subject matter is an animal—then you have to dissect that animal, kill it, and there's blood. It's messy. So I decided to go into insects because you don't see blood. Well, they have blood, but it's not red.

To create a termite baiting system, you need a pesticide that is slow-acting, that won't kill them right away, one the termites can eat and bring back to the colony and feed to the others. When I came to the University of Florida in 1985, I wrote a letter to many chemical companies, and I said this is the kind of chemical I'm looking for. Some chemical companies responded. Some didn't. Eventually, Dow Chemical told me they have this chemical called Hexaflumuron. I tested it, and it worked.

I told the Dow Chemical people what we found, and they invited me to the headquarters to give a presentation. I told them that I put a wooden stake in the ground and prepared a sawdust bait in there, with the compound they gave me, and the termites eat it and the whole colony gets killed. I thought they would get really excited, but they kind of looked at me and said: "Dr. Su, we cannot sell wooden stakes. That's not a product."

That night, I come home. Well, if a wooden stake is not a product, what can I do? So I think sometimes when I pulled the wooden stakes out, the ground would collapse, so why don't I put the stake in a sleeve, a plastic sleeve, that has a hole in the side for the termites to get in and out? I drew a picture of it and sent it to Dow, and they go: "Yeah, yeah, yeah. That sounds good. We have a product now." That's what became the Sentricon system.

My wife, Jill, she was my partner, my best friend. We met in Japan so we shared the Japanese experience together. We shared a lot. We lived together for thirty-three years. Jill's murder was a big, big shocker, not to mention my son went through so much trauma. He's the one who found the body. I used to weep every day. It's still very sad. Everything reminds me of her. Her clothes. I still have her clothes. I don't think I can ever remove any of those things.

Florida has a lot of invasive species. People bring plants and animals here all the time, and the climate is so good, it encourages these invasive species to thrive. The problem is they're replacing native species. Somebody is going to have to pay attention to this. Otherwise these invasive species will take over. Our job is to basically raise our voice and say this is happening—and government really needs to do something about it.

When I was in Taiwan as a kid, I would go outside, no shoes, and run around all day looking for insects, looking under rocks, looking for something that moved.

What you do is more important than money or materialistic gain.

I was fifteen years old, almost sixteen, when my parents decided they wanted to move back to Taiwan from Japan. They asked me if I wanted to go with them or stay in Japan and finish high school by myself and then go to college by myself. Freedom! Initially, I thought I could eat out every day. Well, after one week of eating out, I got so sick of it. I started writing a letter to my mother, "How do you cook this?" So I became a very good cook. Of course, my grades dropped real quick. I had to do the cooking and the laundry by myself in addition to studying. I couldn't compete with those kids who were able to study all the time. Japanese high school is very, very competitive, so I did not do too good, but I learned a lot from that time. I was forced to become very independent.

My son pulled an April Fool's joke on me, and then two hours later I come into my office and receive this email telling me I'm being inducted into the Florida Inventors Hall of Fame. I say, "Can you send me the email again tomorrow?"

Children are very sensitive. If the parent is paying attention to basketball, football games, day and night, the children are going to pay attention to basketball, football games day and night. If you really want the children to pay attention to STEM and science, the parents and society have to change.

Termites captivate me.

I still live in the same house. I'm not going to move anywhere. The house still has a lot of memories. It's the house that Jill and I built. Everything inside, she decorated. She's everywhere in the house. We learn to live with the pain. That's the only thing you can do.

If you are curious about a subject matter, you'll get really good at it.

I'm a tinkerer. I love to design experimental devices. I've started to realize actually, deep inside, that I'm an engineer like my father. I can't fight my DNA. If you look at the Sentricon station, I designed that. It's very simple, but biologists don't usually come up with an idea like that.

If I can, I play tennis every day.

Robert Cade [a UF researcher who invented Gatorade] is a hero. Dr. Cade, if you read what he had to go through to get Gatorade on the market, it's amazing. He was a pioneer. By encountering all of those difficulties, he made it easier for other inventors.

What keeps me young is my students. They are all young and they are so curious.

My wife used to think that I act like a kid sometimes. It's true. Deep inside, I'm still that six-year-old boy chasing the dragonfly and being totally impressed by the beauty of it.

EXPLORERS

JOSEPH KITTINGER

Aviator, Air Force colonel, held records for highest parachute jump (102,800 feet from space) and for being first to make a solo crossing of the Atlantic Ocean in a gas balloon, interviewed in May 2011, when he was eighty-two, Altamonte Springs.

SOME PEOPLE SAY NEVER VOLUNTEER. I say always volunteer. Every great thing I ever did was because I volunteered for it. I'd be in a room full of people and the boss would say we need a volunteer for this, and I'd be the only one to stick my hand up. I'd think, "Gosh, what's wrong with me?" But I ended up with some very interesting projects.

When I got involved in Project Excelsior in 1959, I was working for a visionary by the name of Col. John Paul Stapp. He was a man who knew we were going to go into space, and he knew there was research that needed to be done. We needed to research how to put a man into space, how to protect a man in a space environment, and how to communicate from space. The next part was providing a means of escape from that altitude.

You had to go up to 100,000 feet, and the only way to go up there was a balloon. I actually made three balloon flights, 76,000 feet, 75,000 feet, and 103,000 feet. To get down, I jumped.

The free fall was four minutes and thirty-six seconds. You've got to remember that space is a vacuum. There's no pressure, so when I jumped I accelerated for about the first twenty seconds and reached terminal velocity at 614 mph. From then on, I slowed down. When the parachute opened, I was doing about 150 mph.

There's no way you can visualize the speed. There's nothing you can see to see how fast you're going. You have no depth perception. If you're in a car driving down the road and you close your eyes, you have no idea what your speed is. It's the same thing if you're free-falling from space. There are no signposts. You know you are going very fast, but you don't feel it. You don't have a 614-mph wind blowing on you. I could only hear myself breathing in the helmet.

The goal was not to set the record for the highest jump. The goal was to get the data we needed. But it's still a record some fifty-one years later.

When I was a young 'un, I used to get on my bicycle and ride out to the airport, the Orlando Executive Airport, and watch the airplanes.

That was my field of dreams. When I retired and came back to Orlando, all the area around the airport had been encroached by businesses, and there wasn't any place for a kid to go and watch airplanes land and take off. So, a friend of mine, he and I thought we'd see if we could get some interest in a park for kids. I had no idea they were going to name the park after me, but now the kids have a place to play and watch the airplanes.

If we didn't have air-conditioning, 90 percent of the people in Florida would go back north.

Back in the '60s and '70s, all of the research on space was done by the military or NASA. Now, private industry is doing it. Richard Branson is going to take people up in space. Red Bull is sponsoring a jump from 125,000 feet, and I'm helping them do some research. They're testing a next-generation pressure suit. Thank goodness we have organizations like Red Bull and Richard Branson to sponsor the research that needs to be done.

It takes a team, a good team, to get anything done. You can't do anything in life without a team.

It was 1963 and Project Excelsior was over, so I volunteered for Vietnam. Being a fighter pilot, I felt I owed it to the Air Force and my country to do my part. I actually had three tours in Vietnam: '63–64, '66–67, and then '71–72. On May 11, 1972, I was shot down about 35 miles northwest of Hanoi and spent the next eleven months as a POW.

They kept me at the Hanoi Hilton, first in solitary and then in a very small room with thirty other guys. I lost 40 pounds. The majority of the food they gave us was pumpkin soup. We had pumpkin soup a couple of times a day. There was no meat. We were always hungry, but we would never talk about food because why torture yourself? Today, I would walk 100 miles to keep from eating a bowl of pumpkin soup.

I was tortured for not giving them information, but mainly they just wanted to break me. They knew I had three combat tours, and they knew I shot down a MIG, so I wasn't their favorite person. They never broke me. I'd rather not get into what they did, but it was very painful. They were professionals at it. They knew how to torture without killing you. They were diabolical. They were cruel. They did not adhere to the Geneva Convention. When I hear about waterboarding, it doesn't

bother me a bit because waterboarding would have been the least torture we ever had.

The national debt is atrocious and getting worse. I worry about that
quite a bit.

I had a mother and father who were very loving and very concerned
about my future. They were bound and determined that I was going to
be a success.

I don't think my boys had the advantage that I did because my
mother and father were there all the time and I wasn't. I was in Vietnam. I was doing research, so I wasn't there as frequently as I wish I
could have been. But both of my boys grew up very successfully. I'm
proud of both of them.

When I was in the balloon, getting ready to jump, there were no
second thoughts. No fear. I had confidence in my team. My only thing
was just do the job and get the data. I'm a fighter pilot and a test pilot,
and the one common denominator of every test pilot and fighter pilot
is confidence. You might say that's ego, but that's the personality.

I think I got my confidence from my childhood, going hunting and
fishing, being outside and racing boats. My mother and father would
challenge me constantly to exert myself and take responsibility. They
had confidence in me, and I think that gave me my spirit of adventure,
my spirit of trying to contribute.

As I was falling, I was describing into a tape recorder my sensations,
how stable I was, how the pressure suit was working. I was a test pilot,
and I was getting data we needed.

My wife is a Harry Potter junkie. We've been to the Wizarding World
of Harry Potter a few times. Yeah, I go on the rides. If you go, you've
got to get some of that Butterbeer.

EDGAR MITCHELL

Apollo 14 astronaut, sixth person of twelve to walk on the moon, founder of the Institute of Noetic Sciences, interviewed in July 2009, when he was seventy-nine, Lake Worth. Mitchell died in February 2016.

WHAT MORE COULD AN EXPLORER WANT than to go where humans have never been before, gather data, take pictures, come back and tell the story?

From the moment we stepped out of the lunar module door, we were behind schedule and got further behind schedule every second. There's that momentary thrill, and then it's get back to work because you're running behind. Houston was whispering in our ears, "OK, now you're four minutes behind." A couple of minutes later, "Now you're six minutes behind." That was going on continuously.

The main thing, of course, that we were concerned about was don't fall on your back like a turtle with your feet in the air, because you'd have to have the other guy come help you out. Or don't puncture your suit and blow your air out because that's your death.

Young kids ask, "OK, what's it like to walk on the moon?" and I say, particularly to those who live in northern climates, "It's like Mom lets you go out and play in a snowsuit, but you have two snowsuits on and you're walking on a trampoline." That's what it feels like.

There was very little levity and very little horseplay. Oh, there were some smart-ass remarks, not on the radio, but on the intercom, jabbing each other about this, that, or the other like, "Don't fall in that hole." Stuff like that.

I was coming back to shore duty on October 4, 1957, when Sputnik went up. I realized humans would be right behind robot spacecraft going into space—and that sounded like that would be an interesting thing to do, the new frontier. That was my motivation. My family had come across after the Civil War from south Georgia to west Texas, so we're a pioneering line of folk.

I was on test pilot duty at Edwards Air Force Base when I had applied for and was selected into the Apollo program in 1966. In the group I was in, there were nineteen others selected, and what I was told was there were nineteen thousand applicants.

If you know any astronomy at all and the history of star systems and so forth, you know that our star system is going to burn out here in a couple billion years. It's about halfway through its life cycle, so we've got to be out of here. If our species is to survive, we have to become a universal species. We have to be a part of the universe, not part of the solar system. So we better get on with it.

We have major problems in science at this point because of the clash between general relativity and quantum mechanics. One is the science of the very, very small and Einstein's general relativity, the science of the very, very large, and they don't come together well. And we're going to have to solve that problem before we really can go off into the solar system and outside of it. I say that because we now know we have been visited. We're not alone in the universe, and it is clear from our visitors, that their propulsion systems, the science and technology that they use, is far beyond ours. And they couldn't be coming here if they were limited by the general relativity issues that we think we're limited by.

My major chores were completed. I could be practically a tourist on the way home from the moon. We were flying sideways and rotating. What that caused to happen of course is every two minutes the picture of the earth, the moon, the sun, and a 360-degree panorama of the heavens appeared in the cockpit window. And that's pretty wow.

From my training during my doctoral work in astronomy at Harvard and MIT, I knew that star systems are the furnaces that create matter in our universe. All the molecules of our body and our environment and our planet are created in star systems. And I suddenly realized that the molecules of my body, the molecules of the body of the spacecraft, and the molecules in my partners' bodies were created in stars, and that was a wild experience. It was a visceral experience. I felt it. My molecules and those star systems are one. It's a unity of everything, and this was accompanied by an ecstasy that was just overwhelming. And when I wasn't working and having to watch the gauges or do something to the spacecraft, I'd look out the window, and this experience repeated itself, this wow, this feeling of ecstasy and connectedness. And I realized that our story of ourselves as told by science, scientific cosmology, was archaic and likely flawed.

If indeed the aliens have the technology that we're talking about to get here and we don't, that would be pretty nice technology to have. You can kind of control the world if you have that technology.

My history of this is I grew up in Roswell, New Mexico, which is the site of the so-called Roswell incident of 1947. It appeared in the *Roswell Daily Record* one day as being an alien visitation, and the next day, no, it was just a weather balloon.

It used to be the giggle factor was very high, but it's changing. It's changing quite a bit. Even the Vatican is saying, "Hey, it's OK to believe in an alien presence."

I think the fact that I'm one of twelve people who walked on the moon, yeah, that's history. I would like to think that the work I've done in science will be as important if not more important than simply going to the moon.

JoAnn Morgan

NASA aerospace engineer, first woman to serve as a senior executive at Kennedy Space Center, interviewed in May 2018, when she was seventy-seven, New Smyrna Beach.

My favorite birthday present as a child was a chemistry set.

What started me toward my career path of working in the space-launch world was I saw Explorer 1 launch. I was a senior in high school. Seeing Explorer 1, and reading about it in the newspapers, and the fact that right away a discovery was made—the Van Allen radiation belt—I just thought that this is going to change the world I'm living in, and I wanted to be part of it.

The Apollo 11 launch was the first launch that I stayed in the firing room all the way through liftoff. I had moments when I felt like a goldfish in a bowl, even though I was surrounded by people. It was five hundred men and me.

Biology, math, science—all of those kinds of subjects—were real important to my parents, so I became fearless about math and science. I was never afraid of those subjects, which is something that happened to a lot of girls of my generation.

I worked for the Army Ballistic Missile Agency when I was seventeen. I was assigned to the missile-firing lab, where the big job there was launching the Redstone and Juno rockets. That was Wernher von Braun's laboratory. I went to work on a Monday. I worked on my first launch on Friday. I was given a tracking device and trained along with two soldiers, and we each stood out at night on the tarmac outside of Hanger D at Cape Canaveral, mapping when the first and second stages separated. The only reason I got to do it was one of the German scientists gave us all a hand-eye-coordination test and I was the youngest and I had been a piano player, so I had the best hand-eye coordination.

I've set a physical fitness goal that I want to be able to ski every year. I want to be skiing when I'm eighty.

In the firing room during an Apollo launch, we were on television all the time, and that television could be viewed in Houston or California or Washington or wherever, so I did get obscene phone calls at my console and some other weird things happened because not every man who was there thought that I deserved to be there or should be there because I was a woman.

A television guy, one time he came down, and he said: "JoAnn, I have to tell you something. When somebody brings paperwork to you and they want you to lean over your console to sign it, make them come around to you. Just sit there. Don't get up. Make them come to you, because when you get up the TV techs get inquiries to zoom in the television camera on your butt." I was horrified. My husband was horrified, too.

I'm very disappointed in Florida's lack of preserving some of its precious environment. You know, when I was in high school, I could go to the Indian River in Titusville, and the water was crystal clear. You could swim and see the manatees and pompano. Pompano haven't been in the Indian River in many years, decades maybe.

Basically, I'm a child of war. I was born in 1940, and the very earliest memories I have are of my dad and uncles in their uniforms, going away.

With the Space Shuttle, if I faced directly toward the launch pad, even three miles away, I could feel the shock waves hit my sternum.

I've worked a lot with universities in Florida. I was a trustee for the University of West Florida. I've been on boards at the University of Central Florida and other schools.

I've started working with six or seven institutions to create scholarships to help young women who want to be engineers.

As far as higher education, I feel like that's one of our state's brightest stars.

Part of my bucket list is I'd like to master voice-activated software and get a self-driving car.

I'm so lucky. I never had a dull day. I had bad days—and a bad day in the space business means one of those horrible disasters and loss of life and billions of dollars affected in flight hardware. That part is devastating and hard, but getting back and figuring out what went wrong and making it better is what big achievements are all about.

One of my jobs, I was associate director for Space Shuttle upgrades and advanced development. The Shuttles had been built and designed for either twenty years or one hundred missions. Well, the twenty years was ending, but they hadn't gotten near one hundred missions, but the technology was old and the Shuttles needed upgrades. They were like teenagers with bad skin who needed a brain transplant.

I still play the piano. After that movie *La La Land* came out, I pretty much learned to play most of the piano music from it—and I'm also playing blues harmonica. I went to the John C. Campbell Folk School in North Carolina, and they had a really good harmonica teacher there. I'm a terrible harmonica player, though. All my friends, when I start to play, they'll say, "Oh, spare us!"

Winston Scott

Space Shuttle
astronaut, senior
vice president of
Florida Institute
of Technology,
interviewed in
October 2015,
when he was
sixty-five,
Melbourne.

I'M ON THE FLIGHT DECK, looking out the front window. I'm on my back and the countdown is happening. You can hear it. You can feel it. About seven seconds to go, the main engines start, and you've got all this shaking and vibrating, and smoke and fire billowing up around the windscreen. At zero, the solid rocket boosters ignite and you release from the pad. When you see it on television, it looks like it lifts off in slow motion, just sort of rises up, but in reality it's—boom! It jumps off the pad and kicks you in the butt. It's like riding an old truck along a rocky, dirt road.

Through the ninth grade, I attended segregated schools in Miami. Actually, it had a very good influence on me in some ways. The teachers and the community were very, very dedicated to us youngsters. They wanted to do the best they could for us. Our teachers were really good, brilliant people, as good as any you'd find anyplace else. They were concerned about our future and did everything they could to see that we got the best education that we possibly could. What we did not have, and what we didn't know at the time, was good infrastructure and good equipment.

I have always suspected, and people are now beginning to realize, that art and music and math and science really go hand in hand. Music and math involve the same thought processes.

When I was little, machines fascinated me. I'd open up my toys to see how they worked. I'd cut up Christmas tree lights and hook them up to batteries. I was a kid who naturally should have gone into engineering, but I didn't know what engineering was.

Being a trumpet player, my most favorite jazz artist is Miles Davis.

I think people who allow themselves to be unidimensional are doing themselves a disservice.

At Florida Tech, we have a music program because we realize that students who study math and science and engineering are also quite often very good musicians.

I loved to fly from day one in the Navy, especially fighter jets. I knew I would. I was always the little kid playing with toy airplanes. I still fly. I have a Saratoga, a good traveling plane. Most of my travel, I do myself.

At Florida State, I was studying music, and my roommate was an engineering major. Watching what he was doing, it awakened something inside me. I realized that engineering was what I was supposed to be studying.

I almost didn't apply to be an astronaut. I remember sitting around the dinner table with a Navy buddy of mine and my wife. This buddy, we were both becoming senior enough that we might have to go to D.C. and do the Washington, D.C., part of our military career, and I made an off-handed remark about maybe wanting to be an astronaut, but I didn't know if I had the right qualifications. They both looked at me and said I needed to apply. That whole night, it was in the back of my mind. I went to work the next day, talked to my commanding officer, and he wanted me to apply, too, so I thought I'd do it once and see what happens. Over the next year and a half, when the field kept getting narrowed down, my name kept staying in. Roughly three thousand people started, and I was one of the nineteen selected. It felt like a dream.

In high school, I thought I was going to be a musician. I played rock, jazz, concert music. I thought I'd be a performer and a composer and perhaps a teacher.

I'm always looking to get better. I'm always looking to improve. I'm always stretching.

While I'm not the kind of researcher who will work in a lab and cure cancer, I thought the way I could contribute to bettering life on Earth through scientific research was by becoming an astronaut.

I love being challenged and pushed. I'm always looking to get better.

It concerns me that we don't have enough youth, especially minority youth, going into the engineering, science, mathematics, space and aviation fields.

I particularly like that we've embraced the private commercial space companies—SpaceX, Blue Origin, Sierra Nevada. It's long overdue.

Because of the sheer number of planets, I do believe that there's life somewhere else in the universe.

ENTERTAINERS

ZEV BUFFMAN

Theater producer, actor, partner of the NBA's Miami Heat, interviewed in December 2017, when he was eighty-six, Clearwater.

MY FIRST REAL JOB WAS STEALING CARS. I was thirteen or fourteen, and Israel's war of independence was coming. I was training in every kind of weapon one should know, but I was a great car thief. I was stealing cars because we had no cars. They would send us out to embassies—the ones that had Jeeps—and we would hot-wire them in the middle of night and drive them to the desert, where they were painted in Israeli colors.

I don't celebrate birthdays. I don't celebrate New Year's Eve. I don't believe in anything that acknowledges the passage of time.

This was 1987. I met with David Stern, the NBA commissioner, in New York to talk about bringing an expansion team to Miami. David said: "Zev, you're in the theater. You don't know what you're talking about." He said, "Zev, you're Jewish, I'm Jewish, so I'm not going to offend you, but Florida is a place where old Jews go to die and Cubans come to look for a new life and they are crazy about two things: baseball and boxing—not basketball—so you're offering me a DOA market and you'll never make it." I went back to Miami and told everyone that we have to prove him wrong.

I never take no for an answer. No is just the beginning of a dialogue.

The key is to train your staff and to, eventually, train your board. Boards are so afraid. They're mostly accountants, money managers, and bankers, and they just choke ingenuity and they choke imagination. They want to see all the money up front instead of the design or the idea.

A producer is part shrink. You have to be a great listener. You have to be patient. You must communicate. You just can't be a bull in the china shop.

My dad owned two movie houses in Tel Aviv. I grew up in the back of a projection room. After school, I would rush to a matinee performance, and the projectionist would let me run things.

I came to Hollywood to be a star. I did seven or eight movies, and then I did *The Ten Commandments* for Cecil B. DeMille. I played various parts, including one of Moses's disciples and a slave. Eventually, I realized that my dream of being a star actor was not going to be realized because I was not that good.

Taking a vacation, within two days I get very restless. Although I love to travel, all I can think about is what I can do at work.

When the Russian Revolution was taking hold and the pogroms were becoming very popular in the Ukraine, my family fled. Young Ukrainians along with a handful of Russian soldiers, but mostly Ukrainian civilians, they would storm the villages—and my parents came from a little village called Charkov—and they would beat up the men, rape the women, kill a few men, and take the young men and conscript them into the Soviet army. That's what they did to the Jews then. My parents settled in Palestine, and that's where I was born.

In Florida, economic development and tourism get respect, but education does not.

Despite television, despite movies, despite the iPads and the other devices, there's still that need for live entertainment, that interaction face-to-face, that you cannot duplicate. When you go to a live show and you're able to applaud and scream and cheer, it's a social experience.

When I was a teenager and in the war, I felt invincible. I told myself it was a movie. It wasn't real. We're not really getting shot at. We're not really dying. I was not afraid.

A project happens if it happens fast. If it doesn't happen fast, it doesn't happen. I live by that.

Clearwater brought me back to Florida. St. Petersburg has momentum. It's like San Francisco sixty years ago. It's going someplace. And Tampa has a leader, Jeff Vinik. He'll make it happen there. But Clearwater is the third city, the forgotten city, and that's what attracted me. I came here to build. I'm a builder.

A comic by the name of Danny Kaye was a legend in movies and on Broadway. I loved him. I was crazy about Danny Kaye. I imitated every one of his sketches. I became the Israeli Danny Kaye, entertaining the troops, and it went to my head. I figured I'd be a Hollywood star.

My wife and I have been married for fifty-five years. In show business, that is one of the most amazing miracles. My marriage is like a rock.

Probably the core of what I am today, what I preach and practice and get on the soapbox about, is don't be afraid to make a mistake. Don't be afraid to lead.

I've produced forty-one Broadway shows, the majority of them from the late '70s to late '80s. I've run as many as fourteen performing arts centers around the country, mostly in Florida, at one time. I built four 20,000-seat amphitheaters in the 1990s. My partner was Wayne Huizenga, a good partner, and a good buddy.

Treat everything as an adventure. Otherwise, life can be very boring. One adventure—and I know this is reckless—is I try to beat my old time getting to work. It takes twenty-four minutes, for a normal person driving correctly, to get here from my house. I'm trying to beat seventeen minutes, which is the best time I ever had. Thank God I haven't had a speeding ticket in five years.

If and when the time comes that I cannot continue being the president and CEO of Ruth Eckerd Hall, I want to be a teacher. There's still room in my life to teach.

The lesson I've learned is to lead and not be afraid of it. Welcome it.

BRIAN JOHNSON

AC/DC lead singer, interviewed in November 2012, when he was sixty-five, Sarasota.

THE BEATLES HAD JUST come out and everybody wanted to be in a band, even people who couldn't play. My friends, they were starting a band. The bass player had a bass guitar. His brother had a guitar. Another had a beautiful set of Gretsch drums, orange-spotted, I'll never forget, and they said, "What are you going to do?" I was fifteen, and I sang in the church choir, but that wasn't singing. That was chanting. I asked them, "Can I sing?" and they said: "I don't know. Can you?"

I'm always a believer in taking the path less traveled. It's a scary path, but it can be a very rewarding one.

The first band, me and the boys came up with this name, the Gobi Desert Canoe Club. We thought we were dead funny, really catchy and fabulous. We thought we were dead cool, apart from the fact that our van never started and we didn't have any gigs.

I have a music room at Sarasota Memorial Hospital called the Brian Johnson Music Therapy Room. It's for sick children, terminal children. It's to get them away from the shiny things, the scrubs, the rubber gloves, and the needles. There's guitars, keyboards, drums. Music is good for you.

Florida feels like home. When I go back to England, I feel like I'm visiting.

I'm not a great one for pride, but I'm so happy I've had a grandson so late in life. He's two and a half. What a great tyke. He's the apple of his granddad's eye. He's a little crackerjack. I'm proud of him.

One thing I get angry at is when people tell me that I'm lucky, that the band is lucky. The harder we worked, the luckier we got.

I refuse to watch this X Factor and The Voice and all those bullshit programs. It's cruel. Unfair. They get a person up on stage. They build him up or make a fool of him. They put a group behind him. Then in two weeks' time if they don't win, they're in a Holiday Inn lounge somewhere.

My hero is George Washington. He was the guy. He was a true man of the people, even though he wasn't. They offered him the monarchy of America and he went: "You idiots. We just spent fucking years trying to kick one out and you want to make me king?"

I can't describe how much it means to be standing on stage and see a man of seventy-three, and next to him is his son, and next to his son is his grandson. Three generations, and they're all rocking. We must be doing something right.

The AC/DC boys, we never really got into the drug scene, you know. We were pretty piss-poor at it. Parties. Cocaine. Babes. The next day, that's the problem. It's not good for the voice. It hurts the music. It happened once at a gig. We weren't right, and I said, "Never again."

I hate Facebook. I hate Twitter. What happened to privacy? They give it away. I found out there are eleven Brian Johnsons on Facebook who claim they're me. Bollocks to it.

You can talk yourself up to being a great band, but when the lights go up and you run on that stage and you start belting it out, there's nowhere to hide.

I love getting great people together for dinner parties. I think it's just one of the most wonderful things you can do, to listen to wonderful conversation.

The choir director made me head choirboy, which meant I wore a gold thing and got three shillings and sixpence a week. Big money. I was thirteen. Unfortunately, the ex–head choirboy, who was just losing his voice, got miffed and attacked me behind the church. There we were, behind the house of God, knocking the shit out of each other.

I wanted some fun in the sunshine, where people speak English—and when I say speak English I use the term fucking loosely. I went to Fort Myers first and bought a place on the beach. It was to get away from the tax in England, as well. I wanted to live outside of England. The tax was just crippling, just ridiculous. Way above 50 percent.

When I go back to Newcastle, I become a "used to be man," which means you sit in the car with friends saying there used to be a cinema there, and there used to be a butcher shop there. All the pubs that I used to love have all been knocked down and become wine bars or restaurants selling pork belly, which is a very expensive way of serving you fat with a little bit of meat on it.

I had to come to Sarasota to do a pro-am golf tournament, and I'm driving into Sarasota, and I went to St. Armands Circle, and it was like this place is Monte Carlo. This was 1990. Downtown wasn't as cool then, but I just fell in love with it. Now Sarasota is the worst-kept secret in Europe. It's on the circle of places to be, like Aspen, Gstaad in Switzerland, Monte Carlo.

In England, all the Manchester United fans are ticked off because they got the bloody Glazers: "They take our money and all they do is spend it on the Bucs!" And then all the guys here: "Bloody Glazers. They buy this freaking team in England, and they spend all the money over there!"

France is the center of the civilized world, as far as food and wine.

I didn't join a band to become famous. I joined a band to play music and for my peers to say, "He's a good singer." That's what you do. You want other musicians to admire what you do. The fame part is just fucking horrible.

I hate politics.

Everybody is already dead once they've passed fifty, so just try to have the greatest time you can. On my sixty-fifth birthday, I went, "Yeah, I fucking made it!" I'm fit as a butcher's dog. I race cars all over the world. I've got some good solid pals, great family, and a great wife who really looks after me. When I race, I race to the maximum because I don't care. I've already had a great life.

SHERRILL MILNES

Operatic baritone, interviewed in September 2017, when he was eighty-two, Palm Harbor.

A LARYNGOLOGIST CAN'T LOOK at your throat and say, "Oh, you're good." They can't. They don't know. Singing is a mystery, and that's one of the wonderful things about it.

I grew up on a dairy farm in northern Illinois. Wintertime there, that's part of the reason I like Florida: 15 degrees below zero, milking cows, bare hands, manure. I mean that's down and dirty stuff.

In college, my freshman year, I was pre-med. Hard curriculum. I didn't have time to play my violin in an orchestra or sing in my mother's church choir. When I didn't have music, that's when I realized how important it was to me.

I tried hard to be the best in the world. As I've told various younger baritones, I made it as hard on my successors as I could.

A huge irony in career singing, meaning earning a living from singing, is you can't have a big career without being terrific, but being terrific doesn't guarantee a career.

I'm a full-stomach singer. There are lots of singers who don't want to have a big meal before a performance, but I did. Otherwise, I would start to get weak. Probably 5:00, 5:30 p.m. before an evening performance, I'd eat everything I could cram in, including milk and ice cream, all of that stuff that some singers stay away from.

We often are singing in a language that we don't speak and for an audience who also doesn't speak it. That's a huge load to carry for a singer.

I have music education degrees. I just took off forty-two years to sing around the world, but now I'm doing exactly what I trained to do—and that's teaching and working in our VOICExperience programs.

Social media. People tend to believe what they read, true or not.

People think, from farm to opera, how does that happen? Well, that's a fair question. It does seem like a stretch. But music was always such a big part of my family. So, for me personally, it wasn't a stretch.

Everybody gets better if they study. Not just music. Anything.

I was called the "Bari-Hunk." I was attractive, over six feet, but among the various levels of stardom, opera is pretty far down on the list. Tony Randall was my friend. I sang at his funeral. I also got to know Burt Lancaster. He was a big opera fan. I got to know him the last ten years of his life. Now, he was really famous. Tony was famous, but he could go into a restaurant and he could eat. But Burt, he would only go to restaurants where he either knew the maître d' or the manager. He'd go in the back door with a baseball cap pulled down and sit way in the back. Otherwise, he could never eat. There'd just be a line to get his autograph. That's fame. I was a schmuck—and I had no problem with that.

My wife [Maria Zouves, an opera singer and teacher] is Greek. She's from Pinellas County. The sponge docks in Tarpon Springs, we enjoy going there. The most authentic Greek restaurant? Mykonos. It's a dive, but it's great food. And right across the street, Dimitri's on the Water.

Inhibition is the bane of a singer's existence.

A teacher inspires within reality. As a teacher, if a student is not terrific, you can't say: "You suck. You're terrible. Go away." The old-timers used to do that, but I could never do that. At the same time, you would be totally dishonest if you said, "You're great" and they're not.

I've done a lot of performances at the Metropolitan Opera—654.

You ever see vocal folds? Ugly. Oh, man. It's amazing that beautiful sounds can come from those ugly, little things.

Performing onstage, I loved being there, loved the music, but when the big aria was coming up, my heart started beating faster. Was I immune to nerves? Oh, no. I was as nervous as the next guy. Or maybe more.

You can't sing with a dry throat.

Things change as you become more famous. It's a two-edged sword. You're better all around, but people expect you to be good, and to a certain degree, you're good because they expect you to be good. You do have to deliver, though, and I always did.

Florida's great, notwithstanding the occasional hurricane.

Always, I loved teaching. In fact, every time I did a recital or an opera somewhere, which is forty-two years of earning a living singing, I would do a master class. At the beginning, I would just do them for nothing—just throw it in—with the idea that at some point I would start to charge. I was not totally dumb. So, now as a teacher, I'm expensive. Fame as an opera singer does give you more cachet.

Do something. Even the wrong something is better than nothing.

Words don't mean anything when you describe a voice. Golden? Shimmering? Silver? Yuck. What do they mean? Warm. What does warm mean? It doesn't mean anything. You can use all the words in the world, all meaningless. You have to hear.

BELLO NOCK

Comic daredevil, interviewed in January 2017, when he was forty-eight, Sarasota.

AFTER SEVEN GENERATIONS OF CIRCUS PERFORMERS in my family, my parents told me that I didn't have to follow in their footsteps. I just had to try it out for thirty or forty years.

My parents came to America in the 1950s, one to headline and one to star in the Ringling circus. Father was a daredevil. I'd say he was the Russell Crowe of circus: a very tough guy. Mother was the ballerina, which is why I was in tights taking ballet lessons at age eight. She taught me grace and finesse. Father was the one who said, "Get up there!" But it was mother who said, "Point your toes while you're up there because that's what makes the difference."

I love getting shot out of a cannon.

The biggest misnomer is a daredevil just tries something and sees what happens. That's absolutely not it. You have to practice it, hone it, perfect it, and then, if you can do it one hundred times out of one hundred times at home when no one is watching, that's when you do it during a performance.

When I was growing up in Sarasota, you couldn't throw a rock and not hit a circus performer.

It doesn't matter how much money you make, how much fame you have, what your abilities are. A show is only two hours long. How you live the other twenty-two hours a day is way more important to me.

My daughter, Annaliese—she's twenty, and she's the next generation. She performs in the Whirling Wheel of Death, although we prefer to call it the Whirling Wheel of Wonder. She's in Guinness World Records for doing the most somersaults inside the wheel in under a minute. She did four. She does sky walks. She does trapeze. She's an aerialist. She's probably done everything but get shot out of a cannon.

I have fun no matter where I'm at or what I'm doing. Whatever comes at you, good or bad, grin it, bear it, and keep going.

My father was friends with Evel Knievel and Karl Wallenda. I can remember one day they had a lunch, the three of them sitting at a table, and I was just young and smart enough to sit in a corner listening. They talked about fame, money, what they could do, what they would do next. It was in a friendly way, but they were going at each other. Evel Knievel said, "I'll be more famous than either one of you guys if I have to break every one of my bones." Karl Wallenda spoke out of the side of his mouth. He said, "Ya ya, I'll be more famous even if I have to die trying." And I can remember my father—in his deep Swiss accent—saying, "I love this business, but I'm not willing to break my bones or die for it." My dad died pretty young, but of natural causes—not a single broken bone in his body.

There are very few people you can recognize by their silhouette alone. I'm one of them—because of my hair. I have iconic hair.

I don't live recklessly. I don't live foolishly, but I'm a performer who lives life to its fullest.

Florida does tourism well. It does it better than Paris, France. It does it better than Switzerland. It does it better than just about anywhere else.

I fit into a lot of worlds: clown, circus, daredevil, stuntman, comic, show producing, teaching. You know why? I don't believe in boxing someone in. If you feel like you can do it, you can do it.

Could you have chalked me up as a kid who was hyper? ADD? Full of energy? Yes to all of the above. Attention and an audience—that was me. It was a good thing I had parents who didn't put me on Ritalin. Trampoline? Yup. Wire? Keep practicing. They found resources for me to burn off that energy.

Don't bite off more than you can chew, but dream big.

The decline of the circus—numerous circuses have closed or are closing in America and around the world, I'm sorry to say—but it's not anyone's fault but their own. You have to be willing to adapt and change. You have to remain relevant. Stay true to your core but pay attention to what's changing.

I could eat steak or spaghetti with clams, either one of those, seven days a week. Also, I've never passed up a crème brûlée—never, ever.

The most important job any of us will ever have is being a parent. Being a parent is a high-wire walk.

This may sound very egotistical, but I'm a very driven person. If I hadn't become a performer, I would have been an Olympic swimmer, and I would not have quit until I had a couple of gold medals.

I'm sorry if this sounds cold, but if you know that everything has been done—all the planning and all the practice—whatever happens, happens. That's life. If it's your day, it's your day.

As my wife's grandmother said—she's from Germany—"We get too quick old and too late smart." I say those words every single day of my life.

Burt Reynolds

Actor, interviewed in April 2012, when he was seventy-six, Jupiter. Reynolds died in September 2018.

My father was the Riviera Beach chief of police. He arrested me twice. Once he put me in jail for fighting, and he came in and said to the other guys: "Your father's here, you can go home. Your father's here, you can go home." And then he looked right at me and said, "Your father didn't show up."

I dared to go into Costco the other day. I thought, "What the hell," so I walked in. Everything was fine until I was trying to find a little tiny paintbrush and some paints, and I turned around and there were eight people staring at me. I was in line to check out, and the manager came over and said, "Can I help you get through this?" And I said, "No, no, I'm fine." Suddenly, I'm signing autographs, and if you sign one, you have to sign another, and people are getting PO'd because you're stopping the line, so you have to step out of the line, but you can't go back in, so you have to go to the back of the line. Eventually, I said to the manager, "I'll take you up on that offer."

When I was a kid, people called me Mullet, a fish used for bait mainly, and in order not to be called Mullet and to not hit somebody in the mouth, I found if you put some pads on and hit somebody in the mouth, they thought you were wonderful. So I started playing football, and they stopped calling me Mullet and started calling me Buddy.

Sometimes, the worst reviews are what fuel you the most.

I was walking with Marilyn Monroe on our way to the Actors Studio, and she just had on an old football jersey and pair of slacks, no makeup, and we're walking on Broadway. We're just coming up to Childs Restaurant, and I say to her: "You know, this is amazing Marilyn. We've been walking four blocks and nobody is bothering you." And she went: "Oh. Want to see her?" I said, "What?" She says, "Do you want to see her?" Now, she didn't take off any clothes. She didn't do anything, except change her posture. We took about four steps, and it was damn near a riot. We needed the police to get us out of there.

Growing up, I was enormously shy. I would hide behind being a jock.

My freshman year at FSU, I started two games. My sophomore year, I was a starting left halfback, but before the first game, in practice, a guy hit me—the play was over and he just came in and cut me on the side—and I ended up eventually needing four knee operations. It really was devastating emotionally and in every other way. It was very difficult for me to get it through my thick head that there was possibly something else you could do at the university besides play football and chase Pi Beta Phi's.

I came home, recovering from the knee operation, and they wanted me to pick up some credits because I was going to try to come back and play. I enrolled at Palm Beach Junior College. I was in an English literature class, and like all good football players, I was on the last row. Watson Duncan, the teacher, was talking about Byron, Shelley, Keats, and he waved me to the front of the class. I thought: "Oh no, I'm in trouble. What did I do?" He said, "I want you on the front row," and

I said, "Why?" And he said, "Because you're going to be an actor." I thought he was crazy, but I thought maybe I'd get a good grade, so I sat on the front row. And then he said, "At twelve o'clock tomorrow, we're having readings for a play, and I want you there."

The play was *Outward Bound*, which is a magnificent play. He gave me the part of this tragic character who was an alcoholic, and I was in a perfect mood to play the most tragic character on the planet. I was never a drinker because of being a jock, but I understood the part about having your dreams come to an end and feeling totally impotent and hopeless. Opening night, it felt like when I was nine or ten years old and I walked on a football field the first time. I thought, "I'm home."

I think it's a tragedy what's happening to our beaches, that we're not taking better care of them. The sea turtles come ashore, and it becomes a show. Some people think it's funny to turn them around the wrong way, and that makes me crazy.

The other time my father arrested me I was stealing donuts. It was a silly thing, you know, but it's still stealing. The donuts were set out at five o'clock in the morning at the stores, and my friends and I, we'd go by and take some donuts. It wasn't like stealing jewels out of Doris Duke's house, but it was getting a couple of donuts and giggling about it and going down to the beach and watching the sun rise out of the ocean. When I wasn't fighting, I was eating donuts and looking at sunrises.

I know a lot of actors who become a character they played. They decide I'm better as this character than I am as me, so I'll be this character for the rest of my life.

You walk into a room, some people are thinking, he likes the attention. Some people don't even give a damn whether you came in the room or not. Some people are happy you're there. What I'm thinking is if I can get past the first ten minutes, everything is going to be fine. But that first ten minutes is hard.

I live in Jupiter because people here aren't constantly talking about show business.

We just had our fortieth reunion of *Deliverance.* Jon Voight and Ned Beatty, they still think I'm Lewis, the character I played. Regardless of their success—Ned has been nominated for an Academy Award and Jon has won one—regardless of that, they say: "Where are we going for dinner, Lewis? Can we go to dinner?" I have to tell them what to do.

I can play a cop. I've played my dad hundreds of times. I played a lot of people in my life. I'll take that walk. I'll take that smile. All actors are thieves.

Playing college football was a wonderful time for me. When I think of it, I have nothing but great memories, despite the fact that it was brutal. It was hard to watch guys getting hurt and being cut, and their dreams, since they were old enough to dream, were suddenly over.

I remember when I was in high school, my football team went over to play St. Pete. It was my senior year. My girlfriend and I were walking around the city and seeing how many of those green benches we could sit on in the space of a half hour. We got up to one hundred.

If I hadn't become an actor, I would have become a teacher, and I would have been a coach, a football coach. That was my calling.

My part in *Deliverance*, Lewis, was the most gratifying, because it was the most difficult character to play. He was such an egomaniac that the only thing that was forgivable was that he really was as good as he thought he was.

You never have to be rude, even if people are rude to you.

In high school, I dated a girl from Palm Beach, and, I'll never forget, the second night I had a date with her I went to the door and rang the doorbell. Her mother, who was very attractive, came to the door and said, "From now on, Buddy, when you come to pick up Mary Alice, please come to the service entrance." And I said: "Well, that's all right. That's what I had in mind, anyway."

Filming *Smokey and the Bandit* was the most fun, and I formed lifelong friendships. Jackie Gleason was my mentor and friend forever. Nobody made me laugh more. He was in tremendous pain at that time, but you never knew it on the set. Sally Field, of course, I fell in love with her.

Being shy helps you in the sense when you get a character to play who is not shy; you revel in it. You just love the fact that this guy has no problem walking into a party and just taking over. That guy is somebody I had no idea was lurking inside me.

Florida is a football factory. If you can out-recruit everyone in the state of Florida, you can win a national championship.

You know, Ted Williams was not the kindest guy to fans. I had the honor to go bonefishing with him in the Keys. He was a great fisherman, a great sportsman, and I loved being with him, but that period of time when I got out of the car to when we were fishing, I hated that time, before and after the fishing, because I knew that somewhere along the line he was going to say something that I can't repeat to people who came up and asked him for his autograph.

Smokey and the Bandit has a life that I can't explain. It goes on and on. When we did the picture, sales of Trans Ams went up 700 percent, so GM gave me a Trans Am every year. Well, I gave one to my niece. I gave one to my nephew. I gave one to someone else. After five years went by, I didn't get my Trans Am. I didn't want to be one of these schmucks who calls up and says, "Where's my Trans Am?" But I thought maybe something happened in the delivery or something, so I called GM. They put me through to one guy, then another, then another, and I finally ended up talking to the president, and he said, "I'm the new president, and I didn't like that movie." I never got another one.

MEL TILLIS

Singer, entertainer, interviewed in September 2015, when he was eighty-three, Ocala. Tillis died in November 2017.

I CAME HOME FROM my first day of elementary school, and I said, "Mama, do I stutter?" She said, "Yes, son, you do." I said, "Mama, they laughed at me." And she said, "Well, son, if they're going to laugh at you, give them something to laugh about." I went back to school the next day, and that was my very first day in show business.

My uncle had a bakery down in Pahokee, Florida, and he called my daddy and said he needed help with the bakery, so we moved from Plant City to Pahokee, and that's where I grew up. I still consider Pahokee my hometown.

There was an empty lot up from where we lived and some people come in there and put up a tent, Church of God folks. We're Baptists, but my mom wanted us to go because there'd be music. I sat on the front row. They come out there with them banjos and guitars, and I thought that was the finest thing in the world. It really inspired me. From then on, I started trying to sing, and I realized I could sing without stuttering. I'd listen to Bob Willis on the radio and the Grand Ole Opry, and I'd sit there with that dog-gone radio, and I learned them songs. I was only about six years old.

Stuttering opened doors for me. I know that. I know people came to my shows to laugh at me—and I let them laugh. The next thing I knew, I did thirty-nine Johnny Carson shows—and *The Mike Douglas Show*, *The Merv Griffin Show*, *The Dinah Shore Show*, *The Dean Martin Show*, a bunch of movies and TV shows.

Florida's got hundreds and hundreds and thousands of lakes, and those lakes used to be so clean and pure. I'm concerned about the lakes now. So many of them are polluted up.

If you can laugh, son, you've got it made. It's the best medicine in the world.

I graduated from high school in 1951 and attended the University of Florida, and I was there for three months. I went home for the Christmas holidays, and I told my Daddy, "I ain't going back to school, Daddy." And he said, "If you ain't going back to school, you're going to work in the bakery." And I said, "Daddy, I don't want to be a baker." So, I signed up for the Air Force. I had my training, took an aptitude test to find out what I was suited for, and waited for my orders. The orders came in and said for me to report to the Fourth Army Baking School in San Antonio, Texas. I tell folks I served my country: I served them cakes and cookies and pies and donuts and bread.

Stuttering made me a stronger person.

I was in a few of them Burt Reynolds movies. I did *Smokey and the Bandit II*. I had a scene with Jackie Gleason. That was fun. I really liked him. I did *Cannonball Run*, one and two. Burt's from West Palm Beach, and I'm from Pahokee, about 35 miles away. He always called me Pahokee trash.

My parents taught me how to behave. I got a little switching now and then. You can't switch your children no more, but it worked on me.

I was working with Minnie Pearl and her band, and we opened in Melvin, Iowa. In those days, I really stuttered bad. Roger Miller came out and introduced me, and then, after my song, Roger came back out and said, "Melvin says thank you." This went on for two or three days.

Miss Minnie didn't know I stuttered at the time. Nobody told her, and I didn't do too much talking, but she noticed something was wrong. She took me aside and said, "Melvin, I notice you have some kind of speech problem." She said: "Melvin, if you're going to be in our business, you have to introduce your own songs. You need to thank the folks and you need to sign autographs." I said: "Miss Minnie, I can't do that. They'll laugh at me." She said: "No they won't. They'll laugh with you." From that day on, I started talking onstage a little bit at a time.

I've been around kids who stutter. They come around to my autograph line. I try not to stutter around them because I want to inspire them and help them. I'll keep in touch with a lot of them.

Growing up in Pahokee, it was just like I was Huckleberry Finn. We had Lake Okeechobee to play in. It was like we had our own lake and we shared it with the birds.

My daddy stuttered a little bit, and my brother, he stuttered a little bit, and I stutter. Until I went to school, I thought that was just the way people talked.

I met Al Pacino when we both got a national medal of the arts award a couple years back. He's got that northern accent. He said to me, "You talk funny." I said, "Shit, you do, too."

That's what you do it for, the applause and the appreciation.

I had a guy come through my autograph line not too long ago. He said: "Mel Tillis! I paid thirty-five dollars to hear you stutter, and you ain't stuttered one damn bit!" I said, "I'm trying to quit, sir."

ENTREPRENEURS

George Billiris

Sponge diver, sponge seller, interviewed in February 2016, when he was eighty-nine, Tarpon Springs. Billiris died in September 2016.

GEORGE BILLIRIS

MY MOTHER WAS BIG ON EDUCATION, but I'd go sponging every summer. At fourteen years old, I was making as much money as the local bank president—not only me but all the divers. In the winter, I'd go to school.

The reason I'm in Tarpon Springs is because my grandfather was invited to help develop the sponge industry here. Greece had a sponge industry and was the only country in the world that had sponge divers. It was right around 1900. They found an abundance of sponge here, and immediately the migration started. The industry went from nothing, no boats, to 180 boats, and Tarpon Springs became the sponge capital of the world.

You want success? Help other people be successful. You only get what you give.

If you take a look at the history of the natural sponge, you'll see it goes back thousands of years. Cleopatra would use a natural sponge when she bathed in goat's milk. You'll find a natural sponge in King Tut's grave, embalmed, because it is an animal. And also, when Christ was crucified and he asked for water, they gave him vinegar from a sponge.

Without a sense of humor, you're out of luck. There's a bright side to all of it, regardless of how bad it really is.

In today's world, you have about 1,400 commercial uses for natural sponge. Anything that has to do with the cleansing or the smoothing of an object in the commercial world, they use a natural sponge. The demand for the natural sponge on the world market is twelve times greater than the supply. The problem is lack of supply. The natural sponge does a better job than the synthetic sponge, but, today, in my eyes, the synthetic sponge is a necessary evil.

I listen to the different politicians running for office. I watch them every night on TV—and I laugh every night.

We used to lose eight to ten men a year. When I was growing up, it wasn't odd to go downtown and see forty or fifty divers crippled from the bends.

My father's words to me were: "Work is like medicine. It cures everything."

I believe I have an advantage over someone who is not multicultural because I'm enjoying both cultures.

Tourism has become very important to Tarpon Springs. The youngsters have 102 gift shops, and I think 25 restaurants down here now. They'll do very well, but what they must not forgot and what they must build on is the Greek culture and the sponge industry.

I remember going to school and playing football, of course, and I remember the guy on the PA system. We were playing Clearwater High, and he named all the players, you know, and when he got to Tarpon Springs, everyone was Greek, or 95 to 99 percent of us, so he could hardly pronounce our names. But we had a quarterback out of Palm Harbor, and his name was Smith. The announcer was like, "Oh my God, we have a Smith!"—a name he could finally pronounce.

Let's don't act like something. Let's be something.

The people who came here from Greece came here without money, without knowing the language, without anything, and yet they developed a great industry and made us what we are today.

Every kid has their little cell phone or their little iPads or e-pads or whatever you call them. We're going into a totally computerized world, which is good and not good. We're losing the basic fundamentals of life, and we don't even see it.

We had the BP spill not long ago. That wiped out the sponges in deep water and north Florida, so now the boats are working inshore.

I never wanted to do anything else but work in sponges. I worked in the A&P meat market for a while. I didn't like it.

The populace of America is from all over the world. Because you've been here two generations longer than the next guy doesn't make you a better American. It doesn't make you a better citizen. You cannot, and must not, and should not take a paintbrush and just say, "No more Muslims, no more Greeks, no more this, no more that."

A sponge diver is the type of person who is not afraid.

My father's generation, they lived the law of common sense. They didn't learn anything from books. They learned from living, and that's the way we learned. There were sayings for everything, like, "Don't wait until you're hungry to cook."

Unfortunately, Florida is moving away from its primary resources, which are fisheries and citrus.

I plan to go out this summer for the last time and make one more dive. I'll probably work anywhere from 30 to 40 feet deep, west-northwest of here. It used to be my favorite spot, the place where I got started. I miss it.

ED DROSTE

Hooters cofounder, interviewed in November 2013, when he was sixty-two, Clearwater Beach.

I NEVER COOKED A CHICKEN WING. Not one in thirty years.

Study the market. Study what the market's looking for. Identify the niche, and then evaluate your product objectively and find out if it meets that niche or if you need to modify your product to meet the niche.

In college, I promptly disappointed everyone by struggling through a 2.3 grade point average. The idea of becoming a lawyer kind of went to the side.

When we opened the doors to the first Hooters, nothing. I'm panicking. I had to get it going. I thought advertising, but I had no budget. My partners were like, "Eddie what do you need an advertising budget for?" So my budget was me renting a chicken costume and running around in traffic.

I dedicated a hall up at Iowa State, where I went to college. It's supposed to be like a study hall—the Droste Den. It's really cool, but the last time I was up there everybody's in there sleeping, and I thought: "How appropriate. That's kind of the way I went through school."

Our planning was done on beer napkins.

I've had a lot of luck with a little thing I've done over the years, which is I focus on cultivating my strengths. I know what I'm good at and I want to get better, so I cultivate it. But I also know my weaknesses. In a million years, I'm not going to get really good at financial reporting. I'm not going to get really good at empirical studies. I don't have the discipline for it.

Entrepreneurs worry all the time. You're going to bed a little bit scared and waking up a little scared, but that's why you do it. You like that little fear factor.

I'm a big Ronald Reagan fan. I got to meet him a couple of times. I loved the guy.

Even when we were having legal issues among the partners, we always remained civil with each other. Our attorneys could never understand how we could beat each other up in court and then go out for beers afterward.

My wife, Marsha, is fantastic. She's young, a lot younger than me, so maybe it's not out of the question that we have a kid. The kid would have to call me Grandpa. Right now, we are considering the biggest, biggest decision of our marriage. We are thinking about a dog or maybe two dogs.

We picked this date, November 25, 1995, for the Hooters March on Washington. We put in basically our last resources and we bought ads in the *Washington Post*, the *New York Times*, and *USA Today*. It was a gloomy day. We didn't know if anyone would show up at the press conference. We walked into the room, a gigantic room, and it's mobbed. The walls are covered with cameras. The podium has like fifteen microphones. We were on all the networks. We were in all the newspapers—98 percent of the left-page editorials came out in our favor. We had like four available bullets left in our gun, and we got them with the first bullet. The EEOC dropped the case.

Sen. Connie Mack pulled me into the Moffitt Cancer Center. First, I was just a major supporter. A few years back, I was elected chairman of the foundation's board for a two-year term that I'm now in my sixth year of. I'm passionate about bringing collaboration to the cancer battle—collaboration internally, doctors collaborating with researchers—but even more importantly, institutions collaborating with institutions.

When we first started Hooters, myself and five partners, we kind of represented the niche. The restaurant industry was overwhelmed with fern bars at the time: Chili's. TGI Fridays. Bennigan's. We were all from the Midwest, and so our idea was Midwest meets carefree beach oasis. We tested it on ourselves. We figured if it worked on us, it would work on others.

We don't embrace the term "breastaurant," but it's often said. We were first in the category, but that isn't what we set out to create.

I love golf. I have this foursome with Jon Gruden, myself, Bruce Allen [general manager of the Washington Redskins], and Jim McVay, the Outback Bowl CEO. We play smash-mouth golf. We're all pretty crappy golfers, but we trash-talk. We'll build up a match like it's the Super Bowl.

Marsha came up through the Hooters ranks. She became a trainer. She opened a lot of stores. She was in the calendar a bunch of times. I always voted against her because I thought she had pudgy cheeks. We still laugh about that. Her nickname is Mosh, and I kept hearing about this Mosh—"Oh, you've got to meet Mosh"—because I was single for a lot of years. When I met her the first time, I said: "She's too bubbly. She's too nice. This has to be fake. Nobody's this nice." But she really is.

RICHARD GONZMART

Columbia
restaurant
president,
philanthropist,
interviewed
in December
2011, when he
was fifty-eight,
Tampa.

My GRANDFATHER ALWAYS TOLD ME, when business is slow, that's when you paint the restaurant. It shows strength. It shows you have confidence. Now, during the economic downturn, I'm investing in our properties. We're not downsizing. That's how you improve the economy. You show confidence in your products and people.

When I was twelve years old, I started working in the restaurant washing dishes. My father didn't want me washing dishes, but I wanted to. I learned how hard that work is. The dishwasher is the lowest-paid employee, operating the most expensive piece of equipment, responsible for the sanitation of every eating utensil and glass item for every customer. I hold them in the highest respect.

The way I look at it, and the way I hope my children will look at it, is this business is a legacy started by my great-grandfather. If you sell it, what good is money if you don't have a purpose in life?

I like a traditional hamburger. I don't like these gourmet burgers or these really big burgers. The big burgers are maybe good, but they're not an all-American hamburger, in my opinion, which is about a six-ounce patty, cooked on a hot grill, seared with some crunch.

Back in the '40s and '50s, if you used canned vegetables, that was considered really high-class, luxurious. After I got out of college and came back, the first thing I did was get rid of the canned vegetables.

Our 106 years of success can be ruined by one visit. You're only as good as the last meal.

I learned twenty years ago that I have a learning disability. It was obvious in school, but nobody knew it. I'm dyslexic, and I have ADHD. This is not a weakness. It's my strength, my creativity. But it has taught me that I have to hire people to execute what I want done, because I've got a thousand things going on. I love chaos.

My favorite at lunchtime is boliche, stuffed eye round with chorizo. It's not a good seller, but I won't ever take it off the menu. I just don't understand why it doesn't sell: white rice, black beans, plantains, and this wonderful, rich beef. Maybe I need to change the menu description.

People start treating a family business as their personal bank account. You can't do that. That's the demise of any family business—or company.

My wife and I go to Spain three times a year on business, and I love the food, but I also love Thai and Vietnamese food. I like the freshness of Asian food, the quick preparation, the vegetables.

When the restaurant is really, really busy, it's best for me not to be there because I'll stop everything if I see something I don't like. I'm horrible to have dinner with because I'm totally distracted.

What I dislike is people putting salt on the food before they taste it.

When I was a kid, I was in the 4-H. I had a Black Angus I refused to show in the fair because I didn't want it to get sold and butchered. Some people thought I was going to be a vet because I love animals so much. I don't hunt. I can't stand killing anything. Although I've run with the bulls in Spain, I don't like bullfighting. I admire the bulls, their power.

I'm a comfort food guy.

When I make a decision, I think about how I'm impacting the 850 people who work for us. I can't be careless with their lives. When the economy was going down, my CFO said we have to cut the 401(k). I said no.

I've run sixteen or seventeen marathons. I really hate running marathons.

The Cuban sandwich is really a Tampa sandwich. There's no Cuban sandwich per se. In Miami, they do a Cuban sandwich, but it's different. They don't do the salami. The Tampa sandwich is an immigrant sandwich. The salami is from the Italians. The ham from the Spanish. The pork from the Cubans. The cheese, the mustard, the pickles from the Germans. I have menus from the '40s that called it the mixed sandwich.

Until you love an animal, your soul has not been awakened.

I'm no saint, but I've never asked a woman to show me her boobs. At Gasparilla, we're out there to show respect for our heritage, not to be jerks. So, a few years ago, I took a stand, and I resigned from the krewe that was founded by my father. I'm not in the parade anymore.

We have to make mistakes in business. We may have to make ten mistakes to get to that one success. You just hope the ten aren't fatal.

If it was up to me, I'd have chickens and a dozen dogs at my house.

The day after Lee Roy Selmon died, I prayed to God, I said, "Lord, help me to be kind and gentle like Lee Roy Selmon." Ten minutes later, I was all fired up about something. OK, I'm not a Lee Roy Selmon.

Every morning, I think, "What can I do today?" It drives my wife crazy. I love my wife. I met her when she was fourteen and I was sixteen. I married her when she was eighteen and I was twenty. She wants me to relax. I can't. There will be time to relax when I'm dead.

My education in the restaurant business literally started when I was a baby. The Columbia was my playground.

I can remember feeling stupid because the way I read is different. I always want to read right to left. It makes it tough.

My dogs love me. It's unconditional love. My dog Rusty, he would literally die for me. I only wish I could be half the man my dogs think I am.

People think I don't sleep, but I do. I wake up at one or two in the morning and start sending emails. I sign off my emails, "Here's to life" because that's all we have. Life is short. It's fleeting. That's why I wake up early. I'm trying to get two lives out of one.

Ward Hall

Carnival barker, owner of a traveling sideshow, nicknamed "The King of the Sideshow," interviewed in October 2011, when he was eighty-one, Gibsonton. Hall died in August 2018.

FOR YEARS, I PARTNERED with a marvelous knife thrower. I was a ventriloquist, but I also stood in as his knife-throwing target for seventeen years. I was hit in the head. I was hit in the nose twice, once in each arm and once in each leg. I'd light a cigarette and hold it in my mouth, and he would throw the knife and cut the cigarette in half. When I got hit in the nose the second time, that was it, and we never did the cigarette trick again. The act kept getting shorter and shorter because, anytime I got hurt, we'd take that trick out of the act.

Gibsonton, Florida, used to be worldwide home of the freaks. There were seventy-five to eighty-five human oddities who lived here at the peak, everyone from Sealo the Seal Boy to Percilla the Monkey Girl. We had alligator-skinned people, fat men, fat ladies, dwarfs, giants, people with claws, people with no arms. I can introduce you to all the freaks now in ten minutes. I'll take you to the cemetery. That's where they're all at.

I had just turned fifteen, and I answered an ad I saw in the *Billboard* newspaper that they wanted a sideshow magician and fire-eater for the Dailey Brothers Circus. It was a small circus, and I thought it would be a good place for me to learn, so I answered the ad. I got a telegram back from the sideshow manager offering me the job, and the old nosy landlady in the walkup we lived in didn't give it to me. She waited until my father came home and gave it to him. So he looked at the telegram, and he said, "Well, what in the hell is all of this about?" I said: "Dad, I'm not asking you. I'm telling. I'm going to go with the circus." He said: "Well, you might as well go ahead and do it. You'll get it out of your system and be home in two weeks." Well, I'm eighty-one years old now, and my two weeks still aren't up.

My greatest skill is talking.

Here's how I started my business. It was 1948, and I left one circus because I wasn't getting paid, and I joined this other circus. The manager of the sideshow at that circus had a nice family, two little kids, and his wife was a sword swallower. But he was a terrible alcoholic, and about every three or four days he would get drunk and couldn't work. One time, he was drunk, and I saw the need, so I stepped in for him, called the bally, drew the people in, and opened the show. Afterward, the circus owner came to me and said, "You know, Ward, I can't have that guy getting drunk all the time, and if he does it again I'm going to fire him, and I want you to become the sideshow manager." After about three or four days, the guy got drunk again, and I was the sideshow manager at the age of seventeen.

I moved to Gibsonton in 1967. Before that, I lived in Miami Beach for a while. In all of those years, because I'm on the road so much, I only spent three summers in Florida. No one should ever have to live in Florida in the summertime.

My family? Yes, I have a big family. All of those oddities. They were my friends.

My first job, I was fourteen, and I got hired as a circus clown. Now, I knew that the clowns put something on their face, but I wasn't sure what it was. So, I put on what I thought were some funny-looking clothes and went out and bought a pound of Crisco. I put that Crisco on my face, which made me look more hideous than funny.

I used to love to dance. I'd rather dance than eat. Percilla the Monkey Girl and I used to spend hours on the dance floor. She was a marvelous dancer, and her husband, Emmett Bejano, the Alligator-Skinned Man, didn't like to dance.

We call them the do-gooders, the people against the freak shows. But those people have never talked to a human oddity. If they did, they would know that 99 percent of the human oddities who appeared in sideshows were hams at heart, and they loved the applause.

Today, the carnival is all about the rides. There are so many rides, so many big rides, that there's no longer room for a sideshow. They don't even have room for all of the rides. That's what's really killing the sideshow.

I wouldn't give you fifty cents a week for a fat man today because you can go to any buffet restaurant and in two hours see more fat people who would have qualified to appear at a sideshow than you actually would see at a real sideshow. It's the same thing with tattooed ladies. I wouldn't give you five cents for a tattooed lady.

When I was about eight years old, I did get to see my first circus. When I got home, I'm telling my grandparents about the circus and about what I saw, and my grandfather said: "Ward, that's what you ought to do. You ought to join a traveling circus." I never forgot that.

I'm eighty-one, going on eighty-two, and I want to work until I'm one hundred. Then, I want to retire so I can travel.

The last time I did a juggling act steadily was 1986. About that time, I had to get glasses, bifocals, and you can't juggle wearing bifocals.

It seems like politicians only have two jobs in their life—to get elected and reelected. They literally don't give a shit if they do anything for the public.

I want to see all of the things in the United States that I missed while I was on tour. Most of the time I was going down the highway, and all I saw were the backs of trailers. I have worked in New York City every year since 1960, and yet I have never been to the Guggenheim Museum. I have never been to Ellis Island or the Statue of Liberty. I want to see Yellowstone and Yosemite and all these things I've never seen.

My father always hoped I would be either a trial lawyer or a preacher, and if I had my life to live over again, that's what I would want to do, either be a preacher or a trial lawyer.

It's nice when you get to be as old as I am because you can give lectures, you can tell stories and write things, and you're able to embellish things a little because all the other people who were there are all dead. There's nobody to dispute what you say.

H. Irwin Levy

Attorney, Century Village developer, interviewed in January 2015, when he was eighty-eight, West Palm Beach.

H. Irwin Levy

I'm from Scranton, Pennsylvania. I was going to Cornell Law School, just finished my second year, got married, and came to Florida on my honeymoon in June of 1950. I took a look at Miami Beach and couldn't believe it. What a world it was! I called my father and told him I'm not leaving.

Century Village is the first of its type. From a lifestyle standpoint, we were different. When I was a kid, I remember people going to the Catskill Mountains in New York. Jewish people all went to the Catskills. They went for the lifestyle. There was all kinds of entertainment and fun and this and that, and I thought to myself, "Why shouldn't they want to retire and buy a home in Florida that has all the amenities of the Catskills?" That's the idea behind Century Village.

I'm very involved with Israel, and I'm concerned about its ability to survive. I know a lot of people there. Bibi [Israeli prime minister Benjamin Netanyahu] and I have been friendly for thirty-five years.

My family was in the wholesale shoe business. When I was in high school, my father wouldn't let me play football or anything like that. I had to work in the store.

I travel a little bit, but I like staying home. I love Florida.

We targeted retired schoolteachers, retired policemen, bus drivers—normal working people who made a living, saved a few bucks, had a little pension, had Social Security, and wanted to retire to Florida. Many thousands of people moved here. We had great timing.

I like comedies. I like musicals. I don't like serious things.

There's always a charity that has a problem that's calling me. I get that daily practically. I've been in Palm Beach County so long that almost every Jewish organization here, I was involved in starting it.

I got Red Buttons to do my marketing. He came out of the Catskills. I remembered him from the movie *Sayonara*. He got an Academy Award for that. He was terrific. Everybody knew him. Everybody liked him. He had the greatest sense of humor. He could not be not funny. He was on all the time. No matter what you said, he had a funny remark about it. You couldn't sit with him for five minutes without becoming hysterical.

My daughter is funny. She's a geophysicist. I kid her that she's the only geophysicist in the world who doesn't know a thing about oil. She's an expert on earthquakes and tsunamis. Try to make a living on that!

I'm not as smart as you think I am. I didn't know a damn thing about building, but I was smart enough to ask for help.

Every time I negotiated a deal, I always considered the other side of the fence. What could I do and what couldn't I do if I was in the other guy's shoes? What would I need and what would I not need?

I remember when it was a two-lane road between Miami and West Palm Beach, and there was nothing practically in between.

We bring voting machines into our clubhouses—and that's part of the activities. The residents love it. They get in the bus. They go to the clubhouse, and they vote. Everybody votes. You remember the famous Bush-Gore recount? Those ballots were from Century Village.

I knew Bernie Madoff very well. I used to play golf with him and his wife. After about four holes, he'd say, "You know, I've got a problem and I got to leave, but you continue on," and I would finish the round with his wife. Looking back, I think he knew the day had to come. He was very smart. He knew he was at the end of his rope. His liabilities were getting bigger. His problems were growing all the time because he had commitment after commitment after commitment, and he kept using people's capital. The day that money started slowing down, that was the day he was dead, and he knew it. I lost money, and I'm still waiting to get all of it back. I don't think I'll live long enough to see it, but, look, I've been screwed before. It's not the first time. It's part of life.

TONY LITTLE

Salesman, broad-
caster, fitness
advocate, inter-
viewed in Septem-
ber 2009, when
he was fifty-three,
Tampa.

SOME PEOPLE SAY I DON'T HAVE A FILTER. I say it like it is. You're not going to make everyone happy, but if you're saying the truth and what you believe, why is it wrong?

I've built myself into a brand. There are three business books out there now, maybe four, and they each have three or four pages on me.

During a bad economy, you have to be able to change quickly. You have to diversify. If you know that a category is going to be going down because it's a luxury item, you better friggin' change.

In the early '80s, I won Mr. Florida and won Junior Mr. America and was chosen kind of as one of the big prospects for Mr. America, and then I was hit by a Pinellas County school bus. I got back damage and shoulder damage. I entered Mr. America four weeks later, even though I couldn't train, which was not a good thing, but I still placed fifth. Then everything fell apart. I was out of work for probably about two years, went, "Why me? Why me?" And got addicted to painkillers. I saw Jane Fonda on television, saw her doing her new high-impact aerobic dance–type stuff, and I immediately saw an opportunity to come back in a new profession as a personal trainer.

I like cars. I gotta get out of driving these sports cars, though. I've been lucky—'97 was my last big crash.

Billy Mays could sell anything. I can't sell anything because I can only sell things I truly, truly believe in and I'm involved in. Billy, he was an endorser. Half the stuff I have I take from concept to development. I don't go on and endorse a product unless I own part of the product.

I've turned down at least six reality shows over the years. They want the bad things. They want the dysfunctional. Everyone ends up in a divorce. I don't want that.

My son was overweight when he was young. He was a big kid, and people would say to me all the time, "Are you helping him lose weight?" I wasn't going to push my son. I can be a good role model, but I'm not going to make the kid cry or anything like that. Now, he's like the leanest, meanest jock around, and he did it himself.

I'm a believer that you've got to speak up. You've got to go for it. I can take a lot of no's to get a yes. All you ever need is one.

You do have to realize that on television it has to be very simple to understand. You can't go into technical things. You're not buying a pelvic pillow. You're buying the idea that you can sleep better. It has to serve a purpose. It has to be life-changing.

I love Florida. Best of all, the people in Florida are nice.

Most people think I'm hyper, but I am very low-key and hardly speak at all during the day. Obviously, a couple cups of coffee and an energy drink every once in a while helps stimulate that central nervous system for a better presentation.

I've failed a lot in my life. I just also have a shotgun marketing technique. I find a lot of things, and, if I love them, I do them all at once, and I just need one to work.

My mom was a single mom with four kids, and I was a very hyperactive, unruly child. It was very hard to hold me down. It was very hard for a mom with four kids.

I'm fifty-three, and I still have all my hair, which is a big thing.

I hit a tree at 55 mph. I was getting ready to do the Gazelle infomercial—and everybody knows the Gazelle was a huge hit for me—and the company in Ohio let me go because I had 200-some stitches in my face and we were three weeks out from shooting the show. But I didn't take the "no." I got on a plane and I went to Ohio and I talked to the president of that company. I said to him that I felt that the American public would be more impressed with my infomercial with me having the problem. It was a huge hit. It did $66 million on that one show.

Passion is the big thing. People understand passion.

Home Shopping kept turning me down. They wouldn't buy my videos. The buyers would go, "No, we don't sell videos here." I tried and tried and tried. They wouldn't take me, so do I quit, or do I realize there's always a way? In my mind-set, there's always a way. So, I find out that Bud Paxson's son Todd owns a gym in Clearwater, so I get in my car and I drive over to the gym and introduce myself to Todd Paxson. And I say I used to be a Mr. Florida and a Mr. Junior America and I understand the gym business inside and out. I'd be willing to work with you and help you with the gym business if you can get me fifteen minutes with your dad. And he said, "Hop in your car." So I hopped in my car, followed him, the gates open at this big estate. We drove right in. They open the door. His dad is standing right there. He looked at me and said, "You've got five minutes." I told him about my videos. And he said, "You're the guy who keeps calling." He made a bet. He said he'll take four hundred videos, and if they sell out in four airings on the Home Shopping Network, we'll do some business. It sold out in four minutes. I've been there ever since.

I continually have to sell myself. Nobody else can sell me.

If you're lucky, you have eighty or ninety summers in your life. That's not a whole hell of a lot to be honest with you. So, if I have thirty summers left, why would I not be proactive? Why would I not want the best for my children? Why would I not want to be a superachiever?

If you love something, you should be able to gush about it. There are great salespeople who can sell all day long, selling a product that they might not have anything to do with it. For me, it's the passion of loving something. I don't sell anything I don't love.

My confidence comes from still sitting here after all the times that things tried to kill me.

Being fifty-three, it sucks. The worst thing for me about getting to be fifty-three, other than the pain and stuff that I go through from the accidents, is I don't feel it. I look at other people my age and go, "Do I look like that?"

JOE REDNER

Adult-business entrepreneur, interviewed in June 2016, when he was seventy-six, Tampa.

IF I'M FREE, and if this is a free country, then I should be able to do what I please in private with consenting adults. Being able to do what you want—as long as you don't hurt someone else—is the essence of freedom.

When I see wrong, I'm very confrontational.

In 1976, the club went all nude, and the City of Tampa started coming at me. They'd arrest me. They'd arrest the dancers. They arrested everybody they could. They really went Gestapo, but I was a match for them. I figured out how I could keep operating while they were making all those arrests. I wasn't afraid of getting arrested. I was more afraid of not being able to make a living.

I was on a public access TV show arguing with a guy about my opinions, and he started calling me a liar. But I was giving my opinion, so it can't be a lie. It's an opinion! So I explained to him the difference between a fact and an opinion, that an opinion is the conclusion I came to based on the facts, and I said: "Here's a fact. You're fat!" He got mad, and he got up and he walked around and got a chair, a heavy bamboo chair, and he threw it at me and it hurt me. I was sore for a couple of days.

I won't have a friend who doesn't treat people right. I don't care how good you treat me. That's how I judge people, and it doesn't take me long to find out.

We moved to Tampa when I was eight from New Jersey. I didn't hear anything about race in New Jersey. When we came down here, I noticed the water fountains—colored or white. That was an injustice that just glared at me. Treating people like that, I never understood.

I've run for public office nine times. Tampa City Council. Hillsborough County Commission. State House. And I might run again. It depends on my health. But I've learned it's hard to overcome a reputation. I'm an atheist, and I'm an adult-business owner. That makes it hard to get elected.

Some of them just want company. Some of them will pay a dancer to sit there and talk to them. Some will pay for a back rub. Some just want to look.

I reason very well, but I don't have a good memory, so I have to analyze things over and over.

When I first started in the adult business, I did drugs. I did cocaine. I smoked. I drank—and then I started turning yellow when I drank. It was affecting my liver. So I quit. I didn't touch a drop in twenty-five years. Then Joey got this brewery [his son, Joey, founded Cigar City Brewing in 2009], and I decided I'm going to taste some beer. I drank just a little but didn't like the feeling. I want no part of it.

I'm a rich person, and I say, "Raise my taxes."

If I didn't think a law was just and it didn't serve a purpose, I didn't obey it.

I don't care about Democrats. I don't care about Republicans. I don't care about the political parties. I'm a progressive. That's how I think. I'm a Bernie Sanders man. He thinks just like I always have. He's me.

Having stage 4 lung cancer, I quit smoking marijuana, but I started doing edibles. Man, I went through some chemo and radiation, and it was aggressive radiation because I'm healthy, and that marijuana saved me. The chemo puts you on edge. You can hardly live in your own body, but the marijuana calmed me down.

I'm on a train in Europe, and someone asks me where I'm from, and I tell them I'm from Tampa, Florida, and they said, "Oh, Mons Venus." And I said, "That's me!"

Dancers are smart. You think they're all objects or something, but they're smart.

When I was a kid, I got hit by a car. I was supposed to hold my brother's hand, but I told him I didn't want to hold his hand, and I ran out into the street. I was probably six or seven.

I work out every day, not a heavy workout, not a hard workout, not a long workout, but I work out a body part every day.

Education is the big equalizer, but look at what they're doing to education in this state. They don't fund it. They starve it.

What it takes to be a father, I'm not good at. I didn't spend the time I should have with my children. My son Joey, though, he's a good father, I mean a freaking good father.

Every day, I'm on Facebook. That's how I get the frustration out, by posting political stuff. I don't put family stuff on there. I just attack. I attack what I think is injustice.

I'm a raw vegan. I eat all raw vegetables. Raw fruits. Seeds. Nuts. I use olive oil and balsamic vinegar. I quit eating for taste, although I like the food I eat, and started eating for health.

All my managers are female. They've come up from being dancers. They know. They feel. They care. I have male security but no male managers.

Tradition to me means you can't figure something out, so you do it the same way it has always been done.

Every time the police would come up with a tactic to shut me down, I'd counter that tactic with a tactic of my own. I have always been defiant.

Homebuilder, founder of Arthur Rutenberg Homes, interviewed in July 2011, when he was eighty-four, Clearwater. Rutenberg died in March 2017.

One time we were sitting around, and, literally, my younger brother Dan started drawing on the back of an envelope. He put the master bedroom over to one side and created an entry into the dining room. He was trying to come up with a plan with almost no hallways to provide more square footage of livable space. What he did was develop the first split-floor plan.

My first business, I started when I was twenty-one, with three of my brothers, a retail business, housewares, gifts, and later it morphed into furniture. We made a living. What I learned was it took about the same length of time to sell a ten-dollar item as a three-hundred-dollar item. So I learned that selling higher-priced items is probably a better business than selling low-priced items. That's what pushed me into wanting to build houses.

As an old guy, I've been in this business in every cycle since World War II, and this is certainly the deepest and longest cycle we've had.

Why did it happen? It happened because credit was easy. More homes were being bought by investors than we understood. When your barber tells you he just bought three condominiums, you might expect the markets are a little bit askew.

The lesson we usually learn from something like this is nobody learns. But if you are going to learn anything, it's when assets are running up in price you have to know when to get off the train.

Flying is about the only hobby I still have. I still fly myself, although every year at my physicals the FAA gives me a hard time because I'm reasonably bionic. I've had five bypasses and a couple of stents. But I'm still licensed to fly. What I fly now is a little Cirrus SR22, just a nice single-engine airplane. It's a flying computer is what it really is. You go in there and press the buttons and it flies.

I'm not very much of a political animal, but if I were, my pet peeve would be the amount of government. It can get ludicrous. Approximately one-fourth of every dollar spent on a house has to do with government.

The split plan worked partly because of what was intended—more livable space—but it also became very popular that you could have a little separation from the kids. The master bedroom was on one side, and the secondary bedrooms were all the way on the other.

My father came over to this country in 1903 from what is now Poland, but it was Lithuania at that time. They kept moving the border around. He was eleven years old and worked for a nickel a day. Eventually, he owned his own retail store.

I'm not an architect or really too great at designing houses, but I know when I look at a house plan if it'll work.

Nobody had money during the Depression. My mother was a piano teacher. She would teach the dentist's kids piano, and he would fix our teeth. I had a very industrious upbringing. You learned to work.

After high school, I wanted to go to an engineering school, but Northwestern's engineering school didn't at that time take many Jewish kids because they couldn't place them. There was too much of a bias then toward Jewish employees in the engineering field. I went to the school on a Saturday to look around, and I ran into a guy who wanted to know what I was doing wandering around the halls. No one else was there. I told him I was thinking about applying, and so he took me for a walk around. We sat in his office and talked, and he asked me if I wanted an application. He handed me one, and he initialed it. I found out later he was the dean of the school, so I got in.

My father, being from eastern Europe, liked his meat well done. In eastern Europe, if there's any hint of pink or red showing, that means it's not done, so we had well-done meat. In my household, you didn't waste food. You sat there and you ate it.

To buy a house because it's an investment is probably in my opinion not the best reason to buy a house.

It's not like you get this one big hit, this one big lucky break, and that's how you find success. You have to earn your wings every day. What you've done last week is nice, but if you're building resources that can be brought to bear again, that's the trick.

MICHAEL SAUNDERS

Real estate executive, interviewed in May 2017, when she was seventy-four, Sarasota.

I CAN THROW A CAST NET BETTER THAN I CAN DANCE.

When I first started in real estate and I would travel the country and the world and would talk about Sarasota, people would say: "Oh, Saratoga. You must be into horses." And I'd go, "No, no, no, no, no, Sarasota—the west coast of Florida." I really worked hard trying to put Sarasota on the radar screen as a magical place to be and, thanks to me and many, many others, people listened and found the magic themselves.

I love to cook. Many of my friends today don't cook, so I'm in much demand when I have time to cook. I like comfort foods, whether it's a stew, a meatloaf, spaghetti sauce. You tell me what you like, and I'll try to cook it.

The lack of civility today is frightening to me. Civility is critical in problem solving. If you can't have a civil conversation about major issues impacting us today and into the future, you're not going to find solutions. It trickles down in terms of politics but also the workplace and in schools.

I don't watch television. I've never wanted a television in the house. There are books to read and art to see.

My parents' expectations of me were I could be anything I wanted to be, but I better be the best I could be. Dream the impossible dream, but be prepared to pay the price to make it come true.

Fun for me is business.

I think the cultural assets of the Sarasota community are what set it apart from other sun-kissed, beachfront, golfing areas in Florida and elsewhere. The arts make Sarasota different.

In this business, you have to be a good storyteller. You have to be able to paint a picture of what the lifestyle is like, what living in a particular house will be like.

When I started working, my mother told me to always buy the most expensive jacket I could afford. And she said to find an accessory that changes the look, so the accessory that changes the look for me became scarves. I could dress something up or I could dress it down. That's what began my lifelong collection and love affair with the scarf.

In 1957, my parents moved full-time from Tampa to the north end of Longboat Key. We had a little cottage. Daddy exercised his spirit of entrepreneurship and opened a marina. My earliest, fondest memories are of Longboat Key.

A long time ago, I learned that I don't make the market. I deal with the market I have.

I can teach you this business. This is not a business of rocket science. What I can't teach you are values and a positive attitude. You either have them or you don't, and if you don't, this is not the company for you.

Selby Gardens, I never tire of going there. I never tire of Ringling. I never tire of the beach.

I needed five thousand dollars to start the business in 1976, but as a woman, I couldn't get a loan. A client said he'd co-sign and I gave him my word that, no matter how long it takes, I will pay back every dime. Fortunately, I was able to pay back the bank, and I built the company brick by brick and step by step. I invested everything I made back in the company.

I'm a great, great believer in public education.

Without a strong educational system throughout the state of Florida, we're not going to attract people who have children to raise.

I got a full scholarship to the University of Florida's law school, but I needed a fellowship to attend. When I went to be interviewed for the fellowship, I was very politely told that they didn't give fellowships to women. I said OK. If those are the rules of the game, I need to come home and I need to work. Fortunately, they needed a history teacher at Manatee High School, so I taught for a year.

When I started my business, real estate companies then were a conglomeration of mismatched desks and chairs, and if there were photographs of properties, they were taped to the window and would curl and turn yellow in the sun. And people were not dressed professionally. Agents would come in wearing shorts and sandals. You're helping people make really important decisions, so why shouldn't you reflect that degree of professionalism? It was my goal to establish a real estate company where the offices looked professional and the people dressed professionally.

Probably one of things that I think is most important is the lack of affordable housing in our market area—and I think that's true across the country—but I think it's particularly true here, and I think that's something that as a community we have to face. Sarasota is not as affordable as we would like it to be.

More than twenty years ago, when the Ringling estate's Ca' d'Zan mansion was falling apart, and the balustrades were crumbling, and the roof was leaking, and the paintings on the ceiling were water-stained, I headed the capital campaign to restore it. That was 1995 maybe. It makes me feel full of joy to walk through Ca' d'Zan today.

What makes a real estate market is peoples' confidence in buying.

The Cortez fishermen loved to stop and chat with my father. He was quite the storyteller. We'd wake up in the morning, and one of the Cortez fishermen had left two or three trout on our doorstep or a couple of redfish for breakfast.

I came to real estate from probation and parole work. I worked with females who were on probation or were in abusive situations, and I quickly fell in love with that job because I saw I could make a difference. After that, I forgot about law school.

In the real estate business, you need solid core values and the right people, but marketing was always the underpinning of everything.

INDUSTRIALISTS

ROBERT M. "BOB" BEALL II

Chairman of Bealls
department stores, inter-
viewed in August 2015,
when he was seventy-
one, Bradenton.

THERE ARE MANY FORMS that leadership can take. I'm a quiet person, so my form is probably not as outgoing as many. But if you lead by example and you make more right decisions than wrong decisions, then you're probably going to do pretty well.

Florida's growth and the advent of the shopping center combined to fuel our growth. In the early '50s, the shopping center kind of got off the ground. Publix was doing a lot of shopping centers, and being able to tag along with Publix was really instrumental for us.

I was not in favor of the Bealls' one-hundred-year anniversary hoopla this year. I just thought, "Who would care about our company's anniversary?" But it turned out to be the right thing. Once we got into it, it was fun and enjoyable. I'm glad we did it. It was a mistake to not want to do it in the first place.

My dad's insistence that I work in the store while I was still in school was helpful to me in the long run. I remember—I must have been about fourteen or so—when I became the window washer for the old downtown Bradenton store. Later, when we opened another store, I was kind of promoted to janitor. I'm not sure which was the better job, but I learned from both. I learned to get there on time, even on a Saturday. My dad got very upset when I was late one of the first few days, and that never happened again.

My wife buys most of the family's clothes. She's a Bealls shopper for sure.

I was a little more risk-oriented in the older days. I remember I opened—I forgot the number of stores, maybe six or seven—but I opened enough stores in one year that it was 50 percent more sales space and store space than the previous year. My dad never said anything. I think he was worried. I was young, so I wasn't so worried. If, say, three or four of those stores had been dogs, then I think we probably would have been out of business. I wouldn't do it again.

Amazon is certainly going to continue to grow. They're a great organization. They're very predatory, and I don't use that negatively.

Subconsciously, I must have a style because I gravitate toward the same things. My casual clothes mostly come from Bealls. If I need a jacket or a suit or something like that—usually, when we're in New York for one thing or another once or twice a year—I'll go to Paul Stuart and get that.

Florida has had its little moments, but, in general, the growth has been terrific and very conducive to our sort of business.

The future of retail is going to be difficult, but I'm confident. We were very early to start an e-commerce function, selling goods through e-commerce. That was probably ten years ago. We thought at the time that technology could be the killer of retail. We were quite worried, so we wanted to get that going and we did, and we continue to put a lot of money into technology both in terms of the systems and software, people and so forth. My feeling right now is that if we put a lot of our department stores near the water in resorty sorts of areas, people who are on vacation and visitors who have a lot of leisure time will continue to see shopping as an activity they want to do.

I think we're becoming over time more and more like Europe in a way, maybe learning to enjoy things more and work a little less.

My grandfather started the company one hundred years ago. My dad ran the business, and I followed my dad. I feel like I was a good custodian of our brand, a good builder of it, but I never really thought a lot about being the standard-bearer of the company name. I'm not consciously trying to create a legacy per se. In that way, I suppose I'm like my dad. Our kids, they see what we do. They learn what they like about it and what they don't like about it—and they make their own choices.

The economy in 2008–2009 was very worrisome for me. My blood pressure was up.

I was on the golf team in high school, and that's probably about the last time I played golf. It just took up too much time.

From my family, I learned the importance of honesty certainly. From a business perspective, I learned the value of putting most of the profits back into the business rather than paying ourselves larger salaries.

I don't like the traffic and the crowded beaches and this and that, but I think growth is Florida's destiny.

Albert J. Dunlap

Businessman, philanthropist, nicknamed "Chainsaw Al," interviewed in April 2008, when he was seventy, Ocala. Dunlap died January 2019.

I'VE LIVED IN SEVENTEEN STATES and three countries, so I've lived in a lot of places. We lived in south Florida, which we liked very, very much, but what happened over time is it got a bit built up. We wanted to get a bit of land. Well, you know, they sell it by the inch in Boca. So, we looked in Ocala and found a place we really, really like and bought it. You can have privacy here, yet we're eight minutes from a Walmart. It's the best of both worlds.

I'm a dog person. No horses. I'm kind of an inner-city kid. To me, horses look like dinosaurs. Our neighbors have horses. We feed 'em carrots.

I got to know T. K. Wetherell, Florida State's president. Real nice. And then I got to know Bobby Bowden. I played golf with Bobby and developed a relationship. I respected them. They respected me. They named a practice field after me.

FSU needed a student success center, so the kids could interview for jobs. They had these little-bitty places all over campus, but you come to interview a kid, you sit on a plastic chair in a closet and that wasn't doing very well. They approached me and said they wanted to do this. It's very exciting to see it happening. I truly believe these kids are going to get a lot out of it. The groundbreaking is in September.

I was born in New Jersey. My dad worked in the shipyards. Re-member that movie *On the Waterfront*? Well, that's where my dad worked. Todd Shipyards in Hoboken. My mother worked in a five-and-dime.

After I kind of retired, I did this speaking tour with Mikhail Gor-bachev and Norman Schwarzkopf. We did New Zealand, Australia. Schwarzkopf, he was tough as hell, a big bear of a man. And Gorby was very bright, charismatic, and could be charming, but you knew you were dealing with somebody who wasn't exactly Mother Teresa.

I think all this stuff about Botox and all that is total nonsense. Keep yourself as fit as God allows you. Accept aging as a part of life. Don't do all this nonsense.

When I talk to these students at Florida State or any other college, I always say there's only one barrier in life that you can't get over, and that's the barrier you put there. Once you believe you can't do some-thing, forget it. You have zero chance.

My mother was a very strong person. She would always tell me: "You're a smart boy. You're a good athlete. You've got to make some-thing of yourself." She was kind of a guiding light for me.

I wanted to be the best. I've always been a very committed person, no matter what I did. Whatever the job, I do it full out. I saw people who I thought were smarter than me who didn't do too good because they didn't have that fire in the belly.

I've spoken at fourteen universities. The kids really want to find out how to be successful. Marry a rich woman. That works real good. Be born rich. That works terrific. Or go out and work for it.

There's a price for success, an enormous price. Leadership is very difficult. When you lead, you will be severely and unmercifully criticized when you make decisions. That's why most people don't want to lead.

Opportunity still exists in business, but it has become so technical. I'm essentially an industrialist. I worked in the factories and I learned about the products, like toilet tissue and cups, products you understood. Now you have all this high-tech stuff that nobody can pronounce, and it does something that nobody knows what it is.

If I didn't do what I did, cut back maybe 25 to 30 percent of the people, then the rest of the people, the 70 percent left, would have been out of work, too. Tragically, when you go into battle, you're going to lose some people. The thing is to save as many as you can, but people don't look at it that way. They just say I fired so many people.

We're in an era now where leaders don't want to be criticized. They're not willing to speak out. Myself, Jack Welch, people like that, they don't really exist now. People want to be liked. I always said, in business, strive for respect. If you want to be liked, get a dog.

My wife says that living with me is like being on a roller coaster, but it's a lot more fun than being on a merry-go-round.

I'll ask somebody: "How old do you think I am?" And they'll say, "seventy," and I'll be crushed. I think of myself as fifty.

I'm content. There's this country western song—everybody thinks I'm crazy when I say I like country western music—and it's about this guy living on the street, and another guy comes along and gives him a little handout, and the homeless guy says to him, "You know, I've had my moments." I'm not exactly living on the street, but I've had my moments. The theme is life changes.

We love our animals. We lost one of our dogs just this last year. We went up to Shands. They have an animal hospital up there. It came time to put the dog down. My wife was crying. I said I'll go in and lay on the floor with the dog when he gets the needle. There's a foreign student there. I don't know what his origin is, and I start crying, and I told him I used to be a paratrooper, and I'm sorry I'm crying, and he says to me: "It's alright to cry, Al. I cried when I lost my dog." Then he told me he's in Israeli special forces, and he's over here going to vet school.

I was at a party in England, and John Aspinall says to my wife,

"Where's Chainsaw?" And my wife says, "Who's Chainsaw?" And he says: "It's your husband. He's like a chainsaw. He cuts the fat away from companies and leaves a great sculpture." It was a wonderful compliment from a friend. I came back to the U.S., the media picks it up, and now I'm Chainsaw Al, the crazed killer. Chainsaw was always a nuisance to me because it was taken out of the original context.

Another thing that's enormously important is you've got to keep a sense of humor. Without a sense of humor, you're done.

When I look at what I've been in my life, I've certainly been a soldier. I was a paratrooper, an executive officer at a nuclear missile site, and I'm a graduate of West Point. I've obviously been a businessman in three continents. And I've been an author of a *New York Times* bestselling book. I've been a speaker on international tour. I've been a philanthropist. And I was born poor.

I was with like eleven major corporations. Some of them are not going to happen the way you wanted them to happen. Sunbeam was less enjoyable. Sunbeam, I don't talk too much about it.

When I was with Scott, I moved the headquarters to Boca Raton from Philadelphia, where it had been for 106 years. They had this enormous building, and there was no reason to have it. We got Scott squared away, but, boy, in the process of doing that, the criticism was unmerciful.

My father was a staunch union person. I'm cutting back all these people, and he says, "Why are you doing that?" And I said, "Dad, if I don't do this, they'll all lose their jobs." He reflected for a moment, and he said, "OK, that makes sense."

I loved to go out in the factories. I liked to go in the dining hall and sit at the lunch table. It was hard, though, to make this point—that I was called in as a last resort. And if I fail, you're all done.

It is not pleasant to have to lay people off. It is not pleasant to have to shut down factories. It is not pleasant to move headquarters. There's no joy in that, particularly if you come from a working-class background. I knew it when my father was out of work. He'd be out of work not because he didn't want to work, but because he got laid off. It was so hard on us. I wasn't a privileged preppy. I've seen my mother cry. But later in life, I had to do these things.

I would just go in, very strong-willed, and say we have to do this, this, and this. The early part of my career, I didn't know I was doing turnarounds. It was just go in and do a job. What the heck is a turn-around? But then that's what I became known as, the leading turn-around person in America.

A lot of guys would go from one corporation to another, and everything was already running fine. They didn't have to do a whole hell of a lot. Just don't do anything stupid. I could have taken the easy road. I could have stayed with Kimberly-Clark. Once I squared Scott Paper away, I could have stayed there. Eli Lilly, I could have stayed there after I got it squared away. A nice, easy life. But then what do you do? I'm just going to go through some perfunctory stuff, like a prop. I just have to look nice and wear a nice suit. It wasn't me. It wasn't a challenge. I would stay until the job was done, and about that time somebody would contact me about doing something else.

I like Jack Welch. He was charismatic. He got a hell of a lot of criticism, too. He asked me once to speak to some of his people in New York. I said to them: "You're so fortunate. You've got America's second-best CEO."

A heart doctor goes in and operates on your heart, but you don't want this guy cutting your heart open. It's crazy. But then he says: "OK, fine. If I don't do this, you will die." There's an analogy between that and business. Nobody wants to have a turnaround done. Nobody wants a heart operation. In either case, if the person doing it has the skill, the patient lives.

I didn't go into companies that were just bouncing along. I was never a custodian. Turnaround by definition means you're going to have to make very hard decisions, enormously controversial decisions, and you'll be criticized unmercifully.

Every corporation in the world has a culture. If it's a good culture, try to nurture it and make the necessary changes. But if it has a bad culture, you change it. When you try to change it and they all say, "We can't make that change," that's a culture. If they are not willing to change and you accept that, then you'll be no better than your predecessor.

Why the lion statues? Firstly, I'm a Leo. Born in July. But, secondly, you'll see other predators here. You'll see sharks and eagles, and the reason is I have this theory: a predator has to get its own dinner. It can't order room service. And I've always felt in life that the people I really respected went and got their own dinner. They earned it. They didn't sit back as privileged preppies and order room service. That's why I like predators.

My dad was a good man. My mom was a good woman. But the first mentor I had outside of my family was my football coach in high school. He was tough. He instilled in me that if you play the game, you're going to get knocked on your butt, but get up. He didn't accept any excuses. Just get up and get back in the game.

My whole life, I did what I believed. A lot of people didn't like it.

TOM JAMES

Chairman of Raymond James Financial, co-founder of the James Museum of Western & Wildlife Art, inter-viewed in August 2013, when he was sixty-nine, St. Petersburg.

BACK IN '74, when times were really tough and it looked like we were going broke, I had a written plan for how to shut the business down over a three-month period. When do I stop doing new business and just start delivering the stuff out before I run out of money? I had that plan. Boy, we were close.

How do I relax? Well, the answer is, I don't. I'm an activities-driven person. I fill up time. If I go on vacation, I have a schedule for every minute almost.

My father was one of the world's nice people. He was a really good person, a moral person of high integrity. He's the person who influenced me more than anyone else.

I started playing in a rock band when I was in high school. I went and saw Elvis Presley when he came to St. Petersburg in the 1950s and got really taken with the music. I got a guitar and taught myself how to play.

My wife raised our kids when they were young. If she wasn't there, I couldn't have done what I did.

I could write music when I was younger, but I never really worked hard at that, which is too bad, because I'm not sure I can do it anymore. You've got to have all these emotive juices flowing to write songs. It's good when you're young and thinking about women all the time.

My art education has been in the real world, looking at a lot of art, talking to artists. The more I talked to artists about how they did it, what their modalities were, I just developed more and more taste for what I liked.

It seems to me that most politicians are only interested in getting reelected. That's like number one on the list, and it's also number one through nine. I don't mean they're dishonest or not competent to do things, but they don't. It's unfortunate because we really have some interesting challenges that if they were dealt with now would become minuscule. Instead, everybody just keeps kicking the proverbial can down the road. It's both parties. They won't talk to each other. They won't compromise. What in the world is the matter with these people?

I go to movies once every week or two because, when I go to movies, I just totally lose myself in the movie. It doesn't really matter what it is. It can be an action movie or whatever. I don't think about business problems. But that's the only time.

I'm not afraid to make decisions.

Well, I'm a failure at retirement. I turned over my CEO job three years ago, and I actually have a couple of major tasks to do that I haven't even started. I work just as hard, but on less important things.

I learned very quickly from my father that helping people achieve financial goals was a worthwhile thing, and I also learned from him that the people you associate with are very important.

You want to save religiously. It's most important that you develop the habit of putting aside so much money a year out of what you earn. People say 10 percent, 5 percent. You start with what you can do. It's all about discipline.

I'm paranoid that we would do anything to put the firm at risk. I do everything I can to eliminate what I call branches on the decision tree that have an end point of death.

In college, my band was the Maniacs. We did Chuck Berry, Little Richard, a lot of what we would call real southern rock.

My parents thought it was great that I was in a rock band. I made pretty good money. They didn't have to give me an allowance.

I decided that I wanted to have a western and wildlife museum. Mary and I wanted it right here in the Tampa Bay area. We wanted it to be in downtown St. Petersburg to help St. Petersburg develop a reputation for being a great destination to see art. It'll complement the Dali Museum, which I've had the pleasure of supporting for fifteen to seventeen years now, and the Chihuly and the other museums in the market.

Giving back is a philosophy. I believe that it's consistent with your obligations and your economic best interest to create an environment that is better. I don't think that thinking about shareholders and maximizing profits is inconsistent with pledging part of your profits to charity.

I was an early member of SDS [Students for a Democratic Society], but the minute they had riots in California, I said: "No way. That's not the way you get equal rights for people."

There are tradeoffs you make in life. I didn't take a lot of weekends off, so my kids didn't see me. Remember, I was going to law school at the same time I was starting off in business. So, for ten years essentially, I worked eighty or a hundred hours a week. I really didn't have a lot of time to do a lot of stuff, and when I did, I wanted to go out and hit tennis balls for an hour and a half. I wanted to blow off steam.

We still haven't made the educational infrastructure in Florida as high-quality as it is in a number of other states. That's inexcusable.

This last downturn, it could have gotten so bad that no one would have honored transactions. It got pretty close to that a couple of times. But I actually think the economy is in pretty good shape now. The banking system is stronger than it was before the downturn. Have all of the fixes been good? No. A lot of them are bad, and that's part of the problem. A political system doesn't do a very good job of actually addressing all the causes.

People will pay $150 to listen to a rock group in the forum—and sell it out—but they won't pay a fifth of that to go to the orchestra and listen to classical music, which makes no sense to me at all. We need to do a better job of introducing classical music to our youth.

I wish Jeb Bush had been elected president instead of W, who I like, but he didn't have the skill set to do the job like his little brother.

STEVE RAYMUND

Former CEO of Tech Data, interviewed in January 2011, when he was fifty-five, St. Pete Beach.

MY DAD WAS ALPHA with a capital *A* and really cast a long shadow in the house and was a pretty intimidating presence for me, so I grew up I think quite shy and demure as a result. He was a quirky guy, my dad. Socially, quite inept, I think. He was just sort of a blunderbuss. All hard edges.

Some people know kind of early or they're drawn to at least the idea of a particular profession. I wasn't like that.

I had gone to work for a little while for a bank and didn't like it, so I came back down to live with my parents in Florida after graduate school just to sort out my résumé and crash somewhere and figure out what my next move was going to be.

My dad had this little distribution company that he looked after on the side and said, "Look, we could probably use some help." I didn't have anything better to do, so I said, "OK, what the heck?"

I started liking it and getting to know the people and playing with different parts of the business and so my dad was: "Well, I'll sell you the business. I've got this profit-making enterprise over here that's good for me and I don't want to screw around with Tech Data. It's too small and it doesn't make any money and it'll give you something to do and maybe you can make something of it."

It certainly wasn't a natural instinct or ability for me to go out and sell myself, but there wasn't anybody to do it for me. So I had to learn how to do it, and I got pretty good at it. Necessity is the mother of invention, and it's also the catalyst for personal growth. If I wanted to succeed, I was going to have to stretch my personality and my skill set into a lot of new areas I never knew I could do.

I've given speeches at amphitheaters in front of thousands of people. I couldn't imagine doing that when I was younger. I would have been way too terrified. I still get nervous, but I've done it enough now that I understand the process, the importance of preparation. I can't say it's my most pleasurable experience, but I'm not bad now in front of crowds. I'm not like Obama, a born orator. I'm a born non-orator.

The biggest thing with being Jewish is you're part of a rich cultural and religious heritage that provides a great context and foundation for kids, for families—particularly lifestyle events, like births, bat mitzvahs, and weddings. All my gentile friends would get jealous for bar mitzvahs because they're cool and a really galvanizing event for a family.

I've met a lot of CEOs, and there are all kinds of personalities out there. There are some who look like they come from central casting. They're handsome. They're debonair. They're well-spoken. They're groomed perfectly. They went to the right schools, but I've also met a lot of quirky guys. A guy like Bill Gates, he's a different kind of fellow.

It's good to have a healthy sense of paranoia in business. If you don't, you get complacent, and you will crash.

I tried to be a loving and supportive parent but also one that laid down some pretty clear rules and expectations. I wouldn't say tough love, but there were clearly boundaries. They had to play an instrument. They had to go to Sunday school and be bar mitzvahed. They had to do a sport and give us good grades. That was their job. At the same time, when there was an event at school, like marching in the Halloween parade, I'd be there cheering them on. I really tried to be present as a father, particularly at the events that were important to them. It wasn't so hard. I didn't have to ask permission to leave work. I was the boss.

The role of the corporation is to produce goods and services and make money for its shareholders and provide opportunity for employment for its workers. To the extent that you start deviating from that and encumbering corporations with social missions, you typically see foundering economic growth.

When you're Jewish, you don't know what's going to come next. All we're worried about is, "What's the right way to live now?"

We're in a much more highly regulated environment than ever before. Sarbanes-Oxley, Dodd-Frank, and all this other malarkey has enormously complicated the business of running a corporation. You're constantly looking over your shoulder worrying about violating this rule or that rule, getting sued by the plaintiffs' bar and so on. It's to the point that it's beginning to hurt American competitiveness. We're competing with guys from Taiwan and Shanghai, tough competition, and they aren't laboring under this excessive regulatory burden.

I cycle. I just did my first century—one hundred miles in one day. I'm a big fly fisherman, mostly saltwater, but some freshwater. I go out in a little flat boat and go after redfish. I haven't caught my first tarpon yet.

I'm all for balancing the budget and being responsible, but there are some areas where you need to take a long view and make some investment for social infrastructure that will facilitate growth for future generations. I don't know if that's likely going to happen in Florida right now. I'm a big supporter of high-speed rail, but I don't know if it will survive with the kind of legislative mind-set that we have now in Tallahassee.

I have a daughter Monica, twenty-four, and she's a Hollywood actress. She's in a show called *Lie to Me*. She always did acting as a kid. She was active in the theater program at school, and she did a few summer programs, and it turns out she has a really golden voice. She sings beautifully, and she's pretty and quite talented at acting. My son decided he loves music and wants to be in the music world. He's at the Berklee College of Music in Boston, and we'll see what he does for a living when he finishes. The difference between my kids and me is that I didn't know what I wanted to do, and they do.

We all create our own lives. We all create our own realities.

It was kind of an improbable story, me working with my dad. He and I were not the best of friends. There was always some tension and friction between us, yet we managed to make things work for quite a long time.

JOURNALISTS

David Lawrence Jr.

Chairman of the
Children's Move-
ment of Florida,
publisher of the
Miami Herald, in-
terviewed in April
2018, when he
was seventy-six,
Coral Gables.

AN ENORMOUS NUMBER OF PEOPLE read two items from a newspaper website on their iPhone and think that they've read the newspaper. They have not. We need participatory democracy in this republic, and it's at real risk.

When I was eleven, my parents bought the *World Book Encyclopedia*. There were nineteen volumes. I was the kind of child, as were others in the family, who would sit and read the encyclopedia because it was just fun to learn. I'm not talking about looking up things. I'm talking about turning pages one by one.

Miami's the cutting edge of America. Miami needs to show the rest of America how we give each other the benefit of the doubt, how we celebrate what we have in common, how we learn to respect our differences. I can't imagine being in a better laboratory of the future of America than the community where I live.

I so loved and admired my father, who was a journalist. That's why I went into the newspaper business. And, in fact, my father and I are the only father and son in the Florida Journalism Hall of Fame. The press gallery in Tallahassee is named for my father.

Teaching has become, sadly so, frequently as much about triaging as teaching.

So, in 1996, the governor of Florida was Lawton Chiles, a person I admired deeply and thought was a very special public servant. He asked me to serve on a governor's commission on education, to look at education in the next millennium. There were six task forces that were part of this. One was on school readiness. Now, despite the fact that my wife and I have five children and now seven grandchildren, I didn't know anything about school readiness. I didn't know that 85 percent of brain growth occurs by the age of three. I didn't know lots of the other imperatives of getting children off to a good start in life and then school. I spent two years on this civic assignment. I was still publisher of the *Miami Herald*, but I ended up thinking that the work was so important that I retired from the *Herald* to work full-time on issues of school readiness and so forth.

A newspaper's principal purpose is not as an advertising vehicle. It's to keep people informed in a free society.

The smartest thing you can do—and you can do it during

pregnancy—is start reading with children. You ought to be reading with them from the earliest days.

It's healthy to be a skeptic, but I think it's unhealthy to be cynical—and I see a significant difference between the two.

I grew up on a farm. I was driving a tractor when I was ten. You were expected to work hard. I've always thought that I worked with people who were clearly smarter than I was, but I could work as hard as they could and perhaps harder.

When I was eighteen in 1960, I invited Richard Nixon and John Kennedy to my graduation from Manatee High School. Now, you're going to ask me did they come, and the answer is no, but I have to this day a letter from Nixon, saying he was sorry he couldn't be there, and I have an autographed copy of *Profiles in Courage*, which Kennedy's office sent me. It shows if you have some chutzpah, you can probably do almost anything in this world.

No one who is an informed citizen is getting his or her news from just one source.

I'm a total product of public schools, Manatee High in Bradenton, the University of Florida. To have a public school named for me—90 percent of children in America still go to public schools—that's an honor of a lifetime for me.

Extraordinary learning goes on way before kindergarten. Get the early years right, and chances are, you'll have all the years right.

I don't play golf. I don't play tennis. I don't belong to country clubs. Going with my wife to a movie on a Sunday afternoon is a really good afternoon.

As to charter schools, I have no problem with people having a choice. I think choice is good. I think competition is good. But if you're going to spend the people's money—tax money—on education, then make sure that the programs are high-quality.

The journalism lesson I learned from my father, above all, was to ask questions, and then ask some more, and then ask some more, and then ask some more. And, whatever you do, be fair to other people. You're not in the business for some kind of quick hit. You're in it to come as close as you can to the truth, without arrogantly figuring that you found the truth.

To me, a fundamental in a society of decency is that every child has access to health insurance. We have several hundred thousands of children, literally, who are as perfectly legal as I am who don't have health insurance.

I don't envision a world in which I could retire. It would be very unhealthy for me. You don't know how much time you have. I've lived ten years longer than my father did, so I'm not saving my energy for the next world. I won't need it there.

We live in a state where 40 percent of children at the end of fourth grade can't read at minimally proficient levels. That ought to be a scandal.

A child who is healthy, a child who is not hungry, that child has a much better chance to learn.

I'm more in love with my wife now than when we married almost fifty-five years ago.

To be seventy-six, and to be a lifelong optimist and idealist is an extraordinary blessing. I'm as optimistic and idealistic now as I was when I was sixteen.

LUCY MORGAN

Pulitzer Prize winner, investigative reporter, interviewed in January 2014, when she was seventy-three, Tallahassee.

YOU GET MY ANTENNA UP if I hear about something that is really wrong that nobody's doing anything about.

When I was a child, and my mother began to read me a story, my first question was, "Is this really true?" If it was not a true story, I had no interest in it.

Reading got me my first job as a reporter. In 1965, I was living in Crystal River, married to a high school football coach, and had three children at home. A woman knocked on my door and introduced herself as the area editor of the *Ocala Star-Banner*. Her name was Frances DeVore. She asked me if I would write for the Ocala paper. I said: "Well, I don't know. I've never written anything. Why would you come to me?" She said, "Well, the local librarian tells me that you read more books than anybody else in this town, and I thought perhaps if you read, you could write."

I just had surgery three weeks ago, a lumpectomy, and have breast cancer, and so I have to start chemo and radiation. I'm optimistic I can deal with it. I have no idea what to expect because chemo affects individuals so differently, except I'm probably going to lose my hair.

There is always some corruption, certainly in government, and in law enforcement. If no one looks at it, it gets worse.

I started out working for Ocala, covering west Citrus County and Levy County. At my first Citrus River City Council meeting, I found that the council was very accustomed to telling the reporters who were there, "Don't write this." They would then proceed to do something controversial, and the reporters wouldn't write about it. I just ignored it and wrote about what they were doing, which put me in controversy from the very beginning.

A leader has to be willing to lose an election.

There were times when, as a single mother, that I simply had to take the kids with me. I remember a 3:00 a.m. fire at a hotel in New Port Richey. I ran through the bedrooms and said: "OK, kids. You're going to have to come with me!" My middle son started loading his toys because he thought our house was on fire.

I remember standing outside the courthouse after a nine-year-old was killed by a twelve-year-old, and I was talking to the father of the dead child. At one point, he stopped me and said, "You have no idea what I am going through." And I said: "You're right. I don't because I haven't lost a child." Later, after my son was killed in the traffic accident, I understood.

The thing that made me better known and trusted by the legal establishment and the ordinary citizen was getting sentenced to jail in 1973 because I wouldn't reveal a source.

I think we are in a moment in time when we have no one in either legislative body or in the governor's office who can lead any kind of change.

The reduction of staff at news organizations has dramatically changed the way we cover the news. I think we've lost a great deal. I think we've created black holes, particularly in small counties, where no one knows what's going on until something really erupts.

I had people who would call and ask me to meet in Steinhatchee on the bridge at midnight, and I'd say, "How about the courthouse steps at noon?"

A lot of what I see coming out of our legislative leaders now is merely parroting what they are hearing out of some right-wing think tank somewhere.

The Florida Sheriffs Association had me speak to a convention one year of newly elected sheriffs, and I proceeded to tell them what not to do essentially. I told them I had mixed emotions because it might cut the number of really good stories about the bad things they'd do, but I decided to go ahead because most of them would ignore the advice, anyway.

I am really bothered by the lack of humanity—the lack of civility—among a lot of people.

From the end of 1979 until I took the Tallahassee bureau chief job in 1985, I worked a beat for the *St. Petersburg Times*, the description of which was, "Roam around Florida and cause trouble."

One of the nice things about covering a group of good old boys is they presume that a woman has no brain—and, in my case, they presumed that until it was too late.

It's not easy to govern. It's much easier to run a campaign.

When people tried to intimidate me, it didn't work. Maybe I was stupid, but I kept thinking, because I was a southern woman, that these good old boys were less likely to try to kill me than they would a guy. I could "y'all" just as well as they could.

The biggest award I got out of the Pasco sheriff series was not the Pulitzer. It was the voters of that county throwing that sheriff out.

I've never seen things as polarized as they are now. It disturbs me that so many people will only turn on the newscast that matches what they're thinking at that moment.

The biggest thing I think we could do is get the money out of the political process. It has become a system that reacts to whoever spends the most money.

My son was eighteen. It happened on the Courtney Campbell Causeway, March 1979. There was a knock on our door at like 6:00 a.m., which you know can't be good. My biggest truth I guess came the next morning at 6:30 a.m. My husband had been answering the phone, but he was in the shower, so I picked up the phone, and a woman whose voice I recognized said, "Is this Lucy Morgan?" I said, "Yes." And she said, "Well, I'm glad your son died." I had been covering stories on a trial involving her and her husband and a claim against a builder, and they had lost the trial.

Almost every week brings up a new animal horror story of the way people treat an animal. Those bother me a lot.

I was the Tallahassee bureau chief at the time, and I had all I could handle covering the governor and Legislature, but I got a call from a law enforcement official who said, "There's this sheriff in Gulf County, and he's requiring women in his jail to provide him with oral sex—and we have a prosecutor who doesn't want to prosecute him." Those are hard charges to prove for one thing because, in this case, you're dealing with women in jail whose reputations weren't very good. So, I went over and started interviewing people and did some stories on it. The U.S. Attorney's Office impaneled a grand jury, and twenty-two women went and testified that they had been subjected to this treatment. He was found guilty, and, after the trial, I went back to my office and someone had sent me a dozen roses with a card that said, "From the women you believed." It moved me to tears. That's better than any prize you could ever win.

EUGENE PATTERSON

Publisher, *St. Petersburg Times*, and editor, *Atlanta Journal-Constitution*, interviewed in August 2008, when he was eighty-five, St. Petersburg. Patterson died in January 2013.

WHEN I WAS A BOY, I learned the value of land. My father was a small-town bank cashier, and of course, with the Depression, the bank closed its doors. My mother had a small farm that she bought with money her father had left her, and that became our life raft. When you have a piece of land, you can eat.

I worry about the economy. I worry that our industrial base, especially in automobiles, has been hopelessly out-managed, out-thought, and out-innovated by global competition. All you have to do is look at the makes of the cars on the road and look at the losses that Ford, GM, and Chrysler are racking up—and you wonder how much longer they can last. How did we come to this? How did American management lose its way? This is a story I think we need to look at.

Over the door of the infantry school at Fort Benning is the infantry motto, and it's very simple: "Follow me." Well, that's the way you run a company.

Newspapers are having a difficult time because the electronic media have taken away their advertising, particularly classified advertising, and that's 40 percent of the revenue of a lot of newspapers. And when you lose 40 percent of your revenue, what do you do?

We're in the process of creating an entirely new economic model for newspapers. There's no silver bullet. There's no moment some publisher is going to yell "eureka" and you've got it. It's a matter of one hundred little loose ends that are being explored and pulled together.

Newspapers have something none of the other media have. We have the ability to report and gather news. The written word and carefully reported news must exist or democracy cannot exist.

Growing up where I did in Georgia, hog-killing time was the first cold weather. You'd dress out those hogs, smoke the ham, pack 'em in salt, and eat on them all winter.

Nelson Poynter, who owned the *St. Petersburg Times,* used to say: "If you own eighty newspapers, which community of those eighty do you love the most? The answer is, you don't love any of them. You just love the bottom line." He felt a newspaper was a sacred trust that owed its community its undivided attention.

I still love that farm food. Every chance possible, I get a vegetable dinner. Okra. Corn on the cob. Turnip greens. Squash. On the farm, during the Depression, the only thing we bought in town was salt, sugar, coffee. Everything else, we grew.

After fighting through the Battle of the Bulge, and all the way to the Alps, suddenly I was loaded onto a troop ship in Marseille, and, with a lot of tank and infantry officers, we were sent out to take charge of a new outfit that would hit the beaches of the main, southernmost island of Japan. I knew as we sailed I wasn't going to live through two wars in a row. On the way, the ship's captain came on with one of those wonderful naval announcements: "Now hear this! Now hear this!" and he announced first that a bomb had been dropped on Hiroshima and a bomb had been dropped on Nagasaki, and these were really big bombs, he said. Then he said: "Now hear this! Now hear this! The empire of Japan has surrendered, and the destination of this ship is now Hampton Roads, Virginia." Man, that was a happy group of people.

I was the editor of the *Atlanta Journal-Constitution* during the 1960s, and I wrote a column, with my name on it and my picture on it, seven days a week.

You had to address the issue of race relations because the civil rights marchers were in the streets, the sit-ins were going on, the riots, the fire hoses, the police dogs, the killings. This had to be addressed and not simply by reporting it, but by editors who would stand up and say what we had been doing was wrong and we had to change.

This had a great effect, not because people immediately said: "Oh, that editor is right. I'm going to change my mind." That didn't happen, but they began talking to each other, and the frozen silence that had covered this issue all those years was broken. Even if only to cuss the editors they disagreed with, people began talking, and once you get a community in conversation with itself, you're going to get proper decisions.

You'd get threats. You'd get nasty telephone calls. The hard part was when they'd call my home and talk to my wife or daughter in the most profane ways.

The mayor of Atlanta in the 1950s, a wonderful old man named Bill Hartsfield, called me when I first became editor of the *Constitution*. He asked if I was getting any anonymous phone calls. I said, "Yes, a whole lot." He said he spent years getting anonymous phone calls, and he told me to ignore them. He said anybody who won't tell you his name is a coward, and he's not going to do anything to hurt you. He said the only fellow you have to worry about is the one who never calls.

When my daughter was nine, somebody shot her dog down behind our house. I don't know who it was. She called me at the office. She said, "Come home." She was crying. I came home, and the dog was bleeding. I kept telling my daughter, "Look, we don't know who shot her," but my daughter said she knew, that it was "somebody who doesn't like what you've been writing in the paper." That little girl was taking a beating in school. People would learn her father was the editor of the *Constitution*, and she was constantly coming home with: "They're saying you're a nigger lover." Or: "They're saying you're a communist," and I tried to explain to her. It was tough for a child. The meanness of those people was beyond belief.

I never kept a gun in my office at the *Constitution*, but I had some visitors who became so threatening at times that I worried whether one of them might have one. So I put a ball-peen hammer in the right lower drawer of my desk. I cracked that drawer open a couple of times but never had to get it out.

Martin Luther King Jr. lived in Atlanta when I was there. I got to know him well enough that we would exchange notes. I disagreed with him when he started committing his SCLC against the war in Vietnam. Regardless of whether the war was right or wrong, a good idea or a bad idea, it seemed to me to entangle the American civil rights struggle with a foreign policy disagreement was costly to the civil rights movement—and I said so editorially.

By the time he was assassinated in 1968, Martin Luther King Jr. had lost his headway. The Black Panthers, the Black Power people, the militant-activist wing of the civil rights movement, had pretty much discredited his nonviolent approach. He was right, and they were wrong.

It's hard to believe we came from such times, but it was hard for me to believe that my great-grandfather marched off with the Confederate army, and he and four of his brothers came home in coffins. In my time, the 1960s, I was not in a Confederate uniform. As a matter of fact, I was regarded as a southern turncoat by many of my critics. But I didn't think I was. I thought I was leading us in the direction the South had to go, which was toward justice.

When you look at that little screen on your telephone, it's just like television. It can give you the bulletins. Television has been doing that for fifty years, but that has not wiped out newspapers because we can tell you what's happening and why and what it all means.

America is a wonderful country because it will fool you. One of its major parties has nominated a minority candidate. I didn't think I'd live to see that day.

I took a sabbatical and taught at Duke University for a year and thoroughly enjoyed it. I was what they called a professor of the practice of political science. Translated, it meant I have no advanced degree.

It was a couple of million dollars, as I remember, to buy *Florida Trend*, but we had the money. Here's a state, the fourth-biggest state in the country, and it's totally fragmented from an information point of view. The newspapers in this state, which have traditionally been excellent, got that way by serving their local communities, but they cover just pieces of Florida. It occurred to me in acquiring *Florida Trend* that this is a medium that can cover Florida as a whole.

After I resigned a regular army commission, I went into the newspaper business. I got a job as a reporter at the *Temple Daily Telegram*, which was right close to Fort Hood, Texas, which is where I was based at the time. I covered rodeos, armadillo fairs, city commission, police, fires, hospitals. It was a great experience.

The gap between the haves and have-nots has widened to a point that you worry about a repeat of the time Henry Ford could not sell his automobiles because the workers who made them had no money to buy them.

The extremely low wages of Americans and the extremely high tax benefits for the rich were two of the factors that led to the Great Depression. Maybe, we're not anywhere close to that now, but it's something you have to watch.

With the enormous reduction of the staffs of newspapers, this is bound to cut into their capacity to investigate and spend time developing and explaining the complex developments that the public must know about. It's getting tougher for newspaper staffs to do more with less. I would expect that we are missing some stories that need attention along about now, and this is something that editors need to keep a careful eye on.

We lost our way there with public ownership because with all of the minuses of family ownership—which can get kind of dictatorial at the top—they were not answerable to the stock market. They were answerable to themselves, and I think that's the way journalism should be practiced. I think public ownership of newspapers has been a bad idea.

NATURALISTS

Alto "Bud" Adams Jr.

Rancher, environmentalist, interviewed in February 2016, when he was eighty-nine, Fort Pierce. Adams died in September 2017.

OWNING LAND IS PROBABLY THE BEST INVESTMENT you can make if you can use it and hold it.

My father's father was an orphan of the Civil War. Raised up under Reconstruction, he was never taught to read or write and never learned to sign his name, but he became chairman of the Walton County school board. He sent my father to the University of Florida. All the other boys, he'd give them 40 acres and a mule and start them farming, but my father didn't want that. My father studied law and became the first University of Florida graduate to serve on the Florida Supreme Court.

It's the most natural thing in American business. These cows, they find a bull they like. They breed. They have their calf with no assistance. They eat grass. The calves grow up. We sell the calf.

My granddaughter [LeeAnn Adams Simmons] has been working with the state to put conservation easements on our land so future generations of my family, or anybody else who acquires the land, can never build on it or change it. At my age, that's my priority—to protect the land, to protect the grass, trees, and animals, and to protect our future food supply.

Cowboys have their own sense of humor. Anybody falls off a horse, that'll make a cowboy laugh.

We love the land more than we love the money.

My wife and I built our house when we first got married, and it's still our house. It was built before air-conditioning, and most of the house has still not been air-conditioned. The house has wide overhangs and was designed so well, we really don't need air-conditioning.

Florida is a highly desirable part of the world to live in. It's growing very, very fast. If you do not protect the land as your source of food, clean water, and clean air, you're making a big mistake.

One lesson I've learned is you can't do it all by yourself. The secret to our business is I have a good family and I have good employees. You have to take care of your people and treat them right.

My wife and I have been married since 1949. I married the most beautiful girl at FSU. She has Alzheimer's now, so we stay close to home. I help take care of her, but every day I go out and see the cows and the cowboys. I see my grandchildren. That's my recreation.

Our governor has displeased a lot of people, but he has kept the state solvent, compared to California and some of the others, so I think he's doing all right.

Citrus greening is a serious problem. It's a real question whether you'll be able to get a glass of Florida orange juice anymore.

I ask myself, at my age, "Why do I want to live another year?" I want to see the next calf crop. I want to see the next crop of babies.

If I ever need to go to the Orlando airport, I need a private road or somebody to take me there. I'd say transportation is our state's biggest problem.

In my ignorance, I thought I knew everything I needed to know about cattle, so I studied economics at the University of Florida. It turned out to be a good choice. The first day in economics, I learned the source of all production is land, labor, and capital.

My father never did encourage me to practice law or study law. He could tell I had an interest in the land. Even at age ten or eleven years old, I could comprehend—you have a cow, she has a calf, you sell the calf and get money. I just couldn't quite comprehend how lawyers made their money because they didn't really produce anything or sell anything.

A deer with a rack of horns or a wild turkey, oh, I love to shoot them, but a bear is too much like a man for me to want to go up and shoot him.

Our land is a wonderful habitat for cattle and everything else. Every time you go out, you'll see something a little different—a large alligator, a big buck, wild turkey, all kinds of birds. These wild animals, they have to have a complete ecosystem. Breaking up the land in small tracts, you break up their way of life.

You come back here fifty years from now, you'll still see cowboys and horses and cattle right on this very land. That's my hope.

"Alligator" Ron Bergeron

Developer,
environmental-
ist, interviewed
in December
2014, when he
was seventy, Fort
Lauderdale.

Cumission
lgar Ron Beron

Yes, I wrassle alligators. It's a Florida cultural thing, sort of like
running with the bulls in Spain or fighting bulls in Mexico. That's because, years ago, people ate alligators, so they would wrassle them, tie
them up, and keep them. They didn't have refrigeration, so when they
were ready to eat them, they'd eat them. That's how the culture started.

I actually lived in a house trailer until I was forty-one years old, and
I was a multimillionaire at twenty-five. Success was never about what
it would buy me. Success is about achieving.

We didn't have tennis courts and golf courses in Davie, where I grew
up. Actually, as a little boy, we didn't know what those things were, but
we knew what rodeo was.

Florida had cattle many decades, probably eighty years, before the
West did. In the 1500s, when the Spaniards landed on the west coast of
Florida, some of their horses and cattle got loose, entered into the Everglades, and acclimated to the environment and multiplied by the millions. So, Florida had America's first cow, first horse, and first cowboy.

Leadership to me is the skill of being able to form a consensus.

My grandfather took me on my first airboat ride when I was three.
I can still remember the way it felt, seeing the Everglades of God's

creation, the wildlife, the smells, the sunset. My grandfather introduced me to a beautiful world, and I fell in love with it.

I have a natural resort in the Big Cypress, and I let charities auction it off for people to spend the weekend with me. I introduce them to the beautiful Everglades. I always tell them, "If you want me to wrassle an alligator, I'll wrassle one." So this one group, very prominent people, asked me. I went in the water and started to wrassle one, and I missed his mouth. I'm on his back, and he wrapped his tail around my left leg and death-rolled me with me on his back. He's biting by my ears, but he can't get me, and we're just going around and around and up and down. He twisted around and got my hand in his mouth—2,000 pounds of pressure per square inch. My audience thought this was part of the show. They were actually clapping when all this was going on. I had to use a technique of going his way, go to the bottom, because that's where they want to bring you. They'll calm down because they think they got you, and he did calm down. I'm lying on the bottom of the lake, and I had to trick him into biting the other hand, and he went for it. He opened his mouth, and I got my other hand out. Then I brought him to my stomach and, buddy, I could have whipped Superman's ass. My adrenaline was pumping. I kicked my way to four foot of water, stood up, got his mouth shut, and laid him on the shoreline. I said to the group, "Come on, let's take a few pictures, and then I'm going on to the hospital to get my fingers sewed back on."

I went to Davie Elementary School, the oldest school in Broward County. It was built in 1917. You know how when things happen now, they lock the school down? Well, we had a panther sighting, and I'll never forget this—I was in the first grade—and they didn't lock the school down. They let us go outside to look for the panther.

My family, on my mother's side, entered Florida in the 1840s. So, let's see—great-great, then a great, then a grandmother, mother, and me. I'm a fifth-generation Floridian. And I have children, grandchildren, and great-grandchildren, so that's eight generations of Floridians in my family.

I truly believe that the day we destroy the Everglades our quality of life will change dramatically. I hope I live long enough to see the Everglades uncontrolled by man, flowing naturally.

It was the early 1960s, and I bought a bulldozer and started building driveways and house paths. The boom was coming. I started in business in 1962 and incorporated in 1965—Bergeron Land Development.

When I played football in high school, I was one of those kids who if the coach said to run ten laps, I'd run one hundred. Do one hundred sit-ups, and I'd do five hundred. I remember one day the coach come out on the field, and he was hollering and screaming, and he walked around with a pipe in his hand, and he'd hit you in the helmet, to wake you up, and finally, I walked up to him, and I said, "Coach, what do you want out of us?" And he got right in my face, within an inch of my nose, and he said: "I want every cell in your body. Do you understand that, son?" I'm like, "Yes sir, I understand."

I left home at eighteen with $235.12 in my pocket. I got in a little argument with my mom. She said she's the boss under this roof, and so I left. I ended up working at a gas station for 40 cents an hour and lived in the oil room in the back. Took a bath in the sink. It was pretty tough there for a few months.

The grand slam of the Everglades is when a man or woman sees deer, turkeys, hogs, a bear, and a panther all in one day.

I figured out where the highways were gonna come in the future. I actually got in a plane and looked at how they could connect up the major highways, and I guessed perfect. I bought 50 acres of land, and all of a sudden University Drive comes through. I continued to buy more land all my life.

I catch pythons by hand. I see one, and I just get in there and jump on him. I'm not like most of you guys.

You gotta protect the environment, and so you need regulation, but to duplicate it four or five times makes it hard for businesspeople. In the last four years, I've seen where the state has gotten rid of the duplication, which is good to see.

I work out six days a week, and I'm talking about heavy-duty workouts. Not play-games stuff. An hour on a stair-stepper to five hundred stomach crunches to lifting weights. I realized for me to have a successful life, I've got to be in good shape.

The first panther I ever saw, I was in Boy Scouts. I was eleven years old. You know where this hockey stadium is [the BB&T Center in Sunrise]? Right there.

For Everglades' restoration to succeed, you have to keep your eyes on the global Everglades. You have to decompartmentalize the system to where it has a natural flow from Lake Okeechobee to the central Everglades into Everglades National Park and on to Florida Bay. We can't be divided. Every part has to have shared adversity, shared impacts, and equalization of water levels.

When I first started rodeoing, I was about eighteen years old. I rode bareback horses. That's a young man's sport there. As I got older, I took up roping, and I still rope today.

Bill Nelson is a champion of the Everglades. It's on his radar. He's a fifth-generation Floridian. He is a cracker. Bill is one person who spends enough time there to really understand the issues.

Sure, I read *A Land Remembered*. Truthfully, it made me think of my own family.

I'm a very happy man because I still do the same things I did when I had nothing. I may have a little better roping horse and a little nicer airboat, but the world I live in has never changed.

EUGENIE CLARK, "THE SHARK LADY"

Founder of Cape Haze Marine Laboratory, which later became Mote Marine Laboratory, ichthyologist, interviewed in September 2011, when she was eighty-nine, Sarasota. Clark died in February 2015.

I DON'T WORK AT SOMETHING because I think it's important. I work at things that, to me, are interesting.

When I first heard about the Gulf oil spill, I didn't think it would be as bad as it turned out to be, but now I feel very badly about it. They wanted me to fly over it and see it, but I didn't want to. All I would have seen was oil and animals dying.

When I was nine years old, my mother took me every Saturday to the New York Aquarium at Battery Park, and I just was crazy about the fish. In the back of the aquarium, there was a big tank with some sharks inside. I used to put my face up against the glass and imagine that I was underwater and swimming with them. On rainy days, it was fun because all the derelicts, the bums, would come in from the park and hang out at the aquarium. Some of them would ask me questions like, "Why are you looking at that fish for so long?" Or, "What's that fish doing?" Pretty soon, I had a little audience, and I felt like a teacher.

My health is not too good. I have lung cancer, but I never smoked a cigarette in my life. In 2004, they told me I had four to six months to live.

The medicines don't make me feel so great. I've been through I don't know how many sessions of chemotherapy. They tried a new one on me earlier this year, and it made me feel so sick I lost almost a month of work. I'm pushing ninety, but I still come to work every day that I don't have a doctor's appointment or feel too sick from the chemo.

I didn't worry about the sharks after the oil spill, because I know they swim kind of deep, and they're capable of swimming away during red tide.

The worst danger for sharks right now is overfishing.

In school, when we had to write English compositions, my teacher would tell me: "You know, it's so strange. No matter what topic I give you to write on, you always manage to swing it so that it concerns fish."

In 1955, we opened the Cape Haze Marine Laboratory in Placida, Florida, with two people, myself and a fisherman named Beryl Chadwick. The tourist bureau down in the Englewood area didn't like the people to know how close to shore we set our shark lines to catch specimens, so we told them we went out a number of miles. But really we caught our sharks within a mile of shore. Twelve-foot sharks were common on our lines.

When the *Ziegfeld Follies* opened in New York, in the local paper, they said the most beautiful woman in the *Ziegfeld Follies* was selling cigarettes in the lobby—and that was my mother.

I can't think of anything I regret. Everything I've done, I've enjoyed doing. I've had five husbands, four children. I've done it all, but mainly I've enjoyed studying fish and being underwater with them, being in their natural habitat, looking at the fish and the fish looking at me.

I don't have a normal sense of fear. That's why it's kind of unusual for me to be afraid of Obake. Obake is a Japanese ghost. My grand-mother used to tell me Japanese ghost stories, and Japanese ghost sto-ries are some of the spookiest in the world. My grandmother was an actress. She and my mother worked with Mary Pickford in the movie *Madame Butterfly*. My grandmother loved to play the part of Obake. She would take her long black hair and throw it down in front of her face, and then she'd open her hair, and it was very scary. For the longest time—I think I was in my thirties and had my first child—I was still afraid to go to sleep at night.

Once a shark came directly at me. I was against a coral reef, and I had two bags of fish and shells I had been collecting. I knew the sensi-tive part of a shark's head is the tip of the snout—Beryl used to stun sharks just by taking a Coca-Cola bottle and hitting them square in the snout—and so when the shark came up, I just hit it right in the snout, and it turned and went away. That was the only time I felt a shark was coming at me.

In a way, the movie *Jaws* actually helped our research. We got more money. It became very easy to get a grant to study the behavior of sharks.

It would be nice if we didn't have to drill for oil in the Gulf. We have this shallow continental shelf on the west coast of Florida, and it would be a real disaster if we had a major oil spill there. It would be wonder-ful if we could find some other source of energy.

The other night, I had a dream that it was very hot in bed, and I put my leg over the edge of the bed. I thought I was awake, and a hand came up and grabbed my ankle. I'm sure that's my grandmother's old stories coming back to me. I woke up frightened and thought of Obake.

I want to be remembered as a nice person who didn't hurt people—except my ex-husbands, maybe.

Don Goodman

Founder, Kanapaha Botanical Gardens, interviewed in December 2013, when he was seventy, Gainesville.

At the very beginning, we were using chair legs or table legs for shovels because we didn't have shovels. There was virtually no money for materials. I can remember when we finally had two hundred bucks in the bank, and the first thing we did was go to Hughes Hardware Supply in Gainesville and buy shovels and rakes and all those sorts of things. It was a big day.

My wife and I and our newborn daughter, we took our old un-air-conditioned Datsun and drove down to Fairchild Tropical Botanic Garden in Miami and Marie Selby Botanical Gardens in Sarasota, and we talked with the fiscal officers and the garden directors about the prospect of starting a botanical garden. They didn't laugh at us. They were actually very encouraging.

On this particular day, I had to do some work in the lower pond because it had this really ugly gray mass of algae. A good stiff wind from the west blew it into a crescent on the east side, and somebody—me—had to go in with a net head and pull the stuff out. First thing in the morning, I checked where the alligator was, and he was above the first waterfall, and where I was going to work was below the waterfall. I waded in and worked for a couple of hours and got most of the algae out and then stopped for lunch. During the hour I ate lunch, the alligator moved.

You can never tell where the next break is going to come from or who's going to be your friend and who's not. For example, I got a call from Phil Emmer, who was a very large local builder. Because I thought builders were destroying Florida, I never would have thought about contacting a contractor for help, but he called me. He said he had a lot of extra chain-link fence and asked if I could use it. He also gave us an old travel trailer, which was our very first office. That was kind of a dawning of an understanding that you can't pigeonhole people.

I got into this whole thing because I really like gardening, and I wanted to spend a lot of time gardening—and then I spent years and years putting in boardwalks and fences and irrigation systems.

March 7, 1978, we borrowed a truck from Blount Pontiac, here in town, and drove to Savannah because we could get free bamboo—all we could dig—from the U.S. plant introduction station there. That was when we found out you don't actually dig up bamboo. You do battle with bamboo. We broke our shovels right away. We went into town and bought a couple of axes, and then we finally started getting some bamboo.

After lunch, I walked to the same place where I had been working for two hours, and I walked right into him. He grabbed my arm. I thought once he knew he had a person, and not a great blue heron or something, and I could pound him on the nose, he would turn me loose. When that didn't happen, that's when I realized I was in trouble.

I'm technically retired now, which means I work three days a week instead of five, but I'm finally in a position where I can actually garden.

When the phone rings or bills have to be paid or letters have to be written, my daughter, who's the director now, she does all that. Finally, I have a botanical garden to garden in.

The reason we display giant Victorian water lilies is because I love giant Victorian water lilies. They're one of the world's natural treasures that we can grow in Florida. They're a lot of trouble to grow, but they're worth it.

I like to get factual information about anything I'm involved with, whether it's gardening or botany or zoology or politics or whatever. I'm actually amazed at how many people feel passionate about things they don't understand. I tend not to talk to those people a lot about politics.

We mulch and mulch and mulch, and the mulch breaks down, so there's constantly organic matter going into the soil.

I think the alligator decided I was more trouble than I was worth, so he just took the arm, which was OK with me. I was extremely fortunate to survive. If he had come after me when I turned to walk up the bank, then that would have been it, but he was busy swallowing my arm.

Florida isn't on a good path. I've been worried about the state's environment ever since I got here in 1966. I don't really see it getting better. People tend to look at their pocketbook first and the environment second.

I'm a naturalist, and I've always been an apologist for alligators and snakes because they've really gotten a bad rap. I've always tried to soften that relationship—they were here first, this is their habitat, we have to be responsible, yada yada—and here I am defending alligators and talking about how wonderful they are, then one bites off my arm.

There are definitely people who spend half their time on a cell phone while they're walking through the gardens, and I think that diminishes the experience. The fact is, botanical gardens are even more important at a time when people are distracted by these things. It's very easy to lose contact with the earth when you have all these distractions. At a place like this, there's so much to draw you back.

The phantom pain, it's this kind of grinding pain. I compare it to having your hand in an iron glove one size too small, overlaid by the kind of sensation you get when you have a limb that falls asleep, that sort of buzzing kind of thing, but times ten.

I measure the whole thing in terms of dead versus alive as opposed to one arm versus two arms. I'd much prefer to be right-handed, but I'm just glad to be handed.

There's a very little-known treasure that's in Largo, just outside St. Petersburg. It's called the Florida Botanical Gardens. It's maintained by the county's master gardeners, and it's wonderful.

I'm enough of a committed southerner that, despite the fact that I shouldn't, I love fried catfish. You can get catfish at a lot of places, but unless it's fresh and not frozen, it's just not worth it.

I still love alligators.

BILL HAAST

Owner of the Miami
Serpentarium and
Miami Serpentarium
Laboratories, snake
handler, snake venom
researcher, interviewed
in June 2008, when
he was ninety-seven,
Punta Gorda. Haast
died in June 2011.

FOUR YEARS AGO, I got bit by a Malayan pit viper, and that was the end of my right index finger. The bone just dissolved. Most of my fingers were pretty bad anyway from all the bites, but when that finger went, that was the end. I can't trust my hands anymore. I tried to hold snakes after that, but I couldn't.

These days, what I do mostly is breathe.

Hurricane Charley moved right over our house. I wanted to see it. I stood by the window and put my hand on the glass and could feel it moving.

The FDA always pooh-poohed it, but I think snake venom has the potential to cure disease. Multiple sclerosis, it would put on hold. Arthritis. Polio. This is my unfinished business.

Aging is hard. Sometimes you feel useless. But I always felt I would live this long. It was intuitive. I always told people I'd live past one hundred, and I still feel I will. Is it the venom? I don't know.

I've been bit more than 170 times and maybe almost died 20 or 25 times. I don't count the little bites.

The initial bite is no worse than a bee sting. But when there's tissue damage, it feels like your hand is caught in a vise. There have been times I've been rolling on the floor.

When I was a child, I lived right in the middle of Paterson, New Jersey, in an apartment, and I brought home a timber rattlesnake, my first venomous snake, and I had to promise my mother that I would never open the cage in the house. That's how I got started.

Many times, doctors would transfuse my blood into someone bitten by a snake. It worked, too, so long as the blood type was a match. I have built up such an immunity to snake venom.

I'm not afraid of any animal. I've petted a rhinoceros. I once walked up to an elephant right in the heart of the Congo. If you're really genuinely not frightened, you can walk up to any animal in the wild. They have a sense. They know if they can trust you.

Occasionally, my wife will give me a shot of snake venom. Just a little bit. It burns when it goes in. I think without fail it'll help me make one hundred, easy. I think what it might do, and I don't have any proof, is it makes the heart function stronger and longer.

My blood pressure is normal. My cholesterol is very low. I don't eat much, and I never eat before noon.

My slogan, when I first started the Serpentarium, was, "Venom Production for Venom Research." The attraction was just a vehicle for the research. It was the only way I could make money to support the work. The attraction grew and grew. Being in front of people wasn't particularly fun for me. I wanted to be in the lab, but it was a chore that had to be done.

The boy that fell in the pit, that was rough. It happened in 1977. He was six. I remember I was in the lab doing something, and one of the employees comes running in and said a person fell in the crocodile pit. I remember running. I jumped over the wall and on the crocodile's head. He was partially submerged. I was expecting him to let go, but he didn't. He backed up in the water and took the child with him.

I was up all night. What should I do? What should I do? I debated with myself. The crocodile did only what he knew to do. What should I do? I shot him and buried him in the pit, next to a monument. That was a time I considered closing the Serpentarium.

Will anybody remember me? If they do, what will they remember? And when they die, they take the memory with them. What's the purpose? Memory is a funny thing.

Some of the most important things I've done had nothing to do with snakes. This is during World War II. I was a flight engineer. We took off from Natal, Brazil, in a C-87 transport plane, loaded with detonators, and we were on our way to Dakar in Africa. The moment we got off the ground the captain said we lost hydraulic pressure. We blew a gasket, and the hydraulic oil was gone. We always carried a gallon of reserve hydraulic oil and always fortunately carried chewing gum. I got everybody to chew gum, and then I made a new gasket out of the gum with some cutout cardboard from the back of the log book. It worked. We had our wing flaps. Otherwise, we couldn't have landed. Well, we could have landed, but we would have crashed.

I never got mad at a snake that bit me.

When you're in the wild, in Africa, and a lion roars, even in the distance, the ground shakes. I miss that.

Jeff Klinkenberg

Writer, journal-
ist, interviewed
in March 2018
at the age of
sixty-eight, St.
Petersburg.

By the time I was in high school, I joked I was the founder of the Boys Without Dates Club. I was certainly interested in girls, but perhaps it was the smell of fish on my hands from all the time I spent fishing. We would catch snakes, too, and then you'd have the smell of snake musk on your hands, as well.

I can use Florida as a prism to write about anything.

My parents were not educated people, so there weren't a lot of books in the house, for example, but they were newspaper readers. Back then in Miami, there were two daily newspapers and community newspapers. They were always reading, so I valued newspapers.

In 1951, my parents moved from Chicago to Miami. Like a lot of Floridians, they wanted to make a new start.

I wanted to tell somebody's story as well as it could be told.

The first part of my career, I was a certified workaholic. I went to see a shrink for it. I had to get better at saying no to myself.

When I graduated from the University of Florida, I came back to Miami and was a sports writer for the *Miami News*, which was an afternoon paper that is no more. It was great place to be a young journalist. It was already starting to fail, but there were lots of talented people there, and it had a touch of *The Front Page* era, so I witnessed fistfights and drunkenness and gambling in the newsroom.

I can still find things that excite me. If I see a snake, I'm a happy boy.

My mother had many of the virtues and the vices of the Irish. One of the virtues was, man, she had a gift for gab—like I do.

I've been in a number of hurricanes, including a couple of big ones when I was a kid. Of course, I went down to Miami after Andrew. I know what a Category 4 or 5 can do, and I don't want to be there for that. A Category 4 or 5 is just beyond belief.

John McPhee was a great influence on me.

I'm a crazed cyclist. Yesterday, I did 43 miles. Today, I did 25. I usually do about 100 miles a week. I'm not fast. I'm a tortoise, but I seem to have endurance.

This year, I won the Florida Humanities Council's Florida Lifetime Achievement Award for Writing. That was a huge honor. Previous winners include Carl Hiaasen and Patrick Smith, who wrote *A Land Remembered*, which is the Bible to a lot of Floridians. There are so many great writers in Florida.

When I was growing up, I was a crazed Florida boy who was fishing and doing all that outdoors stuff. I went to parochial school—parochial school during the boxing nun era—and I couldn't pay attention. I used to joke that I invented the rope-a-dope. I wasn't a bad kid. I was just looking out the window, wishing I was someplace else.

In retrospect, my childhood was magical. I grew up like Huck Finn.

I'm really appalled by this narrative of weird Florida. Some of the "Florida Man" stuff and the "Weird Florida" stuff—some of it I have to admit I laugh at—but a lot of it after a while strikes me like dumb blonde jokes or Polish jokes or whatever. It just seems like it's cruel stereotyping.

My dad had been a competitive swimmer in high school, and he liked to do these long open swims on the beach, and when I was old enough—I had a little mask and snorkel—I'd hang onto his trunks and he'd swim along the beach. The Atlantic is much more clear than the Gulf, and it was like looking down into an aquarium.

I was looking for stories that just seemed authentic. I wasn't going to write necessarily about Disney World. I knew out there, away from the interstates, there were these things that were happening that you might not see anywhere but Florida—the critters, the woods, the food, the art, the music. When I started to write those stories, I was like a blind dog in a smokehouse. Wherever I snapped, there was something meaty that I could write about that, most likely, nobody had written about before.

We drove around and we saw our first swallow-tailed kite of the year—they're coming up from South America—and so I knew it was spring.

Writers are famous for not having confidence. The confidence wasn't always in the writing, but it was in the material. I just feared I didn't have the skill to pull things off.

I started reading because I was interested in fishing. I started reading Vic Dunaway in the *Miami Herald*. He was the outdoors editor. I remember reading him as a kid and thinking, "My God, that has to be the best job in the whole world."

I like people. I really feel I can talk to people.

Key lime pie is *the* Florida pie.

I write down inspiring quotes, and I have one from Zora Neale Hurston. She was talking about folklore, and she said folklore is the boiled-down juice of human living. That's what's sort of disappearing from journalism today—the boiled-down juice of what it's like to be alive.

Margaret D. Lowman

Rainforest canopy researcher, author, interviewed in November 2008, when she was fifty-five, Sarasota.

I grew up in Elmira, New York, and my best friend was my neighbor Betsy Hilfiger. She and I used to make little tree forts. I'm embarrassed to tell you this, but we would follow our dads when they mowed the lawn, and we took the worms that got cut in half and tried to bandage them back together. We thought we would be vets, but that career failed because no worms survived. What's funny is she has an older brother named Tommy Hilfiger, and we used to beg him to come out and play with us, but he never would because he was in the basement of their house, sewing bell-bottomed jeans. So, we ended up with our tree forts, and he ended up with a clothing empire that could pay for all my rainforest research.

My parents were very patient with me. I used to shriek for them to stop the car when I saw a wildflower I hadn't seen before. They were really very nice to allow me to be this very strange child.

I went off to Australia for graduate school because I got a very nice scholarship. During my very early weeks over there, the head of the department kindly took me aside and said, "Why on earth are you getting a PhD when you'll only get married and have children?"

Being a woman has caused me to really make sure I'm doing good work, pay attention to detail, be organized, and be productive. I was also a single mom, which is like a scarlet letter, at least I felt it was. I had to make sure I could do my share of research and hold onto my job and be a good parent at the same time.

In the forest, it's very important to cultivate the ability to know where a snake might lurk and be cognizant of that little rustling sound that's a swarm of army ants. That's my work, to be able to recognize those things, which gives me a sense of comfort in the forest. On the other hand, you have to keep me from walking off the curb when the light is red.

I'm not a person who loves to go climbing for recreation. I take it pretty seriously. I'm real careful when I climb. I did have an accident in Australia—I fell about 15 feet—and perhaps that was a really good thing because it taught me to be absolutely careful and not to climb when I'm tired or when the conditions are really wet.

Oreos have become kind of my middle name. I'm pretty famous around the world for bringing Oreos to every village I go to.

I told my children if the world starts to fall apart, we'll move to the Amazon because, quite frankly, any village will take you in. They are so kind and gentle.

I've eaten a lot of insects because they've been offered to me, but I've been in some situations where we actually did run out of food. Once, I survived on raisins for three days, and it was pretty darn OK.

It's really very sobering and I think humbling to go and see people who collect their food from the wild and remind ourselves of where we come from.

My sons came with me on many of my trips. There wasn't such a thing as staying home alone at seven years old. I'll be honest. You try to con your kids: "We will count beetles today and it's going to be really fun!" We turned science into a game, and they became my best field assistants in a sense.

I've really enjoyed working with [Florida CFO] Alex Sink as her climate change adviser because I see now that scientists have to talk to politicians. We have to get in the room and sit at the table if we're going to have good environmental policy. We need to communicate the facts to the policymakers.

I thought of everything, like taking pictures, hiring a monkey and training it, and all this other stuff that would allow me not to climb the trees. But I had to learn. It was 1979, and I was the first person in Australia to do that kind of work.

It was extraordinary. Millions of things were living up there, and we didn't know that back then.

I got involved with the French, designing some of the inflatable gadgets. The hot-air balloon has to be about the most fun thing I've ever done in my life. It's a fabulous sensation to actually be floating among other organisms who are not afraid of you. There are snakes that can almost fly through the canopy. There are monkeys busily hunting fruit and having fun playing. There are amazing, colorful birds and millions of insects. There's a different sense of being a human in that environment. You're really one of them. It's humbling and exhilarating.

Because Florida is facing some very big environmental challenges, we need to be a leader. Communication between science and economics and policy, that's the key.

I won the science fair in the fifth grade and went off to the state science fair, and this was really scary for me. I remember my dad ran out of gas on the way there in our very old jalopy. I was surrounded by all these boys and their physics and electricity and chemistry projects—and I got second prize with my little collection of wildflowers.

Ecotourism is a good intersection of economics and conservation. It's becoming a very good solution in some of the tropical areas where I work. Florida doesn't have a lot of ecotourism inland. That's untapped opportunity, perhaps.

I have a little mantra called: "No Kid Left Indoors."

In Florida, we have invasive species. We have biodiversity threats. We have climate change. We have land-use challenges. We have infectious disease threats. And we have watershed issues. Where this is bad is it's a liability, but it's also an opportunity to get the best researchers to Florida to study these issues.

My favorite tools are a headlamp and a Swiss army knife and little containers because a lot of times I'm looking for little insects.

I have one thousand lamb chop recipes if you ever need any because I was the wife of a sheep farmer for eight years, but all the while I was starving to do my research.

PHILANTHROPISTS

DERRICK BROOKS

Former NFL linebacker, cofounder of Brooks DeBartolo Collegiate High School charter school, interviewed in March 2015, when he was forty-two, Tampa.

I DIDN'T GROW UP WANTING to be a professional athlete. My dream was to be an insurance man. That stems from an insurance man in Pensacola named Mr. Irving. He wore the suit. He drove a nice car and he collected money, so I figured that that was a good job to have. I got the courage one day—I was probably around ten—and I asked Mr. Irving, "How can I have a job like yours?" He told me to go to school, make good grades, and go to college. That was my motivation for a good bit until I got into high school and the football coaches got hold of me.

Every encounter is an opportunity to get better. After this meeting, you and I will have gotten better because we learned something about one another.

I was raised by my stepfather. In terms of books, he had no more than a sixth-grade education. But talk about the education of life. He was an encyclopedia.

My true gift from God is the ability to give back versus the talent God gave me to play football.

In the fifth grade, I was being a class clown. I'd get through with my work, and I'd be bored, and I'd get into a lot of disciplinary troubles because I was bored. My dad warned me and told me if I didn't get it together and stop being a class clown he was going to show me how to get all the laughs I wanted. I called his bluff. I didn't think he'd have time to come to my school. Well, let's say he caught me in the middle of one of my acts. He came in the classroom. Long story short, he took his belt off and whipped me in front of the class. I remember that story so vividly, running home crying, and my mom's home, and she whips me for running home and leaving my dad. I was hysterical, crying. Bad day. But I thank God they loved me enough to do it. No matter how successful you are, you have to learn to treat people with the respect they deserve. I had no right to disrupt a learning environment just because I was bored and selfish. I had no right to disrespect the teacher. I took that lesson to heart, and I basically still use it today. I treat others how I want to be treated.

I was starting to get pretty good at baseball and football, and my dad heard me make a comment about what I did in a game. He said: "Son, if you toot your own horn, you make one sound, but if everybody else is tooting your horn, the sound is endless. Don't let me hear you brag about yourself again."

Education. That's the one word that transcends all my years of living. That one word stands out to me. Education is the great equalizer.

A nice pound cake and butter pecan ice cream. Those are two guilty sins I have in terms of food.

I was sold on Florida State very early in the recruiting process. When Coach Bowden came to the house to visit, he held my little sister in his lap and she fell asleep, and my mom gets up to pick her up and put her to bed, and Coach B's like: "No, no, no. I'm gonna hold her. She's at home." After that, you couldn't tell my mom anything negative about Florida State.

Whatever my edge was, I did the best I could to maximize it.

I was looking for a partner to help me start the charter school. It was a little bit intimidating meeting Mr. [Edward] DeBartolo in a business setting. I was mulling it for a week. "What do I say? How do I say it?" Just before I got ready to meet him—about fifteen minutes before—I had this nice outline, and I crumpled it up in my car on the way to his office. I decided to say what was in my heart. Ten minutes into the conversation, he stops me, looks at me, and says, "Derrick, we're in." All I could do was thank him. I walked outside and wept in my car.

I spent seventeen years in Pensacola and now twenty-two years away from it, but Pensacola's in my blood.

If you want to lead this nation as president, you have to win this state. Not Iowa. You have to win Florida.

My mom was probably the athlete in our family. She was a heck of a basketball player in her day. One of my football coaches told me that she had an opportunity to perhaps play college basketball, but she was pregnant with me. She completed her high school graduation year and gave birth to me all in the same semester.

I'll always be a country boy underneath the coat and tie. I enjoy sitting on a porch, just sitting there for hours. I grew up playing dominoes. I go to Pensacola, one of the first things I do is play dominoes.

The charter school is not about the names on the building. It's about the names in the building. When I visit, I say "thank you" more than anything, just because I understand how seriously I took my education in high school and how education paved my way. This is my passion.

These students and teachers trust my vision, and it's humbling. It's pressure, but it's humbling.

My four kids are very comfortable in their own skin, and that's one thing I'm very proud of.

Monte Kiffin, when he was with the Bucs, taught me this: The three most dangerous words are "I got it" because you never have it. You never, ever have it. There's always an area for improvement. You just have to be willing to find it.

WARRICK DUNN

Former NFL running back, Homes for the Holidays founder, interviewed in June 2011, when he was thirty-six, Tampa.

Warrick Dunn

WHEN YOU DON'T KNOW ANYTHING, it doesn't make sense to go into a room and just start talking. Over the years, I sat back and I listened. I watched. I noticed. I asked a lot of questions. That's how I pick things up.

My foundation helps single parents get homes. Each house is therapy for me. The program is in honor of my mom. Homeownership was her dream, and she didn't have that opportunity, so I'm living her dream through other single parents.

Some of the guys I hung out with when I was younger, they're dead, from just living the fast life. I knew people on drugs. I knew people who sold drugs. Everybody is trying to figure out ways to make it and put food on the table, but that's not the type of life that I wanted to live. You can't be like that when your mother is a police officer.

I started playing football when I was probably seven years old, and I was so small that no one wanted to pick me. But when I played, no one could tackle me. I had a knack for making people miss.

My mom was killed after I had already played my senior year of high school football. We were getting ready to go out on recruiting trips. That semester of school was rough. I can remember at times I was sitting in class and crying.

I'm the oldest of six. A lot responsibility fell on me. It's just a weird scenario that I'm still a kid, and now I'm responsible for five other people.

My mom talked to me a lot about life, about grown-up things. I kid you not, we'd talk about so many different things that I'd think, "Wow, why are you talking about this to me?" The things she talked about started to make sense after her passing. It all just came together, the way that she handled things. It was like she was preparing me for that day.

My first thought was not to go to FSU and play football. I needed to stay home and take care of my brothers and sisters. I was going to try to get a job, but my grandmother said go and she'd make sure everything was OK.

At Florida State, I was trying to be a parent from afar. My deal with Coach Bowden was if I needed to go home, I could go home. He gave me that leeway, so instead of being a typical college kid, my spring breaks and free weekends were spent looking over my family.

You can't hide from depression. You keep everything inside, it's only going to ruin you. I've had to learn that the hard way. It made me hard, made my heart hard.

I had a teammate who was talking about counseling and how another player went to counseling, and I thought it was crazy. But counseling became my saving grace.

When I was playing for the Atlanta Falcons, I spoke to the owner, Arthur Blank, about being upstairs. A lot of times, people think we just want to make money, but I'm thinking bigger. I dropped a little bug in his ear, but I didn't ask. You have to be invited into the ownership group, and he invited me.

Now I'm learning more about the business side of the game, the marketing aspects, the salary cap, putting a team together. Mr. Blank helped start The Home Depot and made it into a global brand. I can learn a lot.

Today, I'm healthy. Who knows how I'll feel tomorrow? I got hit plenty of times, but I always got down. I didn't have any concussions, thank God, that I know of.

Because of counseling, really, which helped me a lot, I got to a point to where I was ready to sit down and talk to the guy who shot and killed my mom. I had to let this individual know how he altered my life. I felt stuck, not being able to have my own family, postponing getting married and having kids. I needed closure so I could move forward.

I went to the prison and sat across the table from this individual. It was crazy. There were no bars. We didn't have anything separating us. Honestly, I didn't feel the need to jump across the table. That wasn't my desire at all. I was able to share a lot of things that I thought I needed to share. I told him how it affected my family, how it affected my life, put my life on hold. It felt good to get it off my chest. He said he didn't do it, but I was expecting him to say that. He told me, you know, that I should move on, that it's time for me to start living my life, to not let it hold me back.

I played the game of football, enjoyed it, loved it. Could I have been a better football player? Yes. I think I could have been. I think a little bit of my joy of playing was taken away.

So far, we've helped more than one hundred single parents become homeowners. We're in Tampa, Atlanta, Baton Rouge, and Tallahassee, but the plan is to get bigger and better. I would like to expand to different markets, hopefully nationally so we can help people across the country.

There are people who knew me before, and they see me now, and they tell me I'm different. I laugh. I smile. I hang out a lot more. I travel. I like to go bowling, golfing. I'm really just starting to live.

WILLIAM R. HOUGH

Investment banker, arts and education supporter, interviewed in August 2010, when he was eighty-three, St. Petersburg.

WHEN I LEARNED MY [$30 million] gift was the biggest private gift the University of Florida had ever received, I told them if I had known that, then I wouldn't have given as much. I didn't want it to be the biggest gift. I'm not that showy.

I'm a conservative person. I believe in paying your own way and not depending on the government.

My mother inherited some stocks from her aunt, my great-aunt, in 1936. I was fascinated by the fact that she got dividends from those stocks. These were blue chips, and they helped us through the Depression. To this day I think that had a lot to do with my entry into the securities business.

Stocks had a bad reputation from the 1929 crash, but most of those were 90 percent margin stocks. The reason the people lost all that money was the margin. Margin was permitted at 90 percent of value, where today it's only permitted at 50 percent. There's a lot of difference between those levels. The lesson was not to be margined too heavily. We're going through the same lesson today because subprime is a matter of borrowing too much money on your house.

I'm a believer in starting off with a savings account, getting a little bit of a backlog of money, and not living beyond your means.

The biggest investing mistake people make? They take a short-term view.

I had a sailboat when I was in my forties. I won the St. Pete to Fort Lauderdale race with it, which is the biggest thrill of my life probably. I got first in fleet out of ninety-four boats, and the fact that there were that many boats is what made it such a big victory.

As a young child, I liked to play Monopoly. I was a pretty good Monopoly player.

I had a paper route when I was fifteen or sixteen. What money I made, I bought war bonds. It's a mentality that a lot of people of my age group still have today. People who had difficult times during the Depression, they like to put money away.

Early on, I was very ambitious. I wanted to make money. I wanted to be in the securities business because I felt that was an area where you had the opportunity to make money.

I don't want to be viewed as a do-gooder. The first thing I will admit is that I like to get the tax deduction. In the case of my gift to the University of Florida, it reduces my federal estate tax.

If you want to accumulate wealth, you should never live beyond your income. You should save something every year, and you should invest that in something that's going to grow. I believe that stock in big companies, blue-chip companies, is the way to go.

I take my briefcase home every night. There's a lot of reading required in the securities business. You're reading annual reports, and you're reading earnings reports. You're reading other research reports. Those reports are long, and you have to pick out what's important. I've been reading these reports for sixty years.

My wife has let me do my own thing. She hasn't nagged me about working all the time. Her influence on me has been getting me interested in the arts. She's very musical. She sings in the choir. I fell in love with her because she was a member of a trio that sang swing hits. I liked that.

What the ordinary person does is they sell at the low and they buy at the high. That's the natural emotion that we as brokers have got to fight.

During my business career, I've probably had three very close shaves. We survived not because we had been conservative. We survived because we had been a little bit of a riverboat gambler. I've never been patient in my decisions in managing the business, but I've been very patient in my own investment account.

This morning, I was thinking about that fact that the ideal life would be living in a small town, where you go to church on Sunday, and you have kind of a structured life. You go to a scout meeting on Monday night, and you go to play softball somewhere on a Saturday.

The stock market commentators are trying to predict what's going to happen in the next day or the next week. The worst thing an investor can do is to watch one of those shows.

Yes, I think some people think about money too much. I think I do. I'm not glad that I do that. I think it's a function of the Depression. I've always wanted to have security, and I don't think that ever goes away. Do you ever have enough money? I tell you what I'm thinking about now. I'm thinking about increasing my income, so I can give more away.

KIRAN PATEL

Cardiologist,
entrepreneur,
interviewed in
June 2014, when
he was sixty-five,
Tampa.

THE QUALITY OF CARE that a patient receives is always dependent on the ethics and morality of the doctor. Nothing else.

At the end of the month, when somebody is struggling to pay the electricity bill, and he finds it within himself to sacrifice and give fifty dollars to a charity, I think that has more value than someone who can write a check for $100,000 and not even miss it.

I was always an entrepreneurial guy, and I knew I would never work for anybody.

My father taught me honesty. Once, I remember, he had me carry a bag of quarters from the bank to his shop, and there was a quarter more. He said that banks can't make mistakes. Count again. I counted again, and the extra quarter was still there. I counted one more time. The bank was probably a mile, two miles away, and he made me walk all the way back to the bank to give that quarter back. I was ten years old.

Philosophically, if a barrier or a wall is in front of me, my theory is either go over it, around it, under it, through it, or whatever, but find a way to get to the other side.

When the HMO concept came, most physicians would look at the insurance and not at the patient. Me, I was worried about the patient and not the insurance. So, by default, when other physicians would not see the HMO patient, I would see the HMO patient. Because I was taking care of those patients and because I have a business type of a mind, I saw an opportunity in managed care. Rather than fight managed care, I embraced it and controlled it. Hence, I got into the insurance business.

If you do something with the only purpose of making money, you might falter. But, if money is the by-product of what you do, then you will see the benefit.

There is a big difference between confidence and arrogance. I am a man of "my way or the highway" only because I am so firmly focused and believe so much in what I want to do that very few people can shake me from my path. So, in that sense, I am rigid. I do listen to people, but that does not mean I will do what they want me to do. Unless they can convince me absolutely that I am wrong, it will be very difficult for me to change my course. My biggest strength and weakness is that.

Spending on health care is highest in the United States, but the outcome is not always the best. Even with all the flaws that we have, I still don't think there is a better system in the world that can replace what we have.

I believe every human being gets up in the morning thinking that he would like to do good for others.

Medicine is one of very few professions where you can make money and serve humanity. You may not become very rich, but you'll never be very poor. If today, somebody comes to me for advice, I would say medicine is the best profession to get into, even with all of the challenges that are there today.

Golf is my passion. I have made a goal of playing at the top one hundred courses of the country and the world. So most of my vacations and traveling, if it is not based on a philanthropic effort, will be for golf. I've probably played fifty of these courses or more. The unfortunate part is the list keeps growing or changing, so I can never catch up.

From childhood, I always wanted to be a doctor.

For me, being a vegetarian is not for health reasons. If you believe that God is omnipotent, omnipresent, then every living thing has God as a part of it. If you can survive without taking the life of another living being, human or animal, then you should do that. In that context, I do not eat meat.

Fortunately for me, I got a very good life partner. I am the accelerator, and my wife is the brake. When I want to do things, she'll stop me and she'll tell me why not. But if I still want to do it, she will not interfere. Once I embrace something, she'll be right there next to me.

Teaching is a noble profession.

My insurance company grew to roughly $100 million a year in revenue, and I was also practicing medicine. I couldn't do both. After a lot of internal conflict, I opted to grow the business and break from practicing medicine. I felt that I could serve humanity maybe better that way. I believe that God gives you some skills or talents, and you have to sometimes make a decision on what is better for you. In my case, history has proven that the option of growing the business was good. It gave me the means to do my philanthropic work, to build hospitals in India and Africa, and to pay for health care for kids.

My father was a very Gandhian guy. He would help anybody who came through the door. Help does not only mean financial, right? He had no differentiation between the poorest of the poor and the richest. Throughout his life, he did not touch alcohol or eat meat. I am the same way.

Nobody tells you that you get good care because you have white skin or brown skin or black skin or whether you're with Humana, Aetna, WellCare, or whatever. When you go to the doctor, he should be looking at you as a human being.

There are people who spend hours and hours of their time on volunteer work. I know many times the recognition may go to the person writing the big check, but who should be praised more?

HOWARD C. TIBBALS

Benefactor of the Ringling Circus Museum's Tibbals Learning Center, interviewed in May 2014, when he was seventy-seven, Longboat Key.

THE CIRCUS INTERESTED ME FIRST because it moved. It was fluid. It didn't have concrete foundations. I liked the fact that they built an organization of thousands—and they did it in such a way that it could be moved from one town to another.

When I graduated from college, my adviser told me I was entering into the toughest employment situation you'll ever find—working for your father. He said you love your daddy and all that soft stuff, but when push comes to shove, he's the boss. Even if you're forty years old, Daddy's still the boss if he hasn't kicked the bucket or retired. So, every time I got pissed with my situation, I'd take a drive. The longest one was fifty miles.

We couldn't get the money we needed for the museum until we changed what we were going to call it from the Tibbals Circus Museum to the Tibbals Learning Center. That's when we got the money from the Legislature. It's just amazing what you can do with verbiage. That taught me a lesson: Be careful what you say in print.

It's amazing the things that came my way just because I was there.

I've been very interested in the circus since I was an itty-bitty fella. Mother's baby book for me says I saw my first circus when I was three.

I've driven people nuts with questions. You can tell when people get tired of you. But if you can ask questions without being a pain in the butt, you can learn a lot.

You look at the people driving down the highway in these 40-foot motor homes. Where in the hell are they going to park those things?

I was born in West Virginia, and my mother and father moved to a small town in Tennessee when I was ten. I wanted to be busy. You can be busy in a small town by being a hoodlum, but I wasn't interested in that. A small town is a good place to build a model circus.

I don't drink liquor of any form. No wine. Nothing. Never. I don't smoke, either.

Dad was always concerned about the longevity of the company, and through the years he would give me more stock to the point that when he died, I already had 51 percent. He knew we were talking about selling. He told me once, in the hospital, the night he died, he said: "Don't sell the company, son. That's a big mistake." The problem was he'd tell me what he thought the company was worth. He gave me a dollar value, and I figured he knew more about what the company was worth than I did. So, some guy came around and gave me twice what it was worth, and I sold it.

I started collecting circus photographs a long time ago. I'd look at the old pictures, and I'd have a strong desire to copy what I was seeing. Name any circus wagon the Ringlings ever ran, and I'll show you twenty or thirty photographs of it.

We love to go to the Grand Floridian hotel at Disney World and spend about two or three days there every spring. It's one of the finest hotels around. And I like antique shows. It's nice to see old-timey furniture.

I started building my model of the Howard Brothers Circus in 1956, and I'm still not done. It turned out to be a lot more time-consuming than I expected.

There was a lady here in town who was the premier Italian cook in the world. She just died. Marcella Hazan. We were very good friends with her. We miss her terribly. The first meal she ever made us was the best meal I ever had in my life. She made pasta. It was the thinnest pasta I've ever seen and softer than a paper page.

I love construction.

Under the tutelage of my father and gradually me, we made our company a success. It was called the Tibbals Flooring Company. We made wood floors. I had a lot of pride in the products we were making. We put the floors in Donald Trump's building in New York City. I had a lot of pride in the woodworking machinery I designed and altered. There's a lot of good commercial woodworking machines in this country, but if you want to change them to do special products and run real fast and all that sort of stuff, that was my specialty—taking existing machinery and adapting it to do more things than it was originally designed to do.

I tried to teach my kids: "Don't do what Granddaddy says. Don't do what Daddy says. Do what you say. You get out there and you find what you want to do. And if you find that you've failed, don't get upset. Try again."

POLITICOS

Susan Benton

Former Highlands County sheriff, first woman to be elected sheriff in a general election, interviewed in October 2016, when she was sixty-seven, Sebring.

Susan Benton

AFTER MY HUSBAND PASSED AWAY and my youngest son graduated from high school, I had to ask myself, "What do you want to do now?" My responsibilities up until then had been, first and foremost, maintaining my marriage, second, raising my children, and third, my profession. So, the first two things were completed, and the thing that was left was my job. Then, after Sheriff Howard Godwin decided to retire, I began thinking that, wow, I could do that job. The biggest hurdle at the time, I thought, was being a woman, and in rural south central Florida, was that going to fly?

A sheriff's deputy needs to have an ethical character and be someone you can trust to do the right thing even when no one's looking.

Early in my life, I began to develop, basically, a calling to service. I didn't know exactly what. Initially, I thought about a religious life. I went to the police academy in Miami in 1974, and after I hit the streets, doing my initial patrol functions, it started to come together. I began to come across intoxicated people, people on drugs, homeless people, and people who chose to do bad things. It was a vocation much like I imagined from the life of Jesus, walking around on earth. He didn't pick and choose who he spoke to or who he helped. That's when it clicked that a career in law enforcement was for me.

Throughout my adult life, I continued to play softball, all the way up to the time I became sheriff. I just ran out of time. I couldn't make the practices anymore.

I ended up in Highlands County because my husband was a state trooper, and he got struck by lightning while working a wreck on the Palmetto Expressway in Miami. Because of that, after he went through extensive rehab, they transferred him to a "less stressful area"—Lake Placid.

Growing up in Miami, I understand and appreciate the importance of diversity. Florida is an amazing place because of its diversity.

I never hesitated to go into that bar fight or search that dark building at two o'clock in the morning. But as a street deputy, if you have the ability to communicate and you use your skills wisely, you won't have to fight too many people. Now, I've had my share of fights. Trust me.

I've been on the lower end of them a time or two, but those are situations that are few and far between.

The primary backbone of Highlands County remains agriculture. It's great to still be able to see guys on horseback, rounding up the cows.

Some folks might not agree with me, but I still think that the economy is driving some of these problems between citizens and law enforcement. We have a lot of folks out there who are hopeless about jobs and having a place to live and hopeless about being able to take care of their kids financially. We have a whole population of folks who are just lost. That's a personal opinion, but I see that in my jail. The majority of people in my jail are either mentally ill, involved with drugs and alcohol, or they're poor.

People who think marriage is easy are naïve. Marriage takes a tremendous amount of effort and nurturing to keep that relationship right.

Being the first woman elected in the state of Florida in a general election to the office of sheriff became a really big deal. I would get letters from young girls. I realized I had much more responsibility than just being the sheriff, operating a big budget, managing lots of people, and protecting and serving. I also was a role model, and that weighed heavy on me to be the kind of person I needed to be so I could be a role model for these young girls.

When I first moved here, it was '78 or '79, and I went to work at the sheriff's office. But, lo and behold, they didn't know what to do with a girl with police powers, so to speak, and I was relegated to working in the office with a crisscross tie on and a Peter Pan–collar shirt. They had no women officially on patrol. At that time, I had four years of experience, I had a bachelor's degree in criminal justice, and so it took a toll on me. I basically cried and told my husband for five years to please take me back to Miami. But obviously in hindsight, there was a plan in place. I found my place eventually.

So, I ran for sheriff in 2004, and it was a tough race. Come to find out, I believe that the biggest push that got me elected was women. It just seemed like the women in this community took me on like the chance they never had—or the chance they want their daughters or granddaughters to have.

When I fish now, it's usually in the ocean, off the east coast, but I was raised in Miami, and a big weekend for us was cane poles and bobbers. When my dad would get a day off, my mom would take the iron frying pan, some Crisco, and some grits, and we'd go out on a canal bank out there in the Everglades, and we'd fish all day. Mom would fry up what we caught and fix up a pot of grits, and we were in hog heaven.

The trust your community has in you as the sheriff is only as good as their trust in you to police yourself.

We've got a couple of great Cuban restaurants here now in Highlands County—finally!

BETTY CASTOR

Former education commissioner, University of South Florida president, state lawmaker, teacher, interviewed in August 2007, when she was sixty-six, Tampa.

AFTER COLLEGE, FROM 1963 TO 1965, I taught secondary school in Uganda. My own family thought I was crazy. They warned me I should not do this. But it was a very idealistic time. I thought I could make a contribution. I wasn't filled with the idea that I had to make big bucks.

At the time, it seemed very safe to me. Now, of course, everybody knows the legacy of Idi Amin, but that came right after my experience.

When I got home, I enrolled at the University of Miami to get an advanced degree in education. I was penniless and decided I had to get a job, so I went to the Dade school district and said I'd like to work, and they said, "Well, if you'd like to work, we're only hiring white teachers for our formerly minority schools." They had a vacancy at Holmes Elementary School, so I said I'd take it. This was a tough school, right in the heart of Liberty City. I had a wonderful experience there. Again, I felt like I could make a contribution.

After a year, we moved to Tampa. I had children and became involved in public affairs, particularly environmental issues. I became president of the League of Women Voters, and that gave me an opportunity to mix and mingle with some of the governmental folks. We decided it was time to reform the county commission, and I invited a group of people over to my home one night to talk about who we could get to run for some of these local offices. And people were saying, "Betty, why don't you do it?" So, after a little bit of persuasion, I figured I didn't have anything to lose, and I ran for county commission.

There were eleven candidates in my primary. I was the top vote-getter, and I had a runoff. I was the only female, and all of my male opponents except for one endorsed my opponent. But I won.

I escape to North Carolina whenever I can. My husband and I are both hikers, and we spend a lot of time hiking. I've recently learned how to play golf—and that's a miserable thing to do.

And then I had that incident when I was asked to leave the University Club in Tampa. It was 1974. At the time, it was an all-male club, and women were not permitted there for lunch. But I was invited by Dick Greco, the mayor then. I went to the back room at the appointed time and sat down. The waitress came in and she looked at me, and I ordered something, and she came back and said, "Mrs. Castor, you'll have to leave." Then, a hostess came back and she said, "Mrs. Castor, you'll have to leave and, if you don't, we'll have to do something." I didn't want to make a scene, so I got out. I didn't know whether to cry or to get mad. I decided I ought to get mad. I went back to the courthouse, and I had a little press conference, and I talked about it. When I was elected later to the Florida Senate, one of my first bills provided that public meetings could not be held in places that discriminated. So I feel like I got the last word. And I've been back there for lunch.

I was the fourth woman ever elected to the Florida Senate, the first woman from the Tampa Bay area. I was elected in 1976 for my first term, and the first black man was elected to the Senate that same year. It was just the beginning of change.

When I was education commissioner, I worked very hard to get the first pre-K programs going, and I think that's very important. It has grown, and I'm very proud of that.

I truly loved being a university president. The only reason you exist is to impart knowledge.

I didn't expect the rough-and-tumble of the U.S. Senate race. I was not prepared for the despicable part of it. I try not to dwell upon it. But I'm glad I did it, and it was a very close race. I've moved on. My daughter [U.S. Rep. Kathy Castor] is in Congress, and I will let her do the politicking in the family.

SAM GIBBONS

Former U.S. congress-
man and Florida leg-
islator, D-Day invader,
interviewed in October
2012, when he was
ninety-two, Tampa. Gib-
bons died three days
after the interview.

I DON'T THINK WE REALLY KNOW who killed John Kennedy. I think Lee Harvey Oswald is the one who fired the shot, but I think the plot was deeper than that. I talked to quite a few members of the investigating committee, and they said that when they started their hearings on investigating the assassination, the FBI came in with one hard line: There was one person, his name was Lee Harvey Oswald, he's dead, and we don't think there was anyone else involved. Well, I don't know.

The war made me a very serious person. I became more interested in the welfare of those around me.

Politicians seem to be having a harder time today. I don't know how much of that is self-inflicted. I really think it's the unlimited amount of campaign money that's the problem.

The first time I ever appeared in a newspaper was in a fishing column. The guy wrote about the two ten-pound grouper I caught in about twenty minutes out in front of my grandmother's house in Haven Beach, by Indian Rocks Beach.

About 100 yards off the front of her home was a reef, a little reef that was just loaded with fish. I'd paddle out there in a canoe. They ran my picture holding these two ten-pound grouper. That was my first public appearance.

When I went to Congress, Florida had about three million people. By the time I got out of Congress, Florida was up to about eighteen or nineteen million people. Florida was addicted to growth, but a lot of the temporary prosperity that comes about from growth just isn't here anymore.

In 1942, I became dissatisfied with the work I was doing in the Army, so I joined the parachute troops. It worried the dickens out of my parents, but I sure knew I would be no worse off than I would be in the regular infantry.

My father was a lawyer. There are thirteen or fourteen lawyers in the Gibbons family. I'm number seven.

I landed in a pasture [in Normandy, France, during the early moments of the D-Day invasion in World War II]. I was all by myself. I had a general understanding of where I was, but I didn't know exactly. When I got out of my parachute harness and got rid of the other stuff I didn't need, I turned over on my belly and started crawling toward the nearest fence line. About halfway, I ran into a very warm cow pie. Ha! I said, "Oh,"—I won't say the next word I said—and then I realized, well, I'm lucky because if there are cows in this field, it sure isn't mined, and land mines were one of the things we were worried about.

Dishonesty gets me angry.

When I was a kid, I liked to dig holes, but they weren't permanent. Nothing's permanent in the Florida sand.

I still like to help people. I try to help them make decisions. When people stop by to chat, they always leave with a little advice.

Our health-care system today is a mess. When I was chairman of the Ways and Means Committee in 1994, I got the first health-care bill approved in committee and got it to the House floor for a vote, but President Clinton decided he couldn't push it through into the Senate, and so we dropped the thing. That's a frustration. You end up with a lot of frustrations when you're in Congress.

I had a rather progressive voting record in the Florida Legislature, and they did not want to run the Kennedy-Johnson campaign through the regular Democratic organization, so Robert Kennedy came around and he said to me, "Well, we'd like you to handle the Kennedy-Johnson campaign in this part of Florida." I said, "What is this part of Florida?" And he said, "As far as you can go."

When I went to Washington, I had the friendship of the president, the vice president, and all of their staff. You can't express what an asset that was. One of the mayors of Tampa—and I won't tell you who it was—he said to me one time, "Sam, you're getting me so much money. I never dreamed there was this much money available at the federal level."

There's nothing worse than Alzheimer's. Fortunately, I haven't had it yet. So far, thank God, I think I've got all my marbles.

The governor, I'd rather not get into that topic. I pray for him. Florida doesn't need a bad governor. We have enough problems without one.

War stinks. It really not only smells bad, but it stinks. I think one of the more important things that Americans must understand is that we are only 4 percent of all of the people on earth. We are not big enough to run the whole world. We've got to have allies and friends. Countries that trade together don't fight each other, so I always tried to promote commerce with foreign countries.

We met at 8:30 Monday morning at MacDill Air Force Base, and I rode with President Kennedy in Tampa. I never dreamed Tampa was such a good Democratic town until I went with him on that motorcade. People came up and stood in lines and waved at him and yelled. I kept waiting to hear a "Hey Sam!" He told me how pleased he was at the reception. Tuesday at 2:00 a.m., we were back in Washington, and I said good-bye to him on the White House lawn. There was a nice limousine waiting to take me to my home. The president and I shook hands, and I thanked him for including me in his entourage. I guess "good night" was the last thing he said to me. Four days later, he was dead.

Like most people who are ninety-two, I have good days and bad days. Today is a good day.

Charles Gray

Attorney, interviewed in March 2012, when he was eighty, Orlando.

I NEVER WANTED TO RUN for political office myself. I found you could put a good person into office and accomplish as much as if you went into office yourself.

In 1964, I was watching TV, a black-and-white TV, and I saw a guy up on a bare stage, talking about what he believed about government in the state of Florida. He was running for governor. His name was Haydon Burns, and I watched him and I listened to what he had to say—and what he said made a lot of sense to me. So, I thought, "Well, I'll support him."

I got all my buddies together, and I chartered a bus—got a keg of beer in the back—and we headed to Jacksonville and talked to Haydon Burns and his wife, Mildred. I pledged our sacred honor—five hundred dollars each, and that was when five hundred dollars was a lot of money—and he asked me to chair his campaign in central Florida. He was the dark horse, a former mayor of Jacksonville, one of six candidates, and he was the least expected to win. But he won, and the win spread from central Florida out. We were responsible for him becoming governor.

I liked working on a ranch. We were outside. I like outside. I really liked the animals. You start castrating bull calves, and it seems a little heartless, but then you get used to it.

After we helped Burns win the election, he called and said, "Charlie, I want to come down and talk to you." He came down and he said to me, "What do you want?" I said, "Well, I want a new university." He said, "You got it." And that's how the University of Central Florida got started.

I really wanted to build something, but I never dreamed the firm would get this big. We've got 260-some-odd lawyers now. I still call it a small firm with a lot of lawyers.

Governor Burns called me and told me he wanted me to be chairman of the turnpike authority, and I said, "What's that?" I didn't know what it was. I got a salary of twelve thousand dollars, and I could still practice law part-time. I had the turnpike authority car at my disposal. I had a twin-engine Aero Commander with a pilot of my choice. This was heady stuff for a thirty-two-year-old kid.

I went to the University of Florida, a wonderful, wonderful university, but it was pretty much a party school for me. As long as I could make my grades, I was having fun.

As chairman of the turnpike authority, I saw there was an area that really needed to have a turnpike, and that was down the west coast of Florida. Well, word got out, and I got a call from Nelson Poynter, the publisher of the *St. Petersburg Times*. He said, "Charles, I'd like for you to have dinner with my wife and me," so I went and had dinner with him. He said, "Charles, I don't want a toll road down the west coast of Florida." I said, "Well, Mr. Poynter, you're not going get an interstate for twenty years, and I can build a toll road in two." This is 1966 or maybe 1965. He said: "Well, I'm very disappointed in your governor. He promised me he would not build a toll road down the west coast of Florida." So, I went back to my office and I called Haydon. I said, "Haydon, did you promise Nelson Poynter you wouldn't build a turnpike down the west coast of Florida?" He said, "I did." I said, "Why did you do that?" He said, "To get elected."

As a child, I wanted to be a cowboy, and I wanted to be a sailor. I've had the good fortune to have done both.

I saw Gemini Springs for the first time in the waning hours of daylight on a Sunday, and I bought it nine o'clock the next morning—and I didn't have any money. I borrowed. It's a public park now, a beautiful public park. We lived there. We raised our kids there. It had a great swimming hole, great fishing, but we never built a home next to the springs because that would just be a sacrilegious thing to do. I always wanted the property to eventually be a park.

During a great deal of the roaring '60s and '70s, I didn't spend enough time with my family. I wish I had spent more time with my children. I guess everybody does, but I have a wonderful wife, and she has been a wonderful mother. Now, I make sure I spend a lot of time with my grandkids. It's like a second chance, and it's wonderful.

When the Disney people first came to the governor, he called me in and he told me and he told them that I was his liaison to Disney. Whatever they wanted, work through me, and I'd get it done. So I worked with them all through the process of acquiring the 27,000 acres. When we finally got it all done—Paul Helliwell was Disney's personal attorney, and Roy Hawkins was his personal real estate consultant—Paul called me. He said: "Charlie, I want to have lunch with you. Meet Roy and I at the Howard Johnson's down on the Orange Blossom Trail." So, I went down there and we had lunch. They said, "Charlie, we want you to know that we are appreciative of you working with us and keeping everything in confidence." They pulled out a map of the 27,000 acres. They said: "We want you to be the first to know where the entrance to Disney is going to be. We have acquired three of the quadrants at the intersection of I-4 and State Road 530 [now U.S. 192], and we think you ought to buy the fourth quadrant." Now, I'm still a struggling lawyer, and I don't have any damn money. I thought about it, but I couldn't figure out what I could put outside the 27,000 acres that Disney couldn't put inside, and I didn't have the money, anyway. The people who did buy it went bankrupt because Disney didn't open until 1971, and this was 1966, and when Disney did open, it took another five or six years for it to really gear up. So, I made a very smart decision not to buy it.

I don't do well without a team. It takes teamwork to do anything. I've got the greatest team in the world with my wife. We sailed our boat around the world together.

Bob Martinez

Former Florida governor, U.S. drug czar, Tampa mayor, teacher, union leader, interviewed in June 2009, when he was seventy-four, Tampa.

IN 1974, I BOUGHT MY UNCLE'S RESTAURANT, the Café Sevilla, in Tampa. That's when you prove your work ethic. The restaurant probably taught me more about discipline than anything else.

I fished with my father religiously until I went off to graduate school. We'd leave at five in the morning to be sure we got to the spot on the bay we wanted by sunrise. One day, it was so cold that we didn't want to put our hands in the bait bucket because the water was just so freezing. There were lots of little whitecaps pounding against the boat. There was a mackerel that must have been near the surface, and the wave action caught it and it landed inside the boat. That was the only fish we caught that day.

I've always been sort of a joiner and active in organizations of one kind or another. I always felt that it was important to get involved with things other than what you do for a living.

Teaching is very demanding. If you want to do it right, you have to be fresh all the time—and by fresh I mean you have to be innovative. You can only capture a student's imagination if you're creative and energetic. Otherwise, they'll spot it and they'll lay back.

By nature, I've been a risk taker, like mortgaging my house to buy the restaurant. When I went off to the University of Illinois to get my master's degree, my daughter was three and my son was six months old. I sold the house for the equity and took money out of my retirement. I showed up in the dead of winter in Urbana-Champaign with no housing. I just kind of rolled the dice. Had I not done that, I don't think the rest would have happened.

You have to listen to the people when you're out there campaigning, but the other side of the equation is you have to have a vision. You have to have some idea how the community will benefit from you being in office.

I love Spanish soups. I grew up with them. My grandmother made a lot of Spanish soups, garbanzo bean soup, collard greens soup, black bean soup. These are soups that taste better the longer they sit in the refrigerator.

Local government is retail—water, sewer, police, fire, street maintenance. You're dealing with the end user directly, which is the citizen. When you're at the state level, you're transferring money. You're regulating. It's like a wholesale business. You're dealing with an intermediary.

I go to Bern's Steak House a lot. I love the Columbia.

When I was mayor, I divided the city in quadrants, and every weekend, either a Saturday or Sunday, I'd get my basset hound, and we'd get in the car and drive and see how the city was functioning in that quadrant. I could see if things were mowed or not mowed, if the streets looked dirty or clean. And every Monday morning, I would make my observations to senior staff.

I named my basset Tampa Mascotte, after the ship, the *Mascotte*, that's pictured in the city seal. That dog was with me all through my public life, mayor, governor, drug czar. He died just when he was about to be sixteen, about four years ago, and it hurt. It really did.

The Shuttle *Challenger* disaster happened when I was campaigning for governor. I happened to be coming out of Broward County, having been endorsed by a number of local officeholders, and I was heading to Brevard County for a fundraiser. I was on Interstate 95, and my driver and I were listening to the radio when all of sudden the music is interrupted with this bulletin. We looked up and saw the plume. We saw that plume the entire drive to Brevard County.

In government, the most difficult thing you deal with—and sometimes it makes you and sometimes it breaks you—is the unscheduled event, whether it's a terrible hurricane, civil unrest, or whatever.

The service tax was my unscheduled event. It had technically been passed before I got there, and it hadn't even come up in the campaign or debates. What was the old World War II movie? *Run Silent, Run Deep.* That's how that issue was.

We implemented about a third of the taxes that had been voted on and left the other two-thirds tax-exempt, but that one-third became the only issue to be talked about. It sucked up all the oxygen. So we repealed it and substituted it with another penny sales tax. We didn't lose the revenue. We went from five to six pennies, which brought in the same amount as the service tax. In hindsight, which is always perfect, probably we should have asked for an extension to become more familiar with the issue and gone around the state talking about it to see what the public thought about it.

There had been a couple of articles and editorials mentioning me as a possible vice-presidential running mate under George H. W. Bush, but that whole service tax thing took a lot of political capital. Whatever might have been kind of went south with that.

When I was drug czar, we worked real hard to stop first-time use. That's your best hope for success. It's a heartbreaking issue. It's an issue that will never end. You go to these drug centers, it's just one terrible story after another. We were just trying to contain it.

I'm not one of those who believe you can force things to happen. You just have to have the guts and the will and the strength to go through a window when it's open. Sometimes, you can't go through it, but when I saw my break, I usually took a shot at it.

I've had a great life. I never thought I would be mayor. I never thought I would be governor. I never thought I would be the country's drug czar. I've had incredible experiences, not only a chance to do something with public policy, but the people I met—presidents, prime ministers of other countries, audiences with the pope, meeting royalty. I had all those opportunities. I thank the public for that.

When I left public life, I knew I would never return to it, even more than I knew I wouldn't return to running a restaurant or to the classroom. When I'm done with something, I just go on to something else. It's always tomorrow with me.

H. Lee Moffitt

Attorney, former
Speaker of the Florida
House and namesake
of the Moffitt Cancer
Center, interviewed
in July 2014, when
he was seventy-two,
Tampa.

You show me a good politician—a good public servant, I should
say—and I'll show you a person who has first and foremost good people skills. The ones who excel are the ones who are not afraid to strike
out on their own and innovate rather than be herded along by some
sort of party policy or party politics or dogma. I like the ones who can
think for themselves.

Nothing has ever come easy for me. It was not easy to graduate from
college. I was working full-time. The same was true in law school. The
key, at least to any success that I have had, particularly with the cancer
center and in politics, is perseverance.

The amount of politics in medicine is always amazing to me. It's
about turf. It's about ego. It's about money. It's really sad that there is

so much infighting. In fact, there is more infighting in the politics of medicine than there is in Tallahassee.

Playing baseball during high school, I crunched my knee sliding into second base, and it always was a problem. And then, later in life when I was twenty-nine years old, I found out that the same knee—I always thought it hurt because of the baseball injury—had a tumor. It turned out to be malignant, and I had to have the tumor removed.

I read a lot and I travel a lot, and when I'm traveling in my car all over Florida I always have a CD or a book on tape that I listen to. I enjoy historical novels and enjoy reading about Harry Truman and Teddy Roosevelt. *The Rise of Theodore Roosevelt* is one of my favorites.

My father was a welder. He tried for years to teach me how to weld, and I was just all thumbs. Jokingly, one day he said: "Well, you're never going to amount to a damn thing. You can't work with your hands, so you may as well be a lawyer."

When you're in elected office, too many people think it's about them. The real reason people should be in public service is to serve the people.

We're a diverse state. When you look at north Florida, compared to Miami, it's very difficult to find a consensus in a state that is so diverse.

There is not a day, and I'm not exaggerating, that goes by when I don't talk to or visit with someone who has either been a patient at the cancer center or wants me to help them get a member of their family into the cancer center. There are some days when I get four or five requests.

When I first floated the idea of building a cancer center, I thought I would receive support. I was absolutely amazed at the amount of opposition. The local medical association, the local hospitals, even from areas around the state that were 100 miles away, did not support it and actively fought it. And when I finally got some money in the budget, just to plan for the creation of the cancer center, the state medical schools went to the governor and got the governor—who was Bob Graham at the time—to veto the first money for the cancer center.

Do you know any of the poetry of Robert Service? There was one particular poem of his that I like, called "Carry On!" that talks about perseverance. You just carry on until you achieve the best you can.

I didn't want the cancer center to be named after me. I didn't want people to think that I was fighting for the cancer center to create a monument for myself. I fought for it because I saw the death of my friends and I saw the state of Florida had either the first- or second-highest incidence of death from cancer in the United States.

My legislative colleagues tried to name it after me when I was presiding one day, actually the next-to-the-last day, I believe, before I retired. They offered an amendment to another bill. I was presiding in the chair at the time, and I ruled the amendment out of order. I brought the delegation up and told them, "Thank you very much, but I really don't want you to do that," and they all nodded and walked away. I thought the matter had been taken care of. Well, unbeknown to me, the next day I was called to the governor's office to put together the finishing touches on that particular legislative session. The governor said he wanted to talk to me about some budget issues. Little did I know it was a plan to get me out of the chair so that they could take the amendment up to name it after me without me knowing about it, which they did. The bill was walked down to the Senate. The Senate immediately passed it, and I didn't even know that it had happened until I read about it the next day in the newspaper. I was outfoxed.

My goal, and our collective goal, is to be able to find ways to prevent and cure cancer so that, someday, the cancer center can be shut down, and we can turn it into another facility that would serve some other public good.

The governor was still not persuaded that a cancer center was a good idea, so I had to turn to some of my friends on the Appropriations Committee to carefully consider the governor's budget. And they saw fit to cut the governor's budget by about a third for the running of the office of the governor. It was amazing. It was so much easier to get the governor's attention for the creation of the cancer center. I gave him his money back to run his office in exchange for his pledge that he would support the cancer center. Sometimes, it takes a meat axe to get things done.

ED PRICE

Legislator, past president Florida Chamber of Commerce, executive vice president of Tropicana Products, interviewed in June 2010, when he was ninety-two, Bradenton. Price died in December 2012.

RUNNING FOR PUBLIC OFFICE TODAY is totally different. In my day, television was no big deal. You'd go door-to-door and meet people. You'd give speeches on the back of a flatbed truck in some parking lot somewhere, and all the people would sit in their cars and honk the horn if they liked you.

I was a Democrat and I'm still a Democrat, but I'm not a Yellow Dog Democrat. I don't vote all Democratic. I vote for the best person.

One thing I've always been against is the power that lobbyists have over legislators.

You have to be able to oppose something when you know it's wrong, even if you might be the only one doing it. It takes courage to do that.

When I served, it was the time of the pork chop legislators. They were rural, very conservative, mainly from north Florida. The pork choppers had a blood oath that they would vote for any bill that another pork chopper put in, period. There were just enough of us—they called us the lamb choppers—to uphold Governor Collins's vetoes of some of their legislation.

People thought the pork choppers were a bunch of bad people. They were not. They were basically representing what they thought was best for their people. While I didn't agree with a lot of them, it wasn't like we couldn't do business. We joined hands and formed a coalition, for example, to build junior colleges throughout the state of Florida. We might fight each other on the floor, but afterward we could go out to dinner.

Reubin Askew asked me to join the Florida Citrus Commission. The commission had some problems that had to be straightened out. I told him I'd do it on one condition: Don't tell me what to do. I went there to eliminate politics from the commission, and I think I did that.

Anita Bryant, she got all involved in the gay situation, which was a bad mistake on her part. Before that, she did a super job for the citrus industry. She could sell orange juice.

It must have been around 1963. I got the representatives from the counties affected to join with me and write a bill to appropriate $250,000 to go to work on this one thing: red tide. The goal was to study red tide, find out what was causing it, and then do everything we could to prevent it. We passed the bill, and the governor signed it. The marine biologists went to work, but the red tide, it still comes.

I was a pilot stationed in England during the war. I flew a B-17. All my missions were over Germany. You were getting shot at every day. It was not unusual to come back with three hundred holes in your airplane. I thought war was a bad thing, and I still do. You hate to be a part of dropping bombs, because somebody is getting killed, but I just wanted to see it get done, get it over with and get home.

In Cologne, Germany, there's a cathedral, and they told us to do everything we could to keep from bombing that cathedral. We didn't. Later, I went over to Germany for Tropicana to sell the first orange juice that was ever sold in bottles in Germany, and I saw the cathedral. It was still standing there in good shape.

Our economy today, we could take a lesson by going back and looking at what Roosevelt did to pull us out of the deep, dark days of the

Depression. Create the jobs, so people can start buying. You can't spend if you don't have a job. And the banks have to start lending.

I believe in hard work.

We didn't have a four-lane highway from southwest Florida to Miami. There was no way to get there from here. The other coast already had a turnpike, and we wanted to utilize some of those federal funds for Interstate 75. We got the chambers from Hillsborough, Manatee, Sarasota, Charlotte, Lee, Collier, Broward, Dade, and so forth, and we got the legislative delegation, and we got the press all working together. And we never stopped working until they built that road.

Even though I strongly opposed renaming Manatee Community College [to State College of Florida, Manatee-Sarasota], I still support the institution because we need the college badly. But I wish they hadn't thrown away fifty-two years of tradition. I worked real hard, along with many others, to get that college put in Manatee County. I would have preferred calling it Manatee State College.

I'm ninety-two years old, and actually I'm still involved in local organizations, but the last year and a half, I took care of my wife 24–7. I was pretty well worn out toward the end. We were married for sixty-two years, and I thank the Lord that we had sixty-two years together. They were wonderful years. The end, it wasn't easy to handle, but I just made up my mind to always remember the good things we had in our life and be thankful.

I still keep an office in downtown Bradenton, and I don't plan on closing it. My landlord wanted to have at least a two-year lease, and I said OK, but with one caveat: If I become incompetent or die, then the lease gets canceled. I'll keep the office open as long as I am.

ALEX SINK

Banker, former chief financial officer of Florida, former candidate for governor, widow of Bill McBride, who ran for governor in 2002, interviewed in March 2017, when she was sixty-eight, Thonotosassa.

I COME FROM A FAMOUS FAMILY, the Siamese Twin family. My great-grandfather Chang Bunker was one of the twins. He had ten children—three boys and seven girls—and my grandfather was the youngest son. I grew up in the house that Chang Bunker built. My father still lives there.

Everybody should make a goal to get one of those "back roads of Florida" books and go exploring. When you drive somewhere, take a different road, a different route. Explore. This is such a phenomenal state.

Banking's a great career. I woke up every day, and I knew I was going to make decisions that were going to make people's lives better.

My parents' expectations of me were that I could do anything I wanted to do, but education was important. I was a really good student. I loved, just loved, learning. I was a sponge. I never made a B all through high school—straight A's. That was my reputation—that I was kind of a nerdy math student.

In Florida, I'm concerned that we take our best and brightest Florida high school graduates, and we put them in these universities with tens of thousands of people. I hear too many stories of these bright young people who can spend a whole semester basically in their apartment in their pajamas taking online courses.

Anytime you have a lockdown of one-party control, that's not good for democracy.

Bill and I met within months of me moving to Florida in January of 1984. I met him at a business lunch, and we had our first date in May. I was living in Miami, and he was in Tampa. We just had so many things in common, so many common interests. We eventually got married, and I moved over to Tampa, and we had two babies right away.

I've been to all of Florida's sixty-seven counties.

When I was running for governor, the loudest applause line I got every time I spoke to a group was, "Why not be known as the Sunshine State because we have more solar power than anybody else?" To this day, do you hear anybody talking about that? What a huge, enormous missed opportunity.

I grew up on a tobacco farm in a small North Carolina town that itself has become iconic. I grew up in Mount Airy, also known as Mayberry.

The Siamese Twins were really sharp businessmen. And my grandfather was an incredible businessman, an amazing businessman, and my own father is an amazing businessman to this day.

Everybody, of course, when you're a candidate, everybody has their own idea of what you should say, what you should look like, what clothes you should wear, how your hair should be. I'll never forget, one time, this guy came up to me and said: "When you're speaking, you squint. You should open your eyes!" And I'm thinking: "I can't. These eyes are inherited."

My mother was a perfectionist. Growing up, everything had to be perfect. That's not so good. I didn't raise my children that way.

At one point in time, Bill was the managing partner of the largest law firm in the state, and I was president of the largest bank. We were both on the cover of *Florida Trend*.

Leadership Florida made a big difference in my life. I was in class four, and I think this year they're up to class thirty-five or something.

It's one of the best and most important statewide leadership organizations in Florida.

The year I lost to Rick Scott, I lost by one percentage point. It was the closest gubernatorial election in Florida history. Every other Democrat that year, because of the Tea Party, lost by 10 points, but it didn't matter. I didn't win. I had all these dreams and hopes and visions for the future, and I didn't get to do it. It was depressing. We had our hopes and dreams dashed.

Being a woman in business, I felt a lot of responsibility to be a champion for diversity.

My favorite book of all time is *A Land Remembered* by Patrick Smith. I just sent a copy to a newcomer to Tampa, and I said, "OK, first thing you have to do is you've got to read this book." It gives you such a flavor for the history of Florida.

I'm hopeful about passing the amendment that demands that we put aside a certain percentage of money into environmental land protection. I'm hopeful about the citizens passing the fair district amendment that demands that we draw our districts in a more nonpartisan way. I'm hopeful about the medical marijuana amendment that passed by 70-plus percent. The flip side is we have a Legislature that doesn't implement the will of the people.

Surveys show that a woman has to be asked seven times before she'll agree to run for office. You ask a guy to run for office, it's like, "Oh yeah, where do I sign up?" We need more women in public life. We need more women in business.

I've always said that, in my next life, I want to come back as a Florida tour guide.

One of the things that makes me most hopeful is the millennial generation. They're not afraid of immigrants. They're not afraid of Muslims. Maybe when the history of this time is written twenty years from now, somebody will say Donald Trump awoke a sleeping giant.

We found Bill dead from a heart attack in 2012. It was totally unexpected. I don't like being a widow. Building a new life is not easy. You wake up every morning and force yourself to get out of bed and put both feet on the ground and keep moving. It's like you've cut your arm off. You look around and say, "Where's my right arm?" It's not there anymore.

PRACTITIONERS

W. George Allen

Attorney, first African American to graduate from UF's law school, interviewed in October 2013, when he was seventy-seven, Fort Lauderdale.

I was born in Sanford, Florida, which used to be a totally segregated community. I was home for a visit and went to the public library to do some research for a project, and I was told that I couldn't come into the white library. I just walked past the lady and found the books I needed and sat down. They whispered and pointed, but nobody beat me up, so I did my research. That's how I grew up. I experienced people being beat up and mistreated because they were black.

It was an injustice that the Florida Supreme Court—all those white justices—kept denying Virgil Hawkins the right to go to the University of Florida. Virgil kind of made a deal that he would give up his right to go if they would admit other blacks, so Virgil sacrificed for me.

I started working in the fields when I was about ten years old. The white farmers would close down the black schools in the winter because Sanford was a farming area, mostly celery at the time, and all of us blacks who were able-bodied had to work in the fields. People were arrested for not working.

When I arrived at the University of Florida, they wouldn't let me live at married student housing because we were black. I would receive telephone calls, saying, "Nigger, nigger we're going to kill you," and I'd tell them to go to hell. My dad gave me a rifle and said, "If they come to your house, shoot them." I had young kids, so I taught them how to shoot. I made it known that I don't believe in nonviolence like Martin Luther King Jr. You bother me, I'm violent.

I fish the St. Johns River and Everglades City on the west coast. I like to fish in Martha's Vineyard, too. My wife and I have a house there. We've been going to Martha's Vineyard longer than Barack Obama.

A friend of mine, Percy Lee, we were working in the fields cutting celery, along with other youngsters. The overseer, the straw boss, his name was Red Tile. He had a bad attitude and hated black folk. He and Percy got into an argument about how Percy was packing the celery. He said Percy sassed him and that "No nigger could talk to a white person this way." So, he got a machete knife, and he said he was going to kill Percy. Percy's mother and my mother and father and a lot of the other grown-ups told him, "No, you won't." They circled Percy, and I was in there with them. We had to get Percy out of the field because the guy was really going to kill him.

I was admitted to Harvard and the University of California at Berkeley, but I'm a native Floridian, and I felt that somebody had to integrate the University of Florida. The racists told me I didn't belong there and I'd never graduate. I got into one or two fights with students who were disrespectful, but I never considered quitting. I made it known that you're not going to run me away. You're not going to scare me. I'm going to out-study all of you, and I'm going to graduate.

In law school, one of the guys asked me if I would be offended if someone used the n-word, and I said yes. It's offensive. It's denigrating. The people who try to popularize that word today are wrong.

The first time I was offered a judgeship, they weren't making a lot of money back then. Nixon was president. I think they were making thirty-six thousand dollars a year, and frankly I was making more. Also, judges have to be impartial, like referees, and I have an opinion about every damn thing.

My father always told me to be careful around white folk and especially white women. Don't appear friendly because that will get you into trouble. So, I was very careful. I knew people who were killed for saying hello.

There was this janitor at UF. He resented the fact that I was a student, because I was black. The bathrooms on campus were just public bathrooms. They didn't have colored and white bathrooms at the law school. So, if I went into the bathroom, he would stand around and wait for me to come out before he would go in. So, this one day, I'm there and he's obviously in distress, needing to use the bathroom, so he came in and looked and saw me, and I stayed in there—washed my hands three or four times—and he kept coming back. And finally, I had my briefcase with me, and I just took out my books and I studied there in the bathroom to keep him from using it. If he won't use a bathroom with a black, then let him go somewhere else. I stayed there about thirty minutes, studying in the bathroom.

Our educational system in Florida is in shambles. This Jeb Bush crap of rating schools and letting all the students who want to leave their school get vouchers to go to good schools just leaves all the schools in the poor communities as F schools. What we've done is we've reverted back to segregated schools in poor communities. Jeb Bush screwed up our educational system. It was never about anything but privatizing education and making money for his friends.

My father instilled in me the attitude that you don't accept injustice. If you have to fight, fight. He was that way. He didn't take any crap.

I was thirty-six, and I saw this yellow Rolls-Royce, and the wife allowed me to buy it. I got stopped a lot by cops, so I got rid of that one and bought a gray one. At the time, I was doing a lot of civil rights work, and the IRS audited me for fifteen straight years. My accountant, who formerly worked for the IRS, told me in order to stop the audits, get rid of the Rolls-Royce. I said fine. I bought a brand-new Checker and the audits stopped.

The Supreme Court of the United States is now killing voting rights. They're trying to undo all the civil rights gains. The fight continues.

In Groveland, Florida, my wife and I built a log cabin. The sheriff who used to be up there, Willis McCall, was really a racist guy, who was involved in that Groveland case. He killed a prisoner and shot another one in the back. Anyway, that was the county where I built the log cabin, and my dad told me I was crazy and tried to talk me out of it, but I said: "Hey, they don't do anything like that now. It's better now." And they burned my cabin, and the sad part was they knew who burned it and never arrested anybody. That was the late '80s, early '90s.

I think there are too many lawyers. I'd hate to be starting out now. A lot of the law schools are just churning them out, but, unfortunately, many of the graduates don't have work when they get out.

CRAIG FUGATE

Former Federal Emergency Management Agency administrator and former director of Florida's Emergency Management Division, interviewed in June 2017, when he was fifty-eight, Gainesville.

PRESIDENT OBAMA NEVER ASKED ME to solve climate change. He was more concerned about how we were adapting to it.

My mom died when I was ten. My dad was in the Navy, so my two sisters and I came to live in Alachua with my grandmother and my aunt. And then, when I was fifteen, my dad passed away. When you lose your parents, it's kind of hard to make plans for the future because you know things can just suddenly change on you.

In disaster response, complexity is not your friend. You need to simplify.

Tubing down the Ichetucknee, throwing a couple of watermelons in the river, and they'd float down with us, and by the time we got out, the watermelons would be cool, and we'd cook hot dogs and hamburgers. The Santa Fe River, Crescent Beach, Cedar Key, eating seafood, swimming at Blue Springs. Those were things I enjoyed growing up.

I figured out that the more people were coming to me with a problem to solve, the more things weren't going well. The less people came to me, the better the team was working.

The worse the disaster, the more likely that the first responder will be your neighbor.

A lot of people get on the ham radio, and they like to talk. I like to tinker. I like to see how far I can reach. I've got a radio built on a Raspberry Pi. You know what a Raspberry Pi is? It's a little microboard computer about the size of a credit card. I was actually hitting Europe with it pretty regularly yesterday.

I don't believe we should go around telling people you can't build on the coast, but I'm also not real comfortable with this idea that we're subsidizing that risk at such a low level that local officials and developers many times are building much riskier properties in ways that aren't sustainable because, ultimately, you the taxpayer take on the risk.

The natural tendency is everyone thinks bureaucrats are assholes, but the government is just like everywhere else. It has its prorated allocation of assholes, but that's not most people. Most of them are hardworking, dedicated servants trying to do the right thing.

What you plan for may not be what happens, but the plan isn't what's critical. It's the team you build and the ability of that team to solve problems you never anticipated.

I was in Future Farmers of America and showed steers in high school. I had four ag teachers there, and they became my surrogate father figures. I thought I'd farm or follow in their footsteps and go to UF and become a vocational ag teacher.

Gainesville is home. I feel like I'm centered when I'm here.

I liked working for Governor Crist. A lot of people, they'll say what they want about Charlie, but I'll tell you, the best thing about Governor Crist is he's an enabler. He'll tell you he hired you to do the best, be the best, don't break the law, don't break the rules, and he had high expectations. He let you do your job.

There are things you're good at and things you're not good at. Don't be something you're not good at. You're just lying to yourself.

Over time, what I found is good emergency managers probably have more in common with baseball managers or good coaches. They build teams. They know what success looks like.

When I was a paramedic, I learned how to talk to people on their worst days. I'm an introvert, so I'm not a people person, but I found a lot of times that, especially when people were having cardiacs and things like that, that if you can just get them to start talking, sometimes that gave them more relief than anything else we were doing.

I grew up as a kid listening to the Gators on the radio.

Probably when I'm cooking, I'll smoke a pork butt or a brisket, put some chicken in the smoker, or grill some ribs. I've got an electric smoker, one of the cheap models, but it turns out one of the keys to good smoking is a constant temperature, a good smoke source and—I had to learn this the hard way—smoke is to perfume the meat, not cure it. You're just giving it flavor. Some people are into apple chips or mesquite or all this other stuff, but good old-fashioned oak and a pork butt is a pretty good combination.

We'd do an annual hurricane exercise—and Governor Bush would always be there. He didn't just show up for a press conference. He was there. He would ask his chief of staff to take roll of all the agency heads and find out who wasn't there and why.

I have to give talks all the time. That's not really what's draining to me. What's draining to me is small talk.

I noticed if there was ever anything open after a disaster, it was always a Waffle House, and that's where the Waffle House Index came from. When we would dispatch National Guard or search-and-rescue teams to where hurricanes were hitting, we say drive until it's bad. Well, how do you know it's bad? If you got there and the Waffle House was open, it's not that bad, keep going. If you got there and the Waffle House was on a limited menu, you've probably got some mass-care issues, power outages, stuff like that, but keep going. You're not to the worst. When you get there and the Waffle House is closed, go to work.

After Superstorm Sandy, I remember going up in a helicopter with the president and Governor Christie, and we're flying over the Jersey shore and Governor Christie's like: "My God, have you ever seen anything like this? I can't believe the devastation." And President Obama's like, "No, I can't believe the devastation." President Obama was pretty sharp, and he looked at me and he says, "You've probably seen this before"—and I'm looking down, and I said, "Yes. It looks like a storm hit."

I learned several things as a paramedic. One, you have to be focused on outcomes, not process. People will tunnel into process and lose the big picture.

The thing you never get back is time.

There's this mythology that introverts can't be good leaders. I've worked for introverts. Jeb Bush is an introvert. Barack Obama is an introvert.

The deadly sin of emergency management is planning for what you're capable of because you will fail your community at its greatest time of need. You have to plan for what can happen, not what has historically happened.

Something that's unique to Florida—you don't find it anywhere else—is our ecosystems, our coastal areas, our spring-fed rivers, the Everglades, even some of our prairies and savannahs. To me, this is what makes Florida cool.

THOMAS "BLUE" FULFORD

Commercial fisherman, interviewed in September 2012, when he was eighty-one, Cortez. Fulford died in March 2015.

THE FISHING GOT KIND OF SLACK in the late 1950s, I guess it was, and I went to work for a construction company for about six months. I got tired of that real quick. The only thing wrong with it was it wasn't fishing.

I helped start the Organized Fishermen of Florida in 1967, and so I'd have to go up to Tallahassee and talk to the politicians about the laws they wanted to pass and all the areas they wanted to close off to commercial fishing. It was extremely frustrating. I was a greenhorn and didn't know the procedures and the terminology they used. I didn't know what they were talking about.

All of the cartilage has gone out of my shoulders. It's extremely painful. All of the cartilage has gone out of my knee. I lost one leg, which doesn't hurt much sometimes. Phantom pain is what they call it. It's all from a lifetime of fishing.

My father was born in Cortez. He died when I was three years old. I had an uncle who took me under his arm. He's who taught me how to fish. That was Tink Fulford. I watched him. He'd never sit you down and tell you this or tell you that. You just watched and learned. I guess if I wasn't going to have a daddy, Tink was kind of a daddy to me.

At a Natural Resources Committee meeting up there, they asked me a question I couldn't answer. W. D. Childers was the chairman. After the meeting, I was sitting there feeling dumb, and Bob Graham, who was on the committee, came over and kneeled down in front of my chair and talked to me. He told me he would help me.

I lost my leg in 1987, September 14, and I went right back to fishing in a month. Somebody visited me in the hospital from the state, wanted to know if I wanted any state help. I said: "No, I don't want any state help. I'm going back fishing."

My mother, when I was tiny, before I could even walk almost, she taught me to say that nursery rhyme—"Little Boy Blue, come blow your horn, the sheep's in the meadow, the cow's in the corn"—and everywhere she'd take me, I had to recite that nursery rhyme. It got to the point that people would say, "Here comes Little Boy Blue." That might be why people started calling me Blue.

My favorite fish is the kind with fins and tails. I eat fish every chance I get.

I had come down from the bridge. It wasn't my job to be where I was. I don't know what I was doing down there. I was standing by the tom weight, a 600-pound weight. I turned it loose, and there she went on her way down, 600 pounds, and everything was fine, and then I moved over and the rope took a loop around my leg and jerked me up. I was hanging spread eagle. It had just about cut my leg off, cut everything except the Achilles tendon. My son come down and was asking if he could cut me down, and I said, "Yeah, I guess." He took his pocketknife and sliced the tendon. That was the start to another phase of my life.

People need to know where their food comes from.

I liked Lawton Chiles. He used to call me Blue. I called him Lawton.

Synthetic fibers were a godsend for people like me. You used to have to work to be a fisherman. Natural fibers, the cotton and linen, bacteria would grow on them and destroy the net. It had to be dried and mended. When people were having to do that, there wasn't a long line of people wanting to become commercial fishermen.

My health is lousy. I'm on my way out.

It was 1953, we were on a shrimp boat, going to Campeche, and we were in a hurricane. That was some experience. I got sick for one thing. I got so seasick I couldn't stay in the bunk. I couldn't stay anywhere. As a matter of fact, I went outside and tied myself to the winch. It was rough. The captain, who was my brother-in-law, said the seas were 55 feet high. Everything started breaking apart. The steering gear broke down. I promised the good Lord then, if he would help me get back to shore, he wouldn't have to worry about me out there in the Gulf anymore. We got home, and I didn't go out that far again. I'm a smooth-water fisherman. Close to the shore. Close to Cortez.

The best way in my opinion to eat mullet is just scale it, filet it, and fry it with the skin on, flesh side down, turn it when it's almost done, and get that cornmeal crust where it's crunchy. Oh man, that's good.

I'll tell you what was a real shock to me when I would go to Tallahassee representing the commercial fishermen. I would sit up in the gallery and watch the Senate or the House in action. They'd be debating a bill, and there'd be three, four guys standing over in a corner talking and joking, reading the funny papers, pinching the girls on the butt, doing everything they thought they could get by with. It bothered me.

Those people were supposed to be taking care of my livelihood. I never pinched anyone on the butt, but I knew the people who did.

If I had my life to live over again, there are some things I'd do differently, but, oh yeah, I'd still be a fisherman. No doubt about that.

"Big Daddy" Don Garlits

Drag racer, museum founder, interviewed in August 2012, when he was eighty, Ocala.

I don't believe in aliens. I know about aliens. There's a difference.

In 1994, I ran for Congress. It cost me $100,000 of my own money, and my wife teased me for years because I always wanted a Dodge Viper, and she says that was your Dodge Viper.

I ran because I'm concerned about the government. I still am. I just realize now there's nothing I can do about it. I thought I'd go to Washington, and I'd be a guy who would stand firm and not be bought, kind of like Ron Paul.

My father was an electrical engineer for Westinghouse, but he retired from that and became a health-food nut. Kook is what they called them then. This was in the '20s. He had a health-food restaurant, and my mother was the cashier.

Aren't those lovebugs hateful? That's why I have what I call a rat-rod. It's a '42 Ford with a real nice engine. When the lovebugs hit, that's what I drive because the paint is terrible and the lovebugs can't hurt it.

In 1970, the transmission exploded in my dragster on the final run, and it cut my foot off and cut the car in two. That's when I drew up plans for what I thought would be a championship rear-engine car. When I got out of the hospital, I immediately started building it. I would go out to the shop in Seffner on my wheelchair, saw stuff out on the band saw, and make the parts.

I should be a farmer, because my mom married a really nice guy after the divorce from my father. He was a dairyman. They built a dairy in north Tampa by Lowry Park. We had about fifty head. My brother and I and my stepdad milked those cows seven days a week. During high school, you got up at four in the morning, milked the cows, cleaned up, went to school, came back from school, milked the cows, did the homework, went to bed, got up, milked the cows. That's how it went. That really puts the work ethic in you.

If we're attacked, I'll be the first to the shore. I'm eighty years old. I'll be there with my guns. But you'd have to kill me to get me to go to the Middle East and shoot somebody I didn't even know. We've got no business over there.

In the beginning, we actually drag-raced the cars we drove to work. There were no spectators. We put lines on the asphalt and raced on a stopwatch. Then it caught the fancy of the general public. People built drag strips and charged a lot of money to get in. In 1958, I got paid $450 to show up with my car in Texas, and I've been winning races and making money ever since.

I try to have my servings of fruit and veggies every day. I stay away from white flour, white sugar. I eat just a small portion of meat, mostly fish, and I drink lots of good water. No soda. A cup of coffee in the morning is OK. No excessive alcohol. I never smoked. None of that stuff. Exercise. Work hard. It works.

I was in high school, and I was taking an accounting degree, and I finished at the top of my class. I went right to work in the accounting department at the Maas Brothers department store in downtown

Tampa. Over breakfast one day—and I always give my stepfather credit for this—he said, "Donnie, I can see you're not happy." He knew me really well. I said: "Why do you say that? Look at my clean shirt!"—because at the dairy, you know, you had those rubber boots because you were so deep in cow manure—"I have a nice little tie. Look at my hands!" He told me: "You want to go through life doing something you love—and you love cars. You should go work at a garage."

Speed is exciting to me. I've been in a lot of wrecks, but I was never scared. Isn't that strange?

My wife has a little bit of all of them, Parkinson's, Alzheimer's, dementia. I have a lady with her in the daytime, but at night I take over. She has moments when she knows exactly who she is and everything is fine, but those don't last long. We've been married fifty-nine years. We celebrated our anniversary in her hospital room this year. I thought I was going to lose her then. The doctor told me she might never come home, but she did.

I'm on a flight from Tampa to St. Louis. TWA. I look out the window and can't believe my eyes. Not more than 1,000 feet away is a saucer with no marks on it. It was an alien craft. Immediately, the seatbelt sign went on, and I put mine on. When I looked back out the window, that thing had moved maybe 50 miles away—and it was just glowing.

Silver Springs is going dry. You know how you solve the water problem? You build no more new houses. If you want to buy a new house, you've gotta buy a house that's already here, tear it down, and build your new house.

The worst wreck was the fire in Chester, South Carolina, in June 1959. No gloves. No facemask. Just goggles. Usually, I would wear just a T-shirt, but fortunately, I had a jacket that my wife had just given me. That jacket saved my life, because the fire would have burned right through my chest. I got out of the car, and the skin just fell off my hands. Three weeks in the hospital. The doctor wanted to take both hands off, but I said I'd rather die. The doctor asked us to leave, and my wife called Tampa Municipal, which is now Tampa General, and they said they'd take me and keep me comfortable while I died. I recovered and went on to race.

We opened a museum in Seffner in 1976 and never had any visitors. We were way out in the country, so finally we decided we needed to be on the interstate. We came up to Ocala and opened the doors in 1983. We had 11,000 people the first year, with no signs or nothing. The next year we had an official opening and had 27,000 people. We're up to 65,000 now, and we're looking to expand. We have the original stuff here. I'm talking back into the '40s. It can't be replaced, and it must be protected, and the only way I know to do that is to build a tornado-proof building.

In 1962, I went to work for Chrysler, and they had this new engine—a wedge motor that ran pretty good on gas—and they asked me to put one of these gas motors in a dragster and compete at the U.S. Nationals using gasoline. And so we did. I was thirty years old and had my two little daughters with me and my wife. Most of the guys who ran their cars on gasoline were sportsman racers, younger guys, and they were kind of making fun of me because I wasn't running good—I didn't usually run on gasoline and didn't know much about it—and they were saying, "Old Daddy Garlits is here with his kids and he can't compete with us." The first thing you know, the announcer is saying, "Here comes Daddy Garlits for another run." Then we set the world record. And the announcer said, "Well, it looks like we're going to have to call him Big Daddy from now on." That's been my nickname ever since.

It was a catchy name, and we made a lot of money on it, but we didn't register it until 1969. I didn't register it at first because there was already a Big Daddy Roth, and we all looked up to him. He built lots of custom cars. Finally, I went out to California in 1968 and I ran into him and I said, "You know they're all calling me Big Daddy, but we don't use it because as far as I'm concerned, you're the Big Daddy." He said: "Don, I'm the Big Daddy of custom cars. You're the Big Daddy of drag racing." It was true because I had just won the nationals two years in a row, so I started the registration process immediately.

I've just always been very competitive. When I was in school, I wanted to turn in the best paper. I wanted to have the fastest bike. My stepdad would give me a calf and give my brother a calf, and I wanted mine to be the best and the prettiest. I always wanted to excel at everything.

When people ask me what is your greatest contribution to racing, I say the development of the rear-engine car. I didn't invent it. I just perfected it.

I'm a mechanical engineer in my heart. I'm self-taught, and I'm a fast learner. When you really love something, then you learn it even faster.

My oldest daughter is a concert pianist. She has a master's degree in that from Florida State. She's really good. She started when she was really young and was taking lessons in Tampa. I had a shop in Tampa then, not too far from where she was taking the lessons, so I took piano lessons, too, for a year to see what it was like. And let me tell you, it's tough.

MARCELLA HAZAN

Cook, teacher, writer, interviewed in October 2009, when she was eighty-five, Longboat Key. Hazan died in September 2013.

I miss the fish of Italy. It has more taste than the fish of Florida. I have to cook the fish here a different way to make it taste Italian. Good fish, you just steam it a little with some very nice olive oil and lemon, because the fish already has so much taste. The Florida fish I like most is pompano. The red snapper, not much taste.

My career was not supposed to be food. I have a doctorate in biology, and I worked in research. I never boiled water in a pot, only in a beaker in the laboratory. But I married a man who was very interested in food. He was courting me, and he was telling me what he ate for lunch and what he wanted to eat for dinner. I was a little surprised because I thought it was not very romantic.

My husband was very smart. When I was first learning how to cook, every time I did something good in the kitchen, he was jumping from the chair to kiss me and tell me how good I was, and so I wanted to do more.

If I have vegetables in the refrigerator, I feel as if I have food. I can cook them many different ways. I can make a sauce for pasta. I can do a soup.

In the morning, we do not have breakfast. We have just double espresso and that's all. They keep saying you should eat in the morning, but we survive very well.

When I test a recipe, I never think about measuring. I do it. I serve it. We eat. If it's good, I try to do it again, and I try to measure. I do it in reverse.

I don't eat Twinkies. All these things that are wrapped, I don't like. One of the things that we teach to children in Italy is to never eat between meals, not to snack, because you ruin your appetite for the meal.

Restaurants, sometimes, they want to embellish the look and the taste of the dishes, so they ruin what is Italian food, really. Italian food is very simple. You have a small portion of pasta without so much sauce. The sauce is a seasoning of the pasta, so you eat pasta with the sauce. You don't eat sauce with the pasta.

You use a very good extra virgin olive oil, and you have a very good dish. Use an olive oil that is not very good, and you ruin the dish.

I could hit myself because I brought the balsamic vinegar to America. Do you know that balsamic vinegar, the real kind, you need at least sixty to seventy years to make it? A small bottle that I have here is only twenty-five years old. It costs $185, so what is this stuff they serve in the restaurants? If you are lucky, it's red wine vinegar where they added caramel.

We always have bread on the table.

Vegetable soup, you have different types of vegetables. You start with the onion, because it's the one with the most taste. You brown the onion in olive oil and in time you peel a carrot and cut it in small pieces and you put in the carrot. You wait until the carrot browns in the onion. You put the onion in first because you want it to give its flavor to the other vegetables. Then you have the celery. When you put the celery in the carrots that have browned in the onion, the celery will take the taste of the carrot and the onion. Don't put in water. Then, maybe, you put in, I don't know, some green beans that you've cut and you do the same thing, and you keep doing this until you reach the potato. You're trying to get the taste of those vegetables into the potato—and then you put in the water. If you put the water in first, you are boiling those vegetables and you don't get the taste.

It's very strange because when I talk to people about restaurants, and they say: "Oh, it was a very nice place. They have very good service. The portions, they're very big, and it's cheap." But they never say the food is good.

The reason that we chose to live in Florida is because we always like to be near the water. For twenty years, before we moved here, we lived in Venice, Italy, which was really living near water.

A dish can look beautiful, but what about the taste?

Don't try to put too many ingredients together. We have a way of saying in Italy that what you keep out has the same importance of what you put in.

If you want to be amused, there are some stars on the television who can amuse you, but you wouldn't want to go into the kitchen to do anything that they are cooking. You wouldn't want to make their dishes. Rachel Ray, she's done in thirty minutes, but everything is frozen and cut into pieces before. I don't understand that. I would never buy all those things she buys to do it. I like her. She's nice. She talks about me very nice, and I thank her, but I would not do that cooking.

There are two things I hate to be asked. People ask me, "What is your favorite recipe?" I hate that. You always want to eat the same thing? No! And also, "What is your favorite restaurant?"

When cooking, the quality is the key. It has to be very good ingredients, the vegetables fresh, not old.

You go into a lot of Italian restaurants, and the first thing you smell is garlic. I use a lot of garlic, but you never smell garlic in my house. My garlic is cooked very, very light. When I'm browning garlic, once I start to smell it, that is enough. Don't go over.

The veal cutlet, the cutlet is pounded and put in egg and flour and fried. When it's fried right, it's crispy and it's tender inside. So, why do they serve it in restaurants with a topping of tomatoes that have juice and that makes the breading so soft? Tell me why.

I'm happy that my son Giuliano [a cookbook author] has followed in my steps. It's like I'm not finished, you know what I mean? It's like something that continues of me and that is nice. It's a continuation of preaching the Italian way.

GENE LEEDY

Architect, original member of the Sarasota School of architecture, interviewed in September 2010, when he was eighty-two, Winter Haven. Leedy died in November 2018.

MY FATHER WORKED FOR A COAL COMPANY in West Virginia, and his boss was an engineer. One rainy day, they were up on the mountain—they were working on a bridge from mountain to mountain—and his boss was wearing a Humphrey Bogart raincoat and a Humphrey Bogart hat, and I looked at him, standing there and doing drawings, and I thought, "God, that's what I want to be." I must have been about ten years old.

There wasn't much to do in West Virginia, you know, so my friends and I used to go in the woods and build log cabins. We'd notch the logs and hold them together with West Virginia clay, so I was in the construction business at a very early age.

Paul Rudolph worked in Sarasota. He was a very famous architect, and everybody wanted to work for him. After college, I went down there and told him I wanted to work for him, and he said, "What can you do?" I said, "Well, I can do your design work." He laughed, and we became friends.

Henry-Russell Hitchcock, one of the great architecture critics in the world, he wrote an article in 1952 for the *Architectural Review* in London, and he said that the greatest contemporary architecture in the world was being done by a group of young architects in Sarasota. I was supposed to put on a big program about what we were doing, and I had to think of a name for the brochure. In those days, they used to refer to the architects in Chicago as the Chicago School, so I called us the Sarasota School, and it stuck.

Walter Gropius had the Bauhaus school, you know, and I would always say that, in Sarasota, we humanized the Bauhaus school.

Sarasota used to be pretty open-minded. There were things you could do in Sarasota that you couldn't do anyplace else. Paul Rudolph was down there doing some real avant-garde stuff, so it attracted a lot of young guys. During the 1950s, Sarasota was probably the greatest place in the world to be an architect. To me, it was like Paris after World War I.

There were about ten or fifteen of us. We were all good friends. No jealousy. In fact, we used to eat at this restaurant downtown for lunch all the time, and we would discuss architecture. I think it was called the Spanish Grill or something. It was our hangout.

Phil Hiss, he was a very wealthy guy, and he came to Sarasota, and he decided he was going to improve the school system, so he ran for school board. He got elected. Well, every vote on the school board was 4 to 1, and he was the 1. He got pissed off, so he went out and campaigned for all his buddies and got them all elected, and he became chairman of the school board. The school board meetings lasted fifteen minutes because he already had it all worked out. He was a very dynamic guy. He hired all of us young architects to do schools. Then those schools got international recognition. Hiss, he appreciated good architecture. He was the catalyst.

I'm in Winter Haven, and Phil Hiss calls me, "Gene, I want you to do Brentwood Elementary School." This is on Friday, and he asks if I can come down to Sarasota Monday and sign the contract and start work on Tuesday. I said, "Yeah!" That's the way it worked.

The public has to be more aware of what they've got, like they just tore down the Riverview High School in Sarasota that Paul Rudolph did. That was a national monument, and they tore it down. We live in a Kleenex society. We use it and throw it away.

Sarasota is a great town, but the architecture in Sarasota today, it makes me want to throw up.

Just about everything you see now is bad architecture. Most of the construction in this state is dominated by the contractor or the developer—and they want it cheap.

I was one of the first architects to start doing my own interiors because so many interior decorators were screwing up my buildings.

Usually, the first-time client is very appreciative, but when the house is sold, that's when the bad stuff starts. I've always said the urge to remodel is stronger than the sex drive.

I spend a lot of time with my clients. When they come in, I know exactly what I'm going to do, but we spend two or three weeks talking about it until I just finally exhaust all of their ideas. Then, when I show them the design, they say, "Hell, that's what I wanted!"

On my sixteenth birthday, I enrolled at the University of Florida to study architecture. I was very inspired by some of the guest lecturers who were real architects, so I feel an obligation to do that myself. I've been an adjunct professor there for forty years. First of all, I tell the students that they have chosen the greatest profession in the world. It teaches you how to solve problems. I tell them, "How else in your lifetime will you be spending millions and millions of dollars of other people's money for your own pleasure?"

I've never done a bad building.

A good building to me is the honest use of materials, straightforward construction, no bullshit. So many architects, especially young architects, they play to the house. They're trying to do something real dramatic. They go over budget, and it doesn't work half the time.

When you walk into a building, you should have a feeling for it. I do a lot of things the client might not be aware of, but subconsciously they are. Everything is in order and detailed nicely to give you a sense of peace.

I treat my buildings like children. I go and visit them.

My philosophy on raising kids is give them lots of love and plenty of self-confidence. When my son Ingram was four years old—he has a very sophisticated computer business in Winter Haven now—some guy came in the office and said to Ingram, "Who are you?" And Ingram said, "I'm Ingram Leedy, and I'm the best kid in the world." The guy said: "Boy, that's impressive. Where did you get that idea?" And Ingram said, "My daddy tells me that every day."

ROLAND MARTIN

Professional fisherman, interviewed in April 2015, when he was seventy-five, Naples.

MOM AND DAD CONSIDERED ME the black sheep of the family because I wasn't in a real profession. My mom was a schoolteacher, and she wanted me to become something other than a fisherman, and my dad—he was a hydrologic engineer—couldn't stand the thought of me being a fisherman. He didn't think I'd amount to much.

I was winning angler-of-the-year awards and decided to use the fishing tournaments as a springboard to get into television. I bought some cameras and some other stuff—and pretty much went broke—but then I got on a national network with *Fishing with Roland Martin,* and things started going pretty well after that.

Ted Williams was a good fisherman. We fished together, and he'd ask a lot of questions. He would look at you and make some stupid insulting comment, and then you had to come back with an insult of your own. He liked that. He was forever getting himself in hot water messing with people.

The perception that I wasn't going to amount to anything was great motivation. It's what drove me to succeed.

I'd get up in the morning at five, starting when I was about thirteen or so, and I'd go down to the river about a mile away and trap muskrats. I trapped muskrats in the dark. The first shotgun I bought, I bought with muskrat pelts. The first rifle I bought, I bought with muskrat pelts. The first car I ever had, when I was sixteen or seventeen, I paid for with muskrat pelts. I could see then that there was money to be made on the outdoors.

I like Jack London's *The Call of the Wild*. I related to it. I envisioned myself like that, living in harsh environments, sort of a man-against-nature kind of deal.

Every fisherman out there on the lake is going to have some lucky opportunity come by, but half of them aren't going to recognize the luck. And half of them aren't going to capitalize on the luck. Really good fishermen capitalize on those opportunities.

My wife gets on me about this. Whenever we have some free time, it's hard for me to do something that doesn't have something to do with hunting or fishing.

When I was growing up, I was a pissant of a kid. I was always doing the opposite of what my parents wanted me to do.

Right now, one of the issues that's kind of grating me a little bit is weed control. What happens traditionally, in Lake Okeechobee for example, is you spray to control some of the weeds like hyacinths that get in the waterways and plug up the locks. So they have a spray program, but now they're spraying too much. The lake was really healthy say three or four years ago, with the great weed cover it had, and now I can take you out and show you acre after acre burned up from the chemicals. They're spraying not only from airboats, but from airplanes, too. It's overkill. An awful lot of the food chain relies on those weeds.

When I was forty, I dreamed about women. Now I mainly dream

about catching big fish, going to Africa and shooting elephants, and stuff like that.

There's a recipe I really like. It's called redfish on the half shell. It's a Cajun recipe. You take the redfish—not a real big one, just a medium-sized one—and you cut one whole side of it off and leave the skin and the scales on. Then you debone it and make sure it's just pure meat, and then you take a grill—a gas grill—and get it to 450. Put the fish down flesh-side up and add some olive oil, maybe some Cajun seasonings, salt and pepper and stuff, and let it grill. The bottom kind of folds up a little like a boat, and all that moisture stays in there. It doesn't take more than twelve or fifteen minutes. The skin and scales become like the plate. It's a tasty meal, but it only works with fish that have thick scales and thick skin.

My parents and I, we were in Brazil for a time, and we're on the way back home, and we stopped in Paris and picked up a new car because the government service allowed for a new car for employees like dad. We got this brand-new Saab, and we were going to go to Sweden to visit some relatives. The car had these new seatbelts, and at that time—this was the '60s—seatbelts were just across the lap, but this was the first time I saw a harness seatbelt. All of a sudden a car comes zooming at us—we're in Brussels, Belgium—and hits us head on and kills Mom and Dad. I was in the front seat. I had just put my seatbelt on.

I do all sorts of hunting—bears, elk, deer—and that's all fun, but hunting turkey is my number one.

Fishing is about being alert and aware. I'm on a lake in Georgia, on the way to a fishing spot, and I see this tree in the water. I ran the boat past it and said, "Damn, that tree wasn't there yesterday." And I saw these little wood chips in the water. A beaver had just brought down the tree! I stopped and thought that tree had to be full of bugs and ants and just think of all the little minnows that are going to come in to feed, which attracts the bigger fish. I pulled up and fished. I ended up catching seven bass out of that tree.

My daughter just got married this last week. You know how it works at a wedding. The bride and groom dance, and then the bride dances with the father. Well, I was really feeling good, and I danced my ass off. About one hundred people came up to me afterward and said that was the best dancing they'd ever seen. I just had the beat and felt like celebrating, you know? My daughter says, "I didn't know you could dance like that." I didn't, either.

TATER PORTER

Rodeo athlete, cowboy, Osceola County sheriff's deputy, interviewed in July 2016, when he was forty-five, Kenansville.

I CAN GET ALONG WITH ANYBODY. It doesn't matter what kind of person. Whether I want to or not, that's a different story, but I can fit in.

Mom was always nervous about me riding bulls, like any mom would be. Dad told me to go ahead if I wanted, but he always told me: "Them bulls will hurt you, boy. They're made for eating. Not for riding."

I was born in Holopaw, which is just around the corner from Kenansville, and then we moved to Deseret Ranch. My dad worked on the ranch, and I was pretty much raised on the ranch.

When I was about five, I went to the Silver Springs Rodeo in town, and that's when I decided that I wanted to be a bull rider. Being on the ranch, they had a practice arena there, and they would buck bulls on Thursday nights, and some of the guys helped me get on a few—and I started liking it. I even wrote it on a kindergarten paper that I wanted to ride bulls.

There ain't nothing at the end of the road for a rancher if you don't own your own land.

I won the world finals in 2000. That was pretty much the highest part of my career. But, at the very beginning, I was just making ends meet. I mean there were times when I'd pay my entry fees and didn't have enough money left to get myself a hamburger at the end of the night.

When I travel, I like talking to people about Florida. Most people don't know that Florida is always in the top five or ten cattle-producing states in the county. We got more cattle in Florida than you can shake a stick at.

I always worked hard for my money. I wasn't afraid to mow a yard or pull some weeds or do something to make a living.

The only thing my parents expected out of me was to be a good, upstanding citizen. The job didn't matter. They said just be yourself and hopefully something'll work out for you.

I'm still a working cowboy, which entails just about everything— working cows, patching fence, tractor work, mechanic, you name it. I love every second of it.

No ifs, ands, or buts about it. I loved riding bulls. I loved every bit about it. I loved the thrill of it. If you do it for the money, you'll never make it.

I'm a person who doesn't take the easy road. Even if I don't know how, I'm still going to go in with both feet. I'm not afraid to learn.

My dad had a friend he really looked up to and respected, and the man's name was Tater, so my dad named me after him.

The bulls are bred to buck, but not all bucking bulls are aggressive. There are a lot of those bucking bulls, when you go in the back pens, you can scrub them on the neck and rub them on the head and pet 'em. There are some that you can't. Bulls have a demeanor just like people.

I don't want nobody rubbing on me, so I'm going to be a little pissed off, but some guys, they like a little petting and rubbing.

Everybody says, "Why did you go with the sheriff's department?" I like the adrenaline. You never know what you're going to get. You pull over a vehicle, it's like opening the gate on a bucking chute.

I ain't afraid. I got stomped. You name it. It happens. All that does is put more fight in me. That bull ain't gonna beat me.

Osceola County is growing so fast that it's going to be hard to preserve what we have. The land is worth so much money. You can't hardly raise a cow or raise an orange grove or sell your hunting rights for what they're going to pay you to put a subdivision on your land. So, the people who own the land—if it's not locked up in a conservation-type easement—as soon as old Grandpa dies, the kids this day and time who get ahold of the land are probably going to sell.

My wife says I don't have a sense of humor.

To succeed in bull riding, you need attitude and confidence. It's 95 percent mental and 5 percent ability. I could win the biggest rodeo today and, tomorrow, go to a different one and get my guts stomped out and end up in the hospital. One day you're the champ. One day you're the chump. You've got to stay confident.

I'm still going strong. I have to. I have to stay in shape to chase the bad guys. I don't work out near as hard as I should, like anybody else, but, if I have to fight for my life today, I want to be able to whoop somebody's ass.

Norman Van Aken

Chef, writer,
interviewed
in October
2017, when he
was sixty-six,
Miami.

AS A KID, I WOULD SIT DOWN AND READ A LOT, by myself, up in a tree, on the bus, anywhere I could soak up the world. If people would have asked me when I was ten years old, what I wanted to be when I grew up, I would say I wanted to be an artist. I didn't want to be a fireman or an astronaut. I wanted to do something that was going to lead me to a greater understanding of why we're here and how we can make the world more beautiful.

The Siamese twin to passion is discipline. You have to have that. Discipline means you have to be organized in such a way that you're not some wild-haired, swearing and yelling guy or girl back there, throwing things around. You've got to be able to have the discipline to be communicative, to be explanatory, to be able to keep your head when everyone else around you is losing theirs.

My early fascination for food was deep, sometimes even argumentative. My father told a story that I heard years later about a night when he and my mother left my two sisters and myself in the care of a babysitter. The babysitter was in tears when my parents returned home. She was fourteen or something, and she told my father that I was outside playing and when I came back in, I said I was hungry, so she fixed me a hot dog. I threw it to the ground and said, "This is not a proper dinner!" What my father said to her was, "Norman has very unrealistic ideas about food, especially in regards to its presentation."

What makes me laugh is what makes everybody laugh, which is the absurdity of something. That's why the Marx Brothers were so genius.

I was peeling some hard-cooked eggs the other day, and I could see my grandmother in my mind's eye, standing over the sink, peering over her glasses, perfectly peeling—no nicks, no scars, no broken parts—hard-cooked eggs.

When I was twenty-one, I was at a party, and it was cold and dark, and during that seemingly never-ending part of an Illinois winter. There were these three brothers I grew up with, and two of them were at the party. It was getting late, and I asked: "Where's Steve? Where's your brother?" and they said he's down in Key West, that he went down there to do something different. I was like, "Wow, anybody want to go?" Ray and Randy said they would, and I said, "When?" and they said, "Let's go now." So we got some concentrated form of caffeine and jumped in the van, and, thirty-six hours later, we pulled into Key West. It felt like I was breaking out of a dark place, a kind of confusion about what I was going to do with my life, and suddenly we were in this place of potential wonder—the smell of the flowers, the smell of the ocean. I fell in love, in love with Key West.

"Celebrity chef" has become a term that has lost its weight, its meaning.

I've managed to be married to the girl I met in the first restaurant that I ever cooked in—forty-four years ago—and that's something that's really amazing in this business. I'm really proud of that.

Most of the people who've known me for any length of time know that I need to be surrounded by books.

I was on this sort of peripatetic journey of crappy jobs. I worked in a glass factory, shoveling broken glass onto conveyer belts. I worked in another factory, where I assembled picture frames. I worked in a carnival for three or four months, then got electrocuted on the Ferris wheel and decided to try something else. I got a job as a hot-tar roofer and got fired because the boss didn't like the fact that a rainstorm interrupted our work and I enjoyed that too much. So I answered an ad in a local circular paper—it said "Short-Order Cook Wanted—No Experience Necessary," and they hired me. It was $3.25 an hour. I started the next day and began to learn what it meant to be a short-order cook. It's an athletic skill, a mental game, keeping track of the orders and dealing with the chaos, the cuts, and the unknown.

The orange industry in Florida is worrying me, how it's being decimated by this disease called greening and by inexpensive imports, primarily from Brazil. The orange is the symbol of Florida, it's what's on our license plate, but it could become a distant memory in a very short period of time.

I always love cooking something I never cooked before.

My father wanted me to be a professional football player or a car dealer. I was a fairly small kid and got my teeth knocked out when I was playing football my freshman year, and I worked one summer at his car lot and hated it. My mom was very open to whatever I was going to become. She had the patience of Job.

One of the great unknown things about *The Godfather* is that you will know when something really violent is about to happen if you see oranges. Like, when Sonny gets assassinated at that tollbooth, right before he gets to the tollbooth, you'll see a billboard advertising Florida orange groves. Like there are oranges on the table before the Abe Vigoda character is killed, and when the Godfather is almost murdered, he's at a fruit market picking up a bag of oranges. It's not a food movie, but, in a way, it became a food movie for me.

My goal is not to feed people. My goal is to create memories.

The mentors, the models for me, have been musicians and writers. I see them responding to the world in ways that are pure. You see depictions of Beethoven losing his hearing and laying his head on the piano to feel the notes. That to me is extremely powerful.

If you can imagine doing anything else, go ahead and do it, because being a chef is a relentless job—the hours, the physicality of it. If you think it's stressful, I agree with you, but, for me, it's what I was born to do.

I'm not the kind of guy who wants to get in a boat and go out 50 miles into the sea and bounce up and down in 40-foot waves. I'm the guy who wants to build a fire on the sand and watch the sun go down.

When a young cook asks me how to become a famous chef, I'm like, that's the wrong question. Fame may never come. You have to look at how to become great.

I love working in Miami. I love the energy of the city, but I'm still really a small-town person.

Watch the plates come back because the plates don't lie. If there's food on the plates, then they're not enjoying it. I look for empty plates.

I don't even know how to this day I had the ability to go buy the book. I certainly wasn't carrying a checkbook. Maybe I had just cashed my paycheck. But I went that day to a bookstore on Duval Street and bought one of Mr. Beard's books—a book called *James Beard's Theory & Practice of Good Cooking*—and it literally changed my life. I went from a person who was kind of catching cooking lessons, one after another in a very willy-nilly way, to a person who began reading books to tell me how to do things. It was a technique book, and it really helped systematize things for me. It was like coming over the ridge of a big hill. This was my art. I finally found it.

DICK VITALE

Basketball
coach, broad-
caster, writer,
interviewed
in December
2009, when he
was seventy,
Lakewood
Ranch.

I LOST MY LEFT EYE AS A KID. I poked it with a pencil. I was three years old. I can't remember. My mother told me, "Don't ever make excuses or feel sorry for yourself because so many people have it worse."

Tourism is great. The snowbirds come, but job opportunities are kind of limited in Florida. I would love to see more industry, more of the corporate world, to attract the young people.

I learned about work ethic from my father. He never complained. Never. I can't remember him ever saying he had a headache or the flu and couldn't go to work. He got up at six in the morning and pressed coats. The more coats he pressed, the more money he made. Then he would come home, eat, and put on his security guard uniform and work until midnight.

He took me in the summer to work at the factory. My job was to feed him the coats. Driving home one day, my dad said: "Richie, Richie"— everybody called me Richie back then—"You don't want to do this. Richie, you're so smart. You've got a brain, Richie. Get a good job. Don't do what I do."

My mother had five brothers who were fanatical sports fans. My Uncle Mike, my Uncle Tom, my Uncle Frank, my Uncle Joe, my Uncle Sam, all five of them were factory workers. They would talk sports. They knew every statistic. They'd fight and argue. Who is the best centerfielder? Mantle or Mays or DiMaggio? I think my uncles helped form the passion I have for sports.

After I was fired from the Pistons in 1979, I get a call from Scotty Connal, and he said he was just named the head of a new network, and he wants me to do its very first big college basketball game, DePaul and Wisconsin. I said: "ESPN? It sounds like a disease. I never heard of it and, to be honest with you, I know nothing about television." About a week later, he calls and asks again. If it weren't for my wife, I wouldn't have done it. She told me I was violating everything I ever preached. I was sitting at home. I was watching *General Hospital*. Luke and Laura. I was depressed. I had gotten fired. I thought it was the end. My wife said: "You're not the first to be fired. You won't be the last. Why don't you go do the game and have some fun?" So I did the game.

People relate to me as an everyday person. People aren't intimidated to come up to me. They're not intimidated to come over for a picture. They feel like I'm their uncle. I'm their buddy, man.

I have a ritual when I do a game. When it's over, I watch the losing coach. I watch him walk to the locker room. I look at him, and I say to myself, "Wow, what he has to face now." When I was a coach, I would let the losing get to me. If it wasn't for ESPN, I would have been a college coach again, and I really firmly believe I would never had made it past fifty. I couldn't handle the losing.

There's a lot you can learn from sports. You learn about sacrifice. You learn about work ethic. You can correlate it to the workforce. If you have people functioning together, working together, you succeed.

I don't drink. My wife was telling people the other day she can't remember the last time I even had a sip. I don't say it's wrong. My buddies will drink. They drink in moderation. As a kid I tried it. I never liked the taste, and I was never going to allow peer pressure to make me drink to be accepted. Accept me for who I am. So at ESPN, they call me Mr. Cranberry Juice. I go to a club or whatever, and I order cranberry juice.

There are people who are going to love you and some are not: "He talks too much. He's loud." You can't take that personally. You can't please everybody, but one thing I'm proud of in my thirty years is I've never ever had a critic say: "He's not prepared. He doesn't know what he's talking about."

I don't feel seventy. You have to tell me I'm that number. I feel like I'm twenty-five. When I start acting my age, I know the party is over.

People come up to me when I'm having breakfast, and I don't get annoyed at all. I love it. I love people. I get annoyed when I see a celebrity with a chip on his shoulder. Somebody comes over for an autograph and he says, "What are you bothering me for?" What kind of attitude is that? I don't understand.

I go to Siesta Key and walk the beach. I've been to Hawaii, Maui, beaches that have been rated so high. To me, there isn't a beach I've been at that can match the white sand of Siesta Key.

My parents were uneducated, maybe a fifth-grade education at best, but they had a doctorate of love.

I try to treat every day like it's the national championship.

There's a camera down my throat, and the doctor says: "There's your problem. You've got ulcerated lesions on your vocal cords and they must come out—and I have to tell you, they could be cancer." Holy cow! To be honest with you, I cried like a baby. The one thing that has been so good to me—my voice—is now going to be the end for me.

Television has allowed me to balance my life, to have my priorities. My family. When the game is over, it's done. The next day I'm not worried about winning or losing. It allows me to have a vacation. I didn't have a vacation when I was a coach. I needed the winner's edge. I always felt like if I were coaching and I'm going on vacation, the competition is getting an edge on me.

For two weeks, until the surgery, the fear of the unknown had me in a state of depression. I had the surgery. The doctor came out and said it's not cancer, but it has to be monitored every four months to make sure the lesions don't come back. It's called dysplasia. Dysplasia is precancer. If the lesions come back, we get them out.

Real happiness comes from love—in good times, in bad times. It's not about money.

I want to give back. In fact, I'm banging my brain about that right now. I told my wife the other day—and I don't know how to go about this—but I want to do something major before I pass on. I want to maybe build a place for kids, homeless kids. I want to do something special.

WRITERS

DAVE BARRY

Humorist, writer, journalist, interviewed in February 2013, when he was sixty-five, Miami.

Apparently, you've run down all the real icons there ever were in Florida. It's a sad commentary on the state that I would be iconic. I can see myself being iconic in Delaware. There's Joe Biden and then who?

A lot of the time, when I ended up writing a humor column about something, the thing that initially spurred it was not funny to me at all. It was like horrible when it happened, but then later on you can go, "Oh, OK, I can write about that." A good example is colonoscopies. I ended up writing a humor column about it, but I don't recall at any point in my colonoscopy experience going, "This is funny."

Rick Scott and Charlie Crist? It's the lizard against the traffic cone running for governor. And people ask why I think politics is funny.

My early years in the newspaper business were as a real reporter and a real editor. I really loved it, actually. It was great fun. I learned a whole lot. I learned everything I know about journalism at the *Daily Local News* in West Chester, Pennsylvania. The only thing is, I realized at some point, that nobody was reading anything I was writing.

Driving in Miami is kind of a spectator sport. It's not unlike roller derby.

My biggest worry is that, because of the career I've chosen, I'm afraid that somebody will go: "Wait a minute. This is what you did with your life?" I'm always afraid I'll have to get a real job.

Key West is a very unusual little place. It keeps changing, and everybody keeps saying, "Oh, it used to be better," but it's just a little pocket of weirdness down at the end of the world, and I really like that.

It's amazing when you think about it: five hundred years ago, there were people in Florida, and we're not really totally civilized yet.

My obvious second career choice—you know, people ask me all the time why I haven't done this already—is to be an international male underwear model.

I'm not a big fan of the Everglades. I know it's a precious ecological resource, but I don't actually believe that. I think it's a swamp. It has a tremendous number of bugs in it and large pythons now and muck. I'm sure it's really vital, but why couldn't it be somewhere else? Basically, it just makes it take longer to get from here to Naples, although I'm sure the people in Naples are glad they have this giant snake-infested barrier between them and Miami. They're afraid we'll come over and steal their dentures or something—which we would.

You're a reporter and you go and cover an organization with a name like the Downingtown Regional Sewage Commission, and the meeting is three and a half hours long and involves something called interceptors, which you, an English major from Haverford College, know absolutely nothing about and never will know anything about, but you have to write 30 inches of story about it with a big headline. If I were to go back and read those stories now, I would think to myself: "What on earth did I think I was doing? Why would anyone care what the Downingtown Regional Sewage Commission had to say about interceptors, and why did you think you were the person to tell them?" But that's sort of the essence of journalism.

There are people I admire and learn from. Carl Hiaasen is the guy closest to me that I would use as an example. The writers I loved growing up as a kid were Robert Benchley and P. G. Wodehouse. When I plot a book, especially *Insane City*, my last book, the writer I most thought about was P. G. Wodehouse. But the Florida element. Nobody does it like Carl.

I was a wiseass as a kid. I was a good student, but I was a little bit of a discipline problem. I was a class clown. I needed attention, and I got my attention by making jokes and trying to get people to laugh. I was really not very good about authority, which was sort of an ongoing problem in my life.

Anybody with completely, wildly out-of-control ambition and no particular views or ethics has a good shot of going far in this state—and that's always been the way. I contend, if he wanted to, Donald Trump, in three years, could be elected governor of Florida.

Kind of the normal state for a writer is writer's block. I don't know anybody who can pour out the words without feeling like, "Wow, this sucks."

I'm a loving parent, but I think my wife is a much better parent in the sense of, you know, remembering to buy clothes and stuff like that. But my children have the gift of sarcasm, a precious gift that I gave them very early. My daughter, she's almost thirteen, but when she was two she knew when I was being sarcastic.

A lot of people get wrought up about the government and worry about it, and I say if you just look at it as entertainment, it's pretty funny. It's like a big-budget motion picture comedy. It's better for your heart probably to look at it that way.

Just everyday life makes me laugh. Miami makes me laugh. The Miami government. The general behavior of people around me in Miami. It's a pretty entertaining city.

I like Disney World. That's not a fashionable thing to say. Carl, I know, will disagree with me. I have a connection with Disney. I've written books for them. But we like to go there and hang out, even just to watch the people and marvel at how large so many of them are, lumbering around eating turkey legs.

CARL HIAASEN

Writer, journalist, novelist, interviewed in June 2015, when he was sixty-two, Vero Beach.

CARL HIAASEN

Mostly, we produce construction jobs in Florida—construction for the sake of construction. That's basically the same mechanism as a cancer cell.

I grew up in what's now Plantation. It was literally on the edge of the Everglades. I'm sure part of it had at one point been in the Everglades. There wasn't a mall, a strip mall, not anything. It had been cow pastures and wetlands, so my childhood was spent outdoors. After school, I'd get on my bike and go snake hunting or fishing, just hanging out and exploring. It was the best possible childhood.

When you're in journalism, they don't pay you to be mellow. They pay you to go out and cover what's happening.

Hoot, the first book I wrote for kids, was a page right out of my own childhood—the little owls and everything. That was me growing up in west Broward County. Near where we lived, there was a lot of open acreage, and it was purchased by a company that was going to build a condominium. There was an actress named Eve Arden, she was the spokesperson and was on all these billboards. The next thing we know there were bulldozers and backhoes, and they cleared the land where these little owls lived, these burrowing owls, and they just buried them alive. That pissed me off then, and it pisses me off today.

When I start a novel, I have no idea where it's going to end. Sometimes, I figure it out sooner. Sometimes, I figure it out later. The later I figure it out, the more miserable I am, and my poor family has to put up with me walking around in a dark cloud while I'm trying to figure out how the hell to wrap up the book.

Amendment One. You have four million people, 75 percent of everyone who went to the polls, saying take this money from doc stamps and conserve our land. They want these special places to still be here for future generations. Well, you saw what happened this last session. That Rick Scott would disregard this should come as no surprise. But the idea that the leaders of the Senate and the House would give basically their middle finger to four million Floridians is so appalling. To see that kind of naked contempt for the will of Floridians is shocking.

When you're a little guy, one way to not get bullied or beat up is to be funny. I figured that out pretty early.

There's no question that there's a glorious abundance of weirdness and depravity in Florida. As a parent and a grandparent, you have to wonder—Is this really where I want my kids to grow up? Is this really what I want my kids to see and experience? But more selfishly, as a writer, you think, "I'm in Heaven."

Joseph Heller had a tremendous impact on me—*Catch-22*—because he was dealing with kind of the darkest of human conditions—war—and still managed to make you laugh.

Think about my job as a newspaper columnist. Look at Tallahassee. Look at that complete festival of horrors up there. I will never run out of material.

It was a big event when the first convenience store opened a couple of miles from where I lived. It was a U-tote-M. My friends and I, we were all excited, and we were going to ride our bikes there. My parents said we don't want you hanging out there—that there was a bad element coming in with the convenience store. Well, basically the whole county's a freakin' convenience store now. The U-tote-M would probably be the cultural highlight of Broward at this point. It's a textbook example of what happens when you let the developers go hog wild.

Florida is one of the most beautiful places in the country, but it's probably too beautiful for its own good. You have this great incoming stampede of people who fell in love with it and wanted to be here and then you have the people who just want to exploit it.

There was nobody in my household saying I had to go out and commune with nature. I discovered this on my own. My dad was an attorney. He worked like a dog. My mom was busy. She had four kids, three others besides me. It wasn't like we were a family of naturalists.

If you get into the business of journalism or the business of writing novels and think you're going to change the world, you're either a madly deluded egotist or you're just mad period. That isn't why you do it. It's enough to know that you've changed a few people's way of thinking or you've plugged into an audience that feels passionate about something.

Right after I finished the golf book, I hurt my back, and I had some surgery about two years ago. It hasn't been right ever since. I tried to play nine holes a few months ago, and I got through about seven. So I haven't been playing much golf, but I'd be much worse off if I had to give up fly fishing.

I don't know any successful writers, and by that I mean novelists and journalists, who were not ravenous readers when they were kids.

When people see their newspapers diminish, and they think, well, so, it put some reporters and editors out of work, no no, it's much worse than that. These are your eyes and ears in the community. Forget whether you agree with the editorial board or if you agree with my column or Leonard Pitts's column or whatever. The point is, if you want to know what's going on in your community, you need journalism. What happens when there are no reporters left to tell you what's happening?

Florida has this incredibly welcoming attitude with regard to corruption. This is by far the crookedest place in the United States.

The last book I read about Florida that knocked me out of my chair it was so good was Karen Russell's *Swamplandia!* It was a beautiful and brilliant book. You know what I read recently that I hadn't read for years? I went back and read *The Yearling* by Marjorie Kinnan Rawlings. Wonderful.

When I started writing about this, no one gave a rat's ass about the Everglades in Tallahassee. Not a rat's ass. And now it's a mom-and-apple-pie issue. Everyone who runs for statewide office has to at least profess a love or passion for the Everglades.

You can go online and see what stories are getting the most hits. If there's a story in the *Herald* tomorrow that says, "Kim Kardashian Grows a Third Ass Cheek" and another story, "Iran Tests a Nuclear Weapon Next to Israel," which one do you think is going to get the most hits? Kardashian's ass every time. That's a bitter pill for all of us who believe people gravitate to what's really important.

Peter Meinke

Author, poet laureate of Florida, interviewed in July 2015, when he was eighty-two, St. Petersburg.

POETRY IS THE KIND OF WRITING that you read again and again, so it behooves the writer to withhold a little something. A good poet buries little surprises in there for the attentive reader.

I'm worried about Florida and global warming. We have friends in Miami. They love the city. They love the Cuban section. They love the food. They love the beaches. But the water's coming up through the streets sometimes, so that's scary.

Florida's poet laureate is an unpaid position. I wanted to get a barrel of sherry the way the English poets did, but that's apparently not going to happen.

It would be a disaster to overemphasize STEM. I'm not against STEM, but we need to teach the arts, too, maybe now more than ever. People who are brought up on STEM, they need something to slow them down a little, both in their reading and in their lives.

I'm not sure what made me want to write. I came from a blue-collar family. We lived in Flatbush, and, like everybody else, I wanted to play second base for the Brooklyn Dodgers.

When poetry works, it makes you better than you are. It makes us more sympathetic, empathetic people.

I have many good friends who are very sturdy Republicans, and we don't have any problems. Occasionally, we'll get into a mild argument, but that's OK because people come from different spots.

One of the things I advise my students is to be ready and take advantage of accidents that seem to be pushing you somewhere. You've got to take a chance now and then.

Early in my career, I sold real estate, and I was showing a lot, not even a house, to a guy, and I'm making small talk. He said he was a teacher over at Mountain Lakes High School, where I went to high school, and I said, somewhat truthfully, "You know, I thought about being a teacher, but didn't know how to go about it." He said, "Oh, what would you have taught?" I told him that I suppose I would have taught English or literature, and he said that was funny because the English teacher at Mountain Lakes just got drafted. It was like I got hit by lightning. I didn't know I was waiting for that. I just left him standing there. I went right to the high school. The principal knew me. I went home and my wife, Jeanne, asked, "How was your day?" And I said: "Well, guess what? I took a job for $4,400 a year teaching at the high school." I had been making at least four times that. That's how I started teaching and I loved it.

When I got to St. Petersburg in 1966, Florida Presbyterian College, which later became Eckerd College, was a really radical, wonderful school, idealistic, no grades, everybody had to study for a time in Europe. It was an exciting place. They wanted to create an undergraduate creative writing program and wanted a poet who had published respectably, but wouldn't be expensive, to do it. That turned out to be me.

Poetry can sometimes be hard to understand. You need to make an effort. You can't speed-read poetry.

My mother had anthologies with poetry. I think she belonged to the Book of the Month Club. I don't remember her reading poetry, exactly, but I found it early on and just liked it, but I kept it a secret. I was a secret poet in Brooklyn. I felt from remarks that people had made that writing poetry seemed to be a sissy thing to do. The talk in Brooklyn was to be tough. We played stickball in the streets. We had little gangs. It was just not a place for poetry, but I liked poetry, anyway.

It says in my high school yearbook: "Peter Meinke wants to be a writer . . . probably will be . . . censored."

Whenever anything important happens—love, triumph, death—people turn to poetry because they realize that regular language doesn't cut it.

I believe in rewriting. This was not always easy in the 1960s and 1970s, when it was, "First thought, best thought." That was the Beat generation. The idea was writing was something that should come out spontaneously. I agree. It should come out spontaneously and be from the deepest part of your heart, but the writing will be a lot better if you rewrite it.

Everyone has loves and fears and excitements and disasters and triumphs, but what makes the poet different is not these particular triumphs and disasters, but the way he writes about them.

I'm interested in the Tampa Bay Rays, particularly since the Brooklyn Dodgers no longer exist.

My wife and I play tennis. That has been very good for us. We used to play four times a week. Now we play twice a week.

I began to publish seriously in the mid-1960s, so, by then, I was in my thirties. John Keats was dead already by then, so I was by no means an early bloomer.

If you're spending your time on social media, you're not spending your time reading good literature. You're not communing with nature. Instead, if you're under a tree, you're on a cell phone, saying, "Nice tree I got here." It's not a good direction.

Poetry is the kind of writing that's closest to music.

Patrick Smith

Novelist, interviewed in July 2013, when he was eighty-five, Merritt Island. Smith died in January 2014.

MARJORIE KINNAN RAWLINGS—I wrote my master's thesis in college on her—she was a tremendous writer, but her novels usually covered one year and that's it. I wrote *A Land Remembered* because I wanted to try to picture life here in Florida over a long period of time. I don't think anyone else had attempted a novel that covered more than one hundred years of Florida.

I was what was called a moonlight writer. That's some guy who works all day and then writes at night. It's a hard way to write. You give up a lot. You have to have the urge.

If I could get out of this bed, I'd like to write a novel about the Indian River Lagoon. It's a waterway that they say is dying. If it would actually die, it would affect not just the wildlife, not just the fish, but everyone.

I met James Meredith a long time ago. I was working for the University of Mississippi in public relations, and he was the first black student. I escorted him to class for the two or three weeks until things settled down. It was an unusual time. I'll say that. My main duty was just to keep the reporters from following him, trying to interview him or go in the classroom. There were a lot of unpleasant things that happened, and I just prefer not to dwell on it or even try to remember it.

When I was in junior high school and high school, I was in charge of our family milk cow. I milked that cow every day, morning and night, rain, shine, whatever.

To me, accuracy is the most important part of writing. A lot of writers, accuracy doesn't bother them very much. If they make a big mistake, they just say, "Oh, this is fiction," but I always tried to write accurately and create a picture of life as it really is and people and things as they really are.

I went down through the Big Cypress Swamp one time and saw all these little chickee huts. It's very unusual to see people living that way. I had an idea I wanted to write something set down there close to the Everglades, so I was just looking around. That turned into my novel *Forever Island*.

In the pioneer days, family was everything. Nothing mattered but family. Everybody wanted to do their part of the work. It's not that way anymore.

The canal behind my house is a playground for manatees.

That's one of the things that young people who have read *A Land Remembered* question me about: Why does everybody have to die? They don't ever want anyone to die! But people die, especially in pioneer Florida.

In the last twenty years, people have become much more conscious in Florida about the environment. It's not rampant destruction like it used to be. Thank goodness.

I've got a copy right here of a Carl Hiaasen book that he wrote not too long ago. I don't have anything bad at all to say about Carl's writing or any of the others, but some of them, you know, are satire. And when people want to read writing about real people, they want something different from satire.

Buddy Ebsen was a big fan of *A Land Remembered*. We talked by telephone about it several times, and then one day he just flew here from California, landed in Orlando, rented a car, and drove over here. He wanted to talk about everything in it. My wife, Iris, took a picture of him, but she cut off the top of his head.

We had a 19-foot Fleetwing boat we kept behind the house here in that canal. We used to go out in the ocean in that thing and up and down the Indian River. I loved it.

Researching the book, I had to read about a dozen books I guess about specific things that happened in Florida, like that great freeze of 1895. You can't just dream that up, you know. I had a lot of old-timers, old pioneer people, tell me stories. I'd sit down and talk to them. They'd tell me about living through those swarms of mosquitoes and alligators and all kinds of things. *A Land Remembered* is not based on a real family. It's based on a dozen real families.

Down in Lake Wales, I love that Chalet Suzanne. Every time I got to that part of the state, I went by there and spent the night.

An article in the *Miami Herald* got me interested in migrant workers. They had arrested one of these independent contractors for enslaving people, and no one would testify against him in court. When I was researching *Angel City*, the novel I wrote about a migrant family, I went down to Homestead and posed as a migrant and lived in the camps. I picked tomatoes and squash and all that kind of stuff. I had to know what it was like.

Right here in Brevard County, up there next to NASA, there's that 140,000-acre Merritt Island Wildlife Refuge. And that's being done more and more places around Florida, taking endangered lands and making them wildlife sanctuaries.

I love what they call soul food, collard greens and corn bread.

Death doesn't scare me. I have emphysema. I broke a bunch of my bones, and before that I had cancer. I also had a really bad stroke. I've been hit so hard by what's got me in this bed that I'm not afraid anymore.

They were supposed to give me that Great Floridian award in Tallahassee, but I couldn't get up there, so the governor came here. It's not every day you have the governor walk in your house. His wife ought to be in Hollywood. I think she's very pretty.

15

ALL OF THE ABOVE

FERDIE PACHECO

Physician, "Fight Doctor" to Muhammad Ali, broadcaster, writer, artist, interviewed in April 2007, when he was seventy-nine, Ybor City. Pacheco died in November 2017.

I FOUND A DOCTOR WHO WANTED to sell me his office in Overtown. They weren't paying him, and I said I didn't care about that. Whoever can't pay can't pay. They'll pay me when they can. I found a stupendous nurse. She really knew how to collect money. I told her try to collect five bucks. If they haven't got five bucks, I told her forget it. There were some who couldn't pay at all.

They burned my office to the ground. That was a gentle hint that I was no longer needed in the ghetto. That was 1980, the McDuffie riots.

I told Ali he shouldn't be in, that I'd leave him if he kept fighting, because he was going to die. He was going to die horribly. And he is dying horribly. I quit when he went to fight Larry Holmes. It was just a joke. The guy couldn't even walk, and they put him in with Holmes.

When I was seventy, I had all my teeth. Never had a toothache. Never had any dental pain that was not incurred by a dentist. Do I floss? No. How many animals do you think floss? They got their tongue. They got their saliva. That's flossing.

I talked to Malcolm X for a long time. I told him he was going to get killed. And he got killed. That was obvious. He knew he was going to get killed.

Coffee, I have an abundance of it in the morning. I have to have it.

I was the doctor for all the fighters at the 5th Street Gym, which the Dundees had. Whenever they got a boxer, I was the doctor, for everyone, hundreds. Ali happened to be one of them.

Ali had won the Olympics. He was looking for a trainer. He was very uncomfortable and confused when he came down to Miami. He won the Olympics, and they wouldn't serve him hot dogs and hamburgers in a regular restaurant.

I would go home at night all those twenty-five years I was in medicine, filled with a feeling of, wow, I did a good job today. I never went home and said, "Oh, fuck it." I worked like hell to save people, and if I saved them, it really felt good.

Working the corner during a fight, it was a lot of fun. Treating wounds. It's what I did in life. Treating cuts. It's just an emergency-room procedure. I loved to work in an emergency room. I was really just a trauma doctor. Broken nose. Broken hands. I liked it.

The whole time I was in boxing, I found it extremely exciting. Very rewarding. Plus the thrill of winning something. You don't get that when you're a doctor. You do your work. You save somebody's life. Go home. That's your job. That's what you're trained to do. But if you win the world championship, you're on the cover of *Sports Illustrated*.

Although I think I'm a very levelheaded guy, I must admit the notoriety appealed to me a great deal. I wanted to be well known.

I only went with beautiful women. I mean gorgeous women. All my life I had gorgeous women. When I got to my present wife, who is the most gorgeous woman I have ever seen in my life, I fell in love with her in one night. I was already engaged to somebody else for four years. But she was so great I said, "That's it, I'm not letting her go." I let the other girl go. We've been married thirty-six years, and that's the greatest choice I've ever made. I say to people, why does it bother you because I like beautiful women? If you can drive a Ford or you can drive a Cadillac, you mean you would drive the Ford instead of the Cadillac? I feel that way about women.

To this moment, I've lived my life doing exactly what I wanted to do. I can't think of anything I left out that I wanted to do. If I wanted to do it, I did it.

I went to the hospital with a stroke, but I only stayed there a couple of days. I talked my way out. My health is excellent. I can't walk like I used to. At seventy-nine, you're not supposed to walk like you used to.

The most important thing is a desire to tell a story. If you don't have that, don't even write. I got stories to tell. I dream them every night.

I'm a patriot. My grandfather would say the most important thing in the world was being an American citizen. He'd say with that and an education, you can conquer the world. And that's what I did.

As long as I'm in control, I'll do anything for you. But if someone is ordering me around, that's not going to work.

A lot of the things that I did peculiarly fit my arrogant view of what I knew. I pretty well knew what I knew. I wasn't hardly ever wrong. Hardly ever wrong.

As a kid, I was smart as hell, and nothing bothered me. My father told me: "You're going to hear this word 'genius'—don't pay attention to it. No matter what they tell you, you have to study hard. Yes, you're smart, but you have to study." People used to say to me, "You must be a genius." I just study hard. Then, later on, when I see all these paintings I've done, the books, who the fuck does all this? These paintings are internationally known. These books. There are fourteen books. In medicine, I saved a lot of lives. A lot of people. So, maybe, I am a genius.

16

A BRIEF HISTORY

THE FLORIDA ICON SERIES in *Florida Trend* did not begin with me. The feature actually started about a year before I went to work for the magazine. The first one—Amy Keller's interview with Wayne Huizenga—was printed in January 2006. And, besides that one, there were plenty of other Icon interviews that I wished I had done myself—Janet Reno and Stetson Kennedy, also by Amy; Clyde Butcher, Andrés Duany, and Gary Mormino by Cynthia Barnett; Willie Gary, Claude R. Kirk Jr., and Al Hoffman by Mike Vogel.

Others got away, too.

Of course, I tried to interview Jimmy Buffett, but, even after many attempts over many years, I never got a call back. Gloria Estefan never got back to me, either, and neither did Stephen King or Tony Dungy. Dickey Betts, the southern rocker, sent word through a go-between that he wasn't interested. Edward DeBartolo Jr. and Mel Sembler said no, too.

Conversely, the people who actually lobbied to be interviewed—either directly or through their representatives—generally didn't end up sitting across from my digital recorders. (I run two at every interview, just to be safe.)

My criteria of what makes an icon is flexible, but I do look for certain attributes—achievement, a purposeful life, a Florida connection, an interesting life, someone who overcame adversity, someone I want to meet.

This book has ninety.

There would be more, but some of the interviews had to be left out for space reasons—Gus Stavros, a St. Petersburg philanthropist; Frank Morsani, a Tampa car-dealership magnate; Doc Dockery, a political observer from Lakeland; Jack Levine, a tireless advocate for children and families; and the late tough-guy novelist Harry Crews. Those interviews can be found at FloridaTrend.com.

ACKNOWLEDGMENTS

Thanks to Andy Corty, the publisher of *Florida Trend*, for allowing these interviews to be published outside of the magazine, where versions of each appeared between 2007 and 2018. A few are reprinted as originally published, but the majority have been supplemented with quotes that were trimmed to make space in the magazine.

Also, thanks to Mark Howard and John Annunziata, my *Trend* editors, and to the splendid writers I've worked with at the magazine—Mike Vogel, Cynthia Barnett, Amy Keller, Barbara Miracle, Jason Garcia, and Amy Martinez—and thanks, as well, to the talented and resourceful art team, Gary Bernloehr and Jason Morton. Gary has always been meticulous in making sure that the portraits that accompanied the interviews were excellent, and many of those photos are in this book. As for the words, each one—from the words written by me to the ones spoken by the interviewees—was examined by proofreaders Susan Murray and Tim Meyer. Their work is very much appreciated.

One floor above my workplace cubicle—*Trend* shares a building with the *Tampa Bay Times* in downtown St. Petersburg—sits Craig Pittman, who encouraged me to pursue this project and introduced me to Meredith Morris-Babb, director of the University Press of Florida. Craig, Florida's best environmental journalist and chronicler of the state's many foibles, is an icon in waiting.

And, of course, if there's any thanking to be done, my wife, Sharon, and sons, Andy and Zach, are first in line—this book is dedicated to them, after all—but it must be noted that, without the interviewees who said yes, this book would never have happened.

Thanks.

PHOTO CREDITS

Wilson Bradshaw. Photo courtesy of Erik Kellar.

Stephen Leatherman. Photo courtesy of Jeffery Salter.

Theresa Manuel. Photo courtesy of Melissa Lyttle/*Tampa Bay Times*.

M. J. Soileau. Photo courtesy of Norma Molina.

Nan-Yao Su. Photo courtesy of Eileen Escarda.

Joe Kittinger. Photo courtesy of Jeffrey Camp.

Edgar Mitchell. Photo courtesy of Jeffrey Camp.

JoAnn Morgan. Photo courtesy of Lido Vizzutti.

Winston Scott. Photo courtesy of Norma Molina.

Zev Buffman. Photo courtesy of Gregg McGough.

Brian Johnson. Photo credit: Fabio Diena/Shutterstock.com.

Sherrill Milnes. Photo courtesy of Bob Croslin.

Bello Nock. Photo courtesy of Chris Lake.

Burt Reynolds. Photo credit: Kathy Hutchins/Shutterstock.com.

Mel Tillis. Photo courtesy of Brandon Alms.

George Billiris. Photo courtesy of Michael Heape.

Ed Droste. Photo courtesy of Michael Heape.

Richard Gonzmart. Photo courtesy of Michael Heape.

Ward Hall. Photo courtesy of Michael Heape.

H. Irwin Levy. Photo courtesy of Scott Wiseman.

Tony Little. Photo courtesy of Brook Pifer.

Joe Redner. Photo courtesy of Michael Heape.

Arthur Rutenberg. Photo courtesy of Steve Widoff.

Michael Saunders. Photo courtesy of Michael Saunders & Company.

Robert M. "Bob" Beall II. Photo courtesy of Alex McKnight.

Albert J. Dunlap. Photo courtesy of Jeffrey Camp.

Tom James. Photo courtesy of Mark Wemple.

Steve Raymund. Photo courtesy of Michael Heape.

David Lawrence Jr. Photo courtesy of Donna Victor.

Lucy Morgan. Photo courtesy of Ryan Ketterman.

Eugene Patterson. Photo courtesy of Jeffrey Camp.

Alto "Bud" Adams Jr. Photo courtesy of Michael Price.

"Alligator" Ron Bergeron. Photo courtesy of the Bergeron Family
    of Companies.

Eugenie Clark. Photo courtesy of Mark Wemple.

Don Goodman. Photo courtesy of Jon M. Fletcher.

Bill Haast. Photo courtesy of Jeffrey Camp.

Jeff Klinkenberg. Photo courtesy of Cherie Diez/*Tampa Bay Times*.

Meg Lowman. Photo courtesy of Carlton Ward.

Derrick Brooks. Photo courtesy of Dirk Shadd/*Tampa Bay Times*.

Warrick Dunn. Photo courtesy of Don Chambers.

William R. Hough. Photo courtesy of Mark Wemple.

Kiran Patel. Photo courtesy of Bob Croslin.

Howard C. Tibbals. Photo courtesy of Alex McKnight.

Susan Benton. Photo courtesy of Chris Lake.

Betty Castor. Photo courtesy of Jeffrey Camp.

Sam Gibbons. Photo courtesy of Bob Croslin.

Charles Gray. Photo courtesy of Brook Pifer.

Bob Martinez. Photo courtesy of Michael Heape.

H. Lee Moffitt. Photo courtesy of Michael Heape.

Ed Price. Photo courtesy of Mark Wemple.

Alex Sink. Photo courtesy of Chris Lake.

W. George Allen. Photo courtesy of Eileen Escarda.

Craig Fugate. Photo courtesy of Bernard Brzezinski.

Thomas "Blue" Fulford. Photo courtesy of Mark Wemple.

"Big Daddy" Don Garlits. Photo courtesy of Brook Pifer.

Marcella Hazan. Photo courtesy of Mark Wemple.

Gene Leedy. Photo courtesy of Brook Pifer.

Roland Martin. Photo courtesy of Walt Reynolds.

Tater Porter. Photo courtesy of Norma Molina.

Norman Van Aken. Photo courtesy of Jeffery Salter.

Dick Vitale. Photo courtesy of Mark Wemple.

Dave Barry. Photo courtesy of Daniel Portnoy.

Carl Hiaasen. Photo credit: WENN Ltd/Alamy Stock Photo.

Peter Meinke. Photo courtesy of Mark Wemple.

Patrick Smith. Photo courtesy of Norma Molina

Ferdie Pacheco. Photo courtesy of Melissa Lyttle/*Tampa Bay Times*.

INTERVIEW INDEX

After graduating from the University of Florida in 1984, Art Levy embarked on an interesting career in newspaper journalism, working along the way at the *Durham (N.C.) Sun*, the *Hendersonville (N.C.) Times-News*, the *Sarasota Herald-Tribune*, and the *St. Petersburg Times*, mostly writing feature stories and winning some awards. He joined *Florida Trend*, a statewide news magazine, in 2006. He lives in St. Petersburg with his wife and two sons.

Photo by James Borchuck.